POINT MADE

POINT MADE

How to Write Like the Nation's Top Advocates

SECOND EDITION

Ross Guberman

OXFORD
UNIVERSITY PRESS

OXFORD
UNIVERSITY PRESS

Oxford University Press is a department of the University of Oxford. It furthers the University's objective of excellence in research, scholarship, and education by publishing worldwide.

Oxford   New York
Auckland   Cape Town   Dar es Salaam   Hong Kong   Karachi   Kuala Lumpur   Madrid
Melbourne   Mexico City   Nairobi   New Delhi   Shanghai   Taipei   Toronto

With offices in
Argentina   Austria   Brazil   Chile   Czech Republic   France   Greece
Guatemala   Hungary   Italy   Japan   Poland   Portugal   Singapore   South Korea
Switzerland   Thailand   Turkey   Ukraine   Vietnam

Oxford is a registered trade mark of Oxford University Press in the UK and certain other countries.

Published in the United States of America by
Oxford University Press
198 Madison Avenue, New York, NY 10016

© Oxford University Press 2014

Library of Congress Cataloging-in-Publication Data
Guberman, Ross
   Point made : how to write like the nation's top advocates / Ross Guberman.—Second edition.
      pages cm
   Includes bibliographical references and index.
   ISBN 978-0-19-994385-2 ((pbk.) : alk. paper)
   1. Legal briefs—United States. 2. Legal composition. I. Title.
   KF251.G83 2014
   808.06'634—dc23
                                                          2013028579

9 8 7 6

Printed in the United States of America on acid-free paper

Note to Readers
This publication is designed to provide accurate and authoritative information in regard to the subject matter covered. It is based upon sources believed to be accurate and reliable and is intended to be current as of the time it was written. It is sold with the understanding that the publisher is not engaged in rendering legal, accounting, or other professional services. If legal advice or other expert assistance is required, the services of a competent professional person should be sought. Also, to confirm that the information has not been affected or changed by recent developments, traditional legal research techniques should be used, including checking primary sources where appropriate.

(Based on the Declaration of Principles jointly adopted by a Committee of the American Bar Association and a Committee of Publishers and Associations.)

To Heidi, Sean, and Meghan

Contents

Preface to the Second Edition

"If it reads easy, it wrote hard."

That age-old writing advice is as true for lawyers as for anyone, but surely writing a brief isn't like running on a treadmill, with its clean line between sweat and calories burned.

Writing a brief "hard" requires smart work, not working-just-to-work. In my first edition of *Point Made*, I tried to turn the "smart work" of brief-writing into fifty concrete techniques.

The reaction to that first edition has been deeply satisfying. I've heard from lawyers and judges all over the world, from Boise, Idaho, to the outer reaches of Bhutan and India. I've reaffirmed my sense that busy lawyers clamor for a step-by-step approach to great advocacy writing—and that busy judges seek help explaining what makes a brief an easy read.

I've also been privileged to speak about the book on three continents and to learn from those audiences what my readers want and need. Although I couldn't integrate every suggestion into this new edition, you'll find a fuller and richer book this second time around.

In just two short years, some of the original fifty advocates profiled have taken on exciting new titles, and others have passed away. In addition to newer examples from the original fifty, I'm excited to introduce eight new lawyers as well, from Solicitor General Don

Verrilli, Deanne Maynard, Larry Robbins, and Lisa Blatt to Joshua Rosenkranz, Texas Senator Ted Cruz, Judy Clarke, and Sri Srinivasan. You'll also find provocative new examples from the Affordable Care Act wars, the same-sex marriage fight, and many other recent high-profile cases.

Three other innovations were suggested by my readers.

First, you'll find much more commentary on the examples themselves, including dozens of style and grammar tips throughout. I've also added more context for some of the examples.

Second, I've expanded the list of transition words and phrases, and I've included a new list of 50 "zinger" verbs.

And third, for those who seek to improve their advocacy skills and for those who simply want a step-by-step guide to making a good brief better, I've ended the book with an all-new set of fifty writing challenges corresponding to the fifty techniques.

On top of the many people I thanked in the first edition, I'd like to thank all the firms, courts, agencies, and governments that have invited me to speak about the book as well as the thousands of lawyers who have shared their thoughts and experiences. I am also grateful for Nichole Best's excellent research assistance, for Daniel Baker and Karin Ciano's fantastic work on the rewrite, and for Noah Messing's helpful comments on the entire first edition.

Happy writing—and reading!

Acknowledgments for the First Edition

A book like this reflects decades of friends, mentors, and influences.

I am grateful to Oxford University Press, particularly to Matt Gallaway for approaching me to write the book and for his sustained support throughout.

I am lucky to have studied writing and the law at such great institutions as Yale University and the University of Chicago Law School. I should also thank the George Washington University Law School for giving me an academic platform and a chance to interact with such motivated and talented law students over the years.

Many people have influenced my own writing and my thinking about writing. My early years as a book translator and editor were superb training, so I thank Jennifer Crewe at Columbia University Press. On the feature-writing side, I learned much from literary agent Lynn Chu and from the *Washingtonian's* Jack Limpert and Bill O'Sullivan. On the legal-writing front, thanks go to Professor C. J. Peters, Judge James Holderman, Judge Henry Coke Morgan, Laura Klaus, and Rob Saunders, all early influences on how I think about advocacy.

I am grateful for my hundreds of Legal Writing Pro clients. And I must also thank the tens of thousands of attorneys and judges who have attended my workshops, shared their experiences, and inspired me to refine my views.

So many people helped with the book itself. I am especially grateful to my close friends Joe Luzzi and Andrew Stewart. Hats off as well to Robert Fiske, John Hayden, Sue Irion, Shannon MacMichael, Gaye Mara, Steve Mullery, Ashley Parrish, Dan Schweitzer, and Wayne Schiess, just to name a few. The Legal Writing Pro team of Ben Olson, Ellen Callinan, Katie White, and Megan Rogers was of great help as well. And my family—Heidi, Sean, and Meghan—gave me needed support and perspective throughout.

Several books deserve mention here, too. I have the highest praise for James Stewart's *Follow the Story* and for Joseph Williams's *Style: Lessons in Clarity and Grace*. And on the brief-writing front, I have long admired Judge Ruggero Aldisert's *Winning on Appeal* and Bryan Garner's *The Winning Brief*.

Finally, I should pay tribute to the fifty-eight lawyers profiled here. In a profession often maligned—and often unfairly—they are all models of great lawyering.

Introduction

When Chief Justice John Roberts was an advocate, he once wrote that determining the "best" technology for controlling air pollution is like asking people to pick the "best" car:

> Mario Andretti may select a Ferrari; a college student a Volkswagen Beetle; a family of six a mini-van. A Minnesotan's choice will doubtless have four-wheel drive; a Floridian's might well be a convertible. The choices would turn on how the decisionmaker weighed competing priorities such as cost, mileage, safety, cargo space, speed, handling, and so on.

I have shared this passage with lawyers all over the world. "Brilliant," exclaim some. "Look how he gets his point across," say others. But they all agree on one thing: "Writing like that is an art."

This book will reveal the craft behind that art. I am convinced that if you learn why the best advocates write the way they do, you can import those same techniques into your own work.

Surging above the norm means making different writing choices, even unusual ones. Take Roberts's car passage. When most lawyers discuss regulations, they fall into an abyss of detail. Roberts offers up the familiar analogy of choosing a car. When most lawyers use abstract phrases like "competing priorities," they stop there. Roberts, by contrast, adds examples of competing priorities, like "cost" and "cargo space," so you can identify with his point right away, nodding your head in agreement.

I will show you how to use such techniques in a chapter called *That Reminds Me*.

Roberts also shapes his sentences in compelling ways. If most lawyers joined "Mario Andretti may select a Ferrari" and "a college student a Volkswagen Beetle," they would chop up their point into two sentences and start the second one with "However." Not Roberts: he uses a semicolon to join the clauses as one sentence, highlighting the contrast. In the list of various "best" cars, he also drops words like "and" and "select," creating a rhythmic effect through techniques known as conjunction deviation and verb ellipsis. And how many lawyers would write "the choices would *turn on how*"? Most would type something slow and flat like "the choices would *be contingent upon the manner in which*."

I'll share similar ways to finesse your style in chapters called *Parallel Lives*, *Good Bedfellows*, and *What a Breeze*, techniques to help you spice up your prose with fresh language, balanced phrases, and creative punctuation.

Many writing books tell you how the author thinks you should write. My approach is more empirical. I began by identifying dozens of the most renowned and influential advocates. Then I dissected hundreds of their motions and briefs. After spotting patterns in their work, I settled on fifty concrete techniques spanning from the opening paragraph to the final footnote. I can't promise that learning these techniques will make you write like John Roberts. But I know they will help you advocate for your clients more effectively.

To help you develop your "theme of the case" and craft a compelling introduction, for example, I'll share techniques in Part One like *The Short List* and *Flashpoint*.

When we turn to the fact section in Part Two, I'll show you examples of *Panoramic Shot*, *Headliners*, and other ways to make your client's story more persuasive.

Part Three focuses on the argument section. We'll walk through such techniques as *Russian Doll* for nesting your headings, *With You in Spirit* for structuring your sections, *One Fell Swoop* for distinguishing cases, and *Lead 'Em On* for framing quoted language.

Think of Part Four as "Fun with Style." We'll explore *Zingers, Size Matters, A Dash of Style*, and many other techniques for freshening your sentences and smoothing your transitions.

Finally, in Part Five, I'll share techniques for conclusions such as *Parting Thought* and *Wrap-Up*.

Before we turn to these fifty techniques, let me explain how I chose the lawyers and examples.

The lawyers profiled count among the most prominent living advocates. I consulted Chambers & Partners ratings, which draw on confidential interviews with clients and colleagues. I also reviewed lists of top lawyers in the *National Law Journal* and other publications that rely on interviews and expert judgment. You will find familiar names like Elena Kagan and Larry Tribe, appellate stars like Maureen Mahoney and Carter Phillips, trial lawyers like Fred Bartlit and David Boies, and former solicitors general and federal prosecutors. Also included are top plaintiffs' lawyers like Joe Jamail and Phil Corboy, specialists like Morgan Chu in intellectual property and Harvey Miller in bankruptcy, legal leaders like President Barack Obama and former American Bar Association President Carolyn Lamm, intellectuals and icons like Larry Lessig and Alan Dershowitz, and the legal directors of the NAACP and ACLU.

In the appendix, I have listed these lawyers along with short biographies. Although many other lawyers write just as well as or better than the ones in this book, I am convinced that these advocates figure among the brightest lights in the profession.

You will also find hundreds of short examples from interesting cases in nearly all areas of practice; I have cut most of the citations and definitions and have made other changes for readability. I have also bolded key language in the excerpts.

Each example is attributed to at least one of the lawyers profiled in this book. Some people ask me, "Aren't most motions and briefs written as a team?" Yes, but my anecdotal evidence suggests that many "famous" lawyers play a much larger role in writing and editing these filings than is commonly believed. In any event, if I include an example, it's because I think it can help you be a better writer no matter who wrote the exact words.

Nor should it matter that some of these lawyers lost their cases. Great writing can trump a conflicting record or adverse case law, but it cannot guarantee victory.

So what's the best way to use the book?

The examples cover everything from Harry Potter to Henry Kissinger, from football to terrorism, and from disputes over jeans to fights over dirty words. The source material includes nearly every type of motion or brief, from routine discovery motions to U.S. Supreme Court briefs.

If you're curious to read the writing of a lawyer you admire, turn to the index. If you need practical tips and models for sections of briefs that are giving you trouble, flip to the relevant section. And if you just want to be inspired by some great writing, read this book as you would a novel.

Whatever your goal, I hope that reading the book will make writing the brief as enjoyable and productive for you as studying the work of these great lawyers has been for me.

PART ONE

THE THEME

Part One will share four techniques for crafting the theme of your case and creating a compelling introduction:

Part One: The Theme

The judge does not possess the luxury of time for leisurely, detached meditation. You'd better sell the sizzle as soon as possible; the steak can wait.

—Former Third Circuit Chief Judge Ruggero Aldisert[1]

Selling the sizzle from the start should be every advocate's goal. And Judge Aldisert's food metaphor is apt: nothing in advocacy is more satisfying than reducing a dispute and its resolution to their essence, almost as if you were preparing a rich sauce.

---

1. Ruggero J. Aldisert, Winning on Appeal: Better Briefs and Oral Argument 142 (2d ed. NITA 2003).

That "essence" is what many judges and litigators call the "theme of your case."

But what should such a "theme" contain?

The openings of great motions and briefs include up to four main ingredients. As with any recipe, you might not need all four, and you can always adjust to taste. But when you're poised to start writing, thinking about these ingredients will focus your mind and help "sell the sizzle."

Not that you should freeze your theme before you write the rest of your brief. Just as you alter the seasoning after sampling what you've cooked, so you can fine-tune your theme as you work through your argument and pore over the case law and record. But then again, it's tough to be a great chef unless you know how you want the dish to look and taste.

In a moment, I'll share examples of the four "theme of the case" ingredients. For now, here's a recipe for your introduction, worksheet-style, with the tools you need to make order out of chaos. If you mold these four ingredients, focusing especially on the first two, the pay-off will be a stellar introduction, a sound theme, and—for both you and the court—a seamless journey through the rest of the brief.

1. *Brass Tacks: The Narrative Lens.* Begin with a paragraph or two that covers what many attorneys never explain at all: *who* the parties are; *when, where,* and *how* the dispute arose; *what* question the litigation seeks to answer; and *why* your client is in the right.
2. *The Short List: The Logical Lens.* List three or four specific points you would make to a judge who gave you only 60 seconds to explain why you should win.
3. *Why Should I Care?: The Pragmatic Lens.* Offer the court a reason to feel good about ruling in your favor.
4. *Flashpoint: The Contrasting Lens.* Draw a line in the sand between two competing views of your dispute.

Let's take those four techniques in turn.

1

Brass Tacks: Explain "who, what, when, where, why, how"

Too often lawyers jump right into the legal nuances of the case without explaining, in clear terms, the legal context in which the case arises.

—*Wisconsin Supreme Court Chief Justice Shirley Abrahamson* [2]

The deeper you are into your litigation, the easier it is to forget what Chief Justice Abrahamson calls the "context in which the case arises." That's why so many lawyers' preliminary statements make you feel as though you're being hit over the head with a hammer.

Imagine you're a judge picking up a motion and you stumble upon this introduction. I've changed only the names:

> Defendant New York Yankees, LLC ("NYY") submits this Memorandum of Law to address the issue of whether paragraph 14.1 of the January 6, 2003 EDG Supply Agreement (the "January 6 Document") precludes testimony by Jay Leno of conversations he had with David Letterman of plaintiff New York Mets ("NYM") concerning the price to be charged by NYM to NYY for EDG. As explained below, because paragraph 14.1 is the classic "general merger clause," and is not a "specific disclaimer," it does not preclude testimony of prior oral conversations between the parties.

---

2. Twenty Questions for Chief Justice Shirley S. Abrahamson of the Supreme Court of Wisconsin, *available at* http://howappealing.law.com/20q/2004_09_01_20q-appellateblog_archive.html.

To avoid this all-too-common chaotic feel, take a deep breath and answer the key questions you would have if you were reading about your case in the newspaper: *Who* are the parties? *When and where and how* did the dispute take place? *What* question is the case trying to answer? *Why* should you win? If you are drafting an opening brief, make those answers the beginning of your filing so you can help orient the court. And if you can spin some of your answers to your client's advantage, all the better.

Judge Aldisert, of "sell the sizzle" fame, suggests that the ideal *Brass Tacks* theme is like how you'd describe your case to a friend in a bar. Here's an example he gives: "This case I had this week. . . . The jury came in against me, but I think I have a good issue on appeal. The trial judge allowed this garage mechanic to testify as an expert witness, and he challenged the design of a new gear box on a $100,000 BMW. I got socked to the tune of a million bucks!"[3]

As Judge Aldisert notes, this short tale makes clear that the court erred in admitting the testimony of an unqualified expert.

Now let's turn to some real-life examples of great opening *Brass Tacks* passages.

When Attorney General Eric Holder was in private practice at Covington & Burling, he litigated a high-profile civil case involving bananas, American missionaries, and extortion in Colombia. He and his team started their introduction to a motion to dismiss with a *Brass Tacks* paragraph telling the court *who* the parties are, *what* happened to the plaintiffs and *when* and *where* it happened, *when* they brought their claim, *what* the families want, and *why* they shouldn't get it. Holder also squeezes in

---

3. RUGGERO J. ALDISERT, WINNING ON APPEAL: BETTER BRIEFS AND ORAL ARGUMENTS 191 (2d ed. NITA 2003).

what the claims do *not* allege, highlighting the weakness of the plaintiffs' case:

Eric Holder, *In re Chiquita Banana*

Plaintiffs in this action are relatives of five American **missionaries** who were abducted for ransom and tragically **murdered** in the **mid-1990s** by a communist **guerilla group** in Colombia, known as the Fuerzas Armadas Revolucionarias de Colombia. Now, **more than a decade later**, they seek to hold **Chiquita Brands** International, Inc. liable for those deaths under the Antiterrorism Act, and Florida and Nebraska tort law. There is **no allegation**, however, that **Chiquita was involved** in the kidnapping and murder of the decedents, that **Chiquita intended** that these despicable acts occur, or that **Chiquita even knew** about them until plaintiffs brought this lawsuit. Instead, plaintiffs allege that Chiquita is liable for decedents' deaths solely because Chiquita's former Colombian subsidiary made **payments extorted** by the FARC **when** this radical **Marxist group controlled** the remote banana-growing regions of Colombia in which Chiquita's subsidiary operated.

In distilling your case in this way, you want to *sound* like a newspaper reporter, not mime the objectivity of one. Holder neglects to mention, for example, that Chiquita had already paid a $25 million fine to settle criminal charges that it had supported the FARC, which was considered a terrorist group. No matter: after just 140 words, we understand why our sympathies for the murdered missionaries might not warrant civil damages against Chiquita.

Joshua Rosenkranz, *American Lawyer*'s 2011 Litigator of the Year, perfects this technique in a brief defending Facebook and Mark Zuckerberg from "failing competitor" ConnectU. This is the dispute that inspired the film *The Social Network*. Note here how Rosenkranz adds a "where" dimension through his "two coasts," explains the "what" with crisp words like "bout," "peace," and "plunge," and slants the "who" factor by mentioning ConnectU's "bevy of lawyers":

Joshua Rosenkranz, *Facebook, Inc. v. ConnectU, Inc.*

This appeal arises from the settlement of rancorous litigation on **two coasts**. On one side were Appellees **Facebook, Inc.** and its founder and CEO **Mark Zuckerberg**. On the other side were Appellants, who founded a failing competitor of Facebook's called ConnectU. The **CU Founders** [the Winklevoss twins] claimed that they had the idea for Facebook first, and Facebook stole their idea. Facebook denied those claims and, for its part, accused ConnectU and its Founders of unlawfully infiltrating its systems, stealing millions of email addresses, and then spamming them. During a global mediation, the parties signed a "Term Sheet and Settlement Agreement." In the interest of achieving litigation peace, Facebook agreed to purchase ConnectU for over a million shares of Facebook stock, one of the **hottest start-ups** in the world. Surrounded by a **bevy of lawyers**, the CU Founders signed the deal. Then they suffered **a bout of settlers' remorse**. They ask this Court to relieve them of the deal they struck to **plunge back** into scorched-earth litigation.

In a single paragraph, Rosenkranz tells us what the case is about and why Facebook is in the right, all in a fast-paced journalistic style.

(Style notes: For parallelism and clarity, add another "that" before "Facebook stole their idea" to clarify that the stealing was the second thing that the Winklevoss twins claimed. And in the final sentence, change "to plunge back" to "so they can plunge back" to clarify that they didn't strike a deal *about* plunging back into litigation.)

Speaking of the journalistic style, let's turn to a third example, this time from a plaintiff-side patent infringement motion penned by star trial lawyer Fred Bartlit, a master of bringing dry, complex facts to life.

And few things are drier and more complex than your typical patent-infringement case. I pulled a random trial motion in one such case, and here's how the introduction starts. I've changed only the names and numbers:

> The Plaintiffs, Acme Corporation, Baker, Inc., and Cary Grant (hereinafter the "Plaintiffs"), commenced this action for alleged patent infringement of U.S. Patent No. 2,748,137, entitled *Visual Enhancement Mechanism* (hereinafter referred to as the "'137 patent"). The Plaintiffs have asserted claims 1 through 3 of the '137 patent.

"Selling the sizzle" this is not. But now compare the following example from Fred Bartlit. Here's the beginning of his introduction for Pinpoint, a Texas company suing Amazon for patent infringement. Pinpoint is unhappy about Amazon's "recommendation engine," the feature that gives you personalized recommendations about which products to buy based on your purchasing history:

> **Fred Bartlit, *Pinpoint v. Amazon***
>
> This is **a case about** online personal recommendation systems. The inventors of the patents in suit **pioneered techniques** to deal with information overload. **They invented systems and**

> **methods** to help users sort out the plethora of information available and to help online shoppers at the "electronic mall" find items of interest.
>
> **Plaintiff Pinpoint, Inc. owns** the three patents in suit.…
>
> **Defendant Amazon.com operates** the world's most successful electronic mall. Amazon also operates the platform that the co-defendants use for their websites.

I'm sure you appreciated Bartlit's direct, conversational tone—a sign of a superb trial lawyer who is able to translate his oral advocacy skills to the page. It may not have the pizzazz of the Facebook example above, but for this patent-litigation matter, it fits the bill.

Let me share two more "This case is about" variations. As Bartlit's example above suggests, before launching into the narrative, sometimes you might want to seize the debate through an opening sentence on what the case is truly "about," as in these jeans (summary judgment) and same-sex-marriage (Supreme Court) openers below:

> **Brendan Sullivan, Greg Craig, and Nicole Seligman,**
> *Calvin Klein Trademark Trust v. Wachner*
>
> **This is a contract case.** The terms of the pertinent contracts, and the material facts concerning their performance, are not disputed. Plaintiffs' principal claim has been that defendants without authorization sold apparel through discount and warehouse club retailers. But the undisputed record shows that the contracts authorized such sales, and that plaintiffs for years fully knew of and profited from them. And now discovery has disclosed in addition that plaintiffs themselves had for years sold eagerly to the same group of retailers of which they now complain.

(If you want to avoid ending a sentence with a preposition, as in the final sentence, make sure to use the right preposition. You complain "about" groups of retailers, not "of" them.)

David Boies and Ted Olson, *Hollingsworth v. Perry*

This case is about marriage, "the most important relation in life," *Zablocki v. Redhail*, 434 U.S. 374, 384 (1978), a relationship and intimate decision that this Court has variously described at least 14 times as a right protected by the Due Process Clause that is central for all individuals' liberty, privacy, spirituality, personal autonomy, sexuality, and dignity; a matter fundamental to one's place in society; and an expression of love, emotional support, public commitment, and social status.

This case is also about equality. After a $40 million political campaign during which voters were urged to "protect our children" from exposure to the notion that "gay marriage is okay," and "the same as traditional marriage," and thus deserving of equal dignity and respect, Proposition 8 engraved into California's constitution the cardinal principle that unions among gay men and lesbians are not valid or recognized as marriages, and therefore second-class and not equal to heterosexual marriages.

As we've seen above, the *Brass Tacks* technique is priceless in an opening brief, but it can be just as useful in an opposition or reply brief as a way to help reorient the court.

Bernie Nussbaum, President Clinton's White House Counsel and a top partner at Wachtell Lipton, takes such an approach in a reply brief for IBP, a meat distributor seeking to require Tyson Foods to acquire it after Tyson tried to invoke a material-adverse-change clause to get out of the deal:

Bernie Nussbaum, *IBP v. Tyson Foods*

This is IBP's Reply Brief in support of its request that the Court continue to enjoin Tyson from prosecuting the Arkansas action—more precisely, that the Court enter a preliminary injunction in follow-up to the two temporary restraining orders it already has entered.

In just one sentence, Nussbaum and his team remind the court *who* is involved, *what* the dispute is about, *where* the proceedings are headed, and *what* the client wants.

A narrative opening can be more than just a way to reengage and reorient: returning to a well-crafted story line can bolster your theme itself. Consider the opening sentence below from a reply brief filed by Larry Robbins. Robbins, a top appellate lawyer, managed to get a conviction overturned for Daniel Bayly, an investment-banking guru convicted during the fallout from the Enron scandal. Robbins makes the "fundamental issue" of the entire case a single-sentence tale:

Larry Robbins, *United States v. Bayly*

The **fundamental issue** in this case **is whether Dan Bayly, during his December 23, 1999 phone call** with Andrew Fastow, **reached an agreement** that Enron itself would buy back Merrill Lynch's barge interest if a third-party buyer could not be located.

All these opening narratives alert the court to what it will need to do to resolve the dispute: they start to sell the sizzle.

Even so, you'll usually want your introduction to run more than just a paragraph. To your *Brass Tacks* paragraph, then, consider adding a short list of reasons you should win.

2

The Short List: Number your path to victory

The top advocates love numbered lists: lists in the facts, lists in the argument, and, most of all, lists in the introduction. Nothing helps a brief hold together better than a list of legal, factual, or common-sensical reasons you should prevail.

But here's the challenge: you don't want those reasons to be circular and thus unpersuasive. In other words, don't list things the judge knew you were going to write based solely on the type of motion or brief you're filing.

If, say, you're moving for a preliminary injunction, writing "The balance of equities favors the petitioner" won't cut it. *Why* do those equities favor the petitioner?

And if you're moving for a protective order, writing "Defendant is on a fishing expedition" won't help you either. All movants for protective orders say that (in researching for this book I must have seen the phrase "fishing expedition" a million times). *Why* is the request unreasonably broad and burdensome and *what* proof do you have that the defendant is seeking irrelevant documents?

So make your reasons more specific than your instinct might suggest. Add the word *because* at the end of each draft reason, and include some detail specific to your own dispute and not to just any dispute with the same procedural posture.

Before we look at examples, here's a table to help you organize and order your reasons:

When the order of your reasons is . . .	*you should . . .*
obvious because the dispute turns on statutory elements, common law factors, or multipart rules, and you need to address them in order or need to start with the one that's dispositive or pivotal,	focus on the key facts that establish each of those elements (or not), weaving in the actual elements or rules rather than making those standards the focus of your list.
obvious because you need to address threshold questions of standing, timeliness, or jurisdiction before addressing the merits,	argue in the alternative ("The Plaintiff lacks standing. But even if the Plaintiff had standing, the claim still cannot be sustained.").
not so obvious because the dispute is complex or fact-driven, or because you're focusing on a broad standard like "materiality,"	add detail to your reasons and order them the way you'd deliver them orally if the judge asked you why you should win.
dictated in part by your opponent because you're filing an opposition or reply brief,	stress why you're still right, and don't just announce that the other side is wrong.

Now let's consider how to handle these four situations.

A. Your list is governed by factors or rules

In common law or statutory disputes, your introduction often needs to track the elements of a cause of action (like the four elements of negligence) or a multifactor test (like the factors for injunctive relief). Ordering your list is the easy part: you track the factors the way they appear in the case law or statute, you address only the factors in dispute, or you address the one factor that makes the other ones moot (as in "no damages, no case").

But in developing that list, avoid doing what most attorneys do: copying the elements and simply declaring that each one has been established—or not.

In this example, former Solicitor General Seth Waxman weaves in the well-known factors for injunctive relief as he seeks a permanent injunction for MercExchange. The dispute arose out of MercExchange and eBay's high-profile patent dispute over eBay's "Buy It Now" feature, which lets eBay shoppers bypass the bidding process and grab the goods they want at a presumably higher price:

Seth Waxman, *MercExchange v. eBay*

The **equities** strongly favor [injunctive relief for MercExchange]. This is a case of deliberate, and by eBay's own assertion, **avoidable infringement**. eBay was not only well aware of MercExchange's patent ("the '265 patent"), but eBay tried to purchase that patent before it started infringing....

MercExchange, on the other hand, will continue to suffer **irreparable harm** in the absence of an injunction. MercExchange, and MercExchange's licensees or potential licensees are, or aspire to be, competitors of eBay. Permitting eBay to continue using MercExchange's technology would irreparably **harm MercExchange's ability to market, sell or license its technology** to these existing or future competitors to eBay....

The **public interest** also favors injunctive relief. In addition to serving the strong public interest in **maintaining the integrity of the patent system** by enforcing patent rights, enjoining eBay also serves the public interest in **promoting competition.**

As you can see, the four factors lurk in the background, not the foreground—at least initially. The brief *later* marches through the four-part preliminary injunction test, but the Introduction is more intuitive and natural.

B. You need to address threshold questions before addressing the merits

Sometimes the order of your reasons is obvious not because you're tracking, say, a four-factor test, but because you have to resolve threshold issues such as standing or mootness before you can address the merits. In those cases, argue in the alternative by following former Solicitor General Ted Olson's "even if" example below. Olson is asking the court to throw out a suit challenging the eligibility of Senator John McCain to be President of the United States. The plaintiff was a leader of the American Independent Party who claimed that McCain was ineligible for the presidency because he wasn't a natural-born citizen (Senator McCain was born in the Panama Canal Zone while his father was stationed there):

Ted Olson, *Robinson v. Bowen*

Plaintiff **lacks standing** to raise his claims for relief, and his complaint demands resolution of a nonjusticiable political question. **But even if** plaintiff could satisfy the justiciability requirements of Article III, dismissal of his complaint still would be required because the injunctive relief plaintiff seeks is barred variously by Article II of the U.S. Constitution, the First Amendment, and the Twelfth Amendment....

(In the second sentence, the first passive construction—"dismissal of the complaint still would be required"—might have been better in the active: "the Court should still dismiss the complaint." But the second passive construction—"the relief plaintiff seeks is barred variously by"—is better left as is: the focus of the passage is on the relief itself. Some legal-writing "experts" take their crusade against the passive voice a bit too far, as we'll discuss in Part Four.)

C. Your dispute is complex or fact-driven

The way to order or structure your list will not always be so obvious, particularly when the dispute turns on contested facts or on a broad standard like "materiality" or "reasonableness" or "competitive harm."

But you can use that structural freedom to your advantage. Starting with a blank slate gives you a chance to think of the three or four points you'd make to the judge if you had only 60 seconds to do so. Those points, listed in the order you'd make them orally if you had to look the judge in the eye, will give you the structure you need.

Keep in mind the gold standard for these lists: in each numbered reason, share something newsworthy.

Take the following example. Supreme Court stalwart Maureen Mahoney defended the University of Michigan Law School against a challenge to its affirmative-action admissions plan. Toward the beginning of her winning brief, she might have listed an unpersuasive circular reason such as "The plan does not violate the Equal Protection Clause." But why else would she be defending a plan against an Equal Protection challenge? Instead, in her Statement of the Case, she lists three specific factual, legal, and policy reasons to leave the plan intact:

Maureen Mahoney, *Grutter v. Bollinger*

First, academic selectivity and student body diversity, including racial diversity, are both integral to the educational mission of the Law School. *Second*, the Law School successfully realizes both goals through an admissions program that is "virtually indistinguishable" from the Harvard plan that five Justices approved in *Bakke*. It evaluates the potential contributions and academic promise of every individual and does not employ quotas or set-asides. *Third*, no honestly colorblind alternative policy could produce educationally meaningful

> racial diversity at present without enrolling students who are academically unprepared for the rigorous legal education that the Law School offers.

The way Mahoney sets up the dispute, you can't win unless you first deny that selectivity and diversity are legitimate educational values, then prove that the Michigan program was materially different from the plan approved decades before in *Bakke*, and finally explain how the university could attain racial diversity without the plan. If you can't, game over. And it was over indeed: Mahoney's side won.

After the Mahoney side won the law school version of the Michigan case at the Supreme Court, the state's voters passed a referendum seeking to undo the result and to prohibit state universities from taking race into account when admitting students. Jennifer Gratz, one of the original plaintiffs who had challenged the admissions policy, moved to intervene in litigation over whether the referendum was constitutional (she believed that it was). In opposing what he calls Gratz's "eleventh-hour motion to intervene," Larry Tribe, best known for his Supreme Court work, starts his trial motion with a numbered list of specific reasons to keep her out of the case:

Larry Tribe, *Gratz v. Bollinger*

First, Ms. Gratz's motion to intervene is untimely. *Second*, Ms. Gratz lacks a substantial legal interest sufficient to support her intervention. At most she has a mere desire to see Proposal 2 upheld for political and ideological reasons. *Third*, Ms. Gratz's purported "interest"...is adequately represented by Attorney General Cox. *Finally*, adding Ms. Gratz to the case at this late stage would serve no purpose other than to needlessly delay the litigation.

In a quick seventy-five words, you can peer at Tribe's goal—to keep Ms. Gratz out of the lawsuit—through four procedural and substantive lenses.

Let's consider how to use a numbered list in an even more fact-intensive example. Now wearing a criminal law hat, crack trial lawyer Brendan Sullivan is seeking a shorter sentence for Walter Forbes, the former Cendant chairman convicted of the largest accounting fraud of the 1990s. Watch how Sullivan follows a legal justification by listing two strong factual ones:

Brendan Sullivan, *United States v. Forbes*

First, while Mr. Forbes does not dispute that the jury verdict permits each of the sentencing enhancements applied by the [Presentence Report], the cumulative, overlapping impact of these adjustments warrants a reduction in the resulting sentencing range, as Judge Thompson found in the case of [Codefendant] E. Kirk Shelton.

Second, Mr. Forbes' admirable character and history of charitable giving warrant consideration in determining the length of his sentence.

Third, Mr. Forbes' advanced age should be taken into consideration, particularly in light of the statutory mandate that a punishment should be "sufficient, but no greater than necessary to effectuate the goals of criminal punishment."

For our final list, let's return to Ted Olson, who also served as the solicitor general for G. W. Bush. Below he helps the federal government in its quest to deny a Freedom of Information Act request to turn over the death-scene photographs of Vince Foster, the former Clinton Deputy White House Counsel who some thought had been murdered. Olson develops here three reasons to reject the lower court's standard for weighing the Foster family's privacy rights against the public interest:

Ted Olson, *Office of Independent Counsel v. Favish*

First, this case stands as a testament both to the ease with which allegations of governmental misconduct can be leveled and the longevity that they can acquire.

Five investigations conducted by officials in the Executive and Legislative Branches, as well as two Independent Counsels, have unanimously concluded—without dissent—that Vincent Foster committed suicide....

Second, even where a FOIA requester makes such a showing, this Court's cases establish that the public interest in disclosure must be evaluated in light of the amount of information already in the public domain. In this case, five expert investigations have resulted in the disclosure of thousands of pages of evidence and analysis and more than 100 photographs associated with the suicide....

Finally, the photographs ordered released bear no substantial nexus to the public interest that respondent asserts. They reveal only Foster's death image; they show nothing directly about the Office of Independent Counsel, which did not take the photographs and was not involved in the investigation until months later....

(The second reason is a sort of argument in the alternative.)

In all these examples, the attorneys reach the goal I proposed at the start of this section: to get across in writing what they would say to the judge in person if they had only a minute to do so.

D. You need to regain the offensive in response to your opponent's arguments

It's all the more challenging—and important—to stick to a list of winning reasons when you're filing an opposition or reply brief. Most lawyers spend too much time resurrecting the other side's arguments before shooting them down, thus letting their adversaries dictate the structure.

Yet some lawyers manage to fight that instinct and stay on the offensive.

One way to do so in a reply brief is to acknowledge your adversary's opposition papers explicitly while insisting that your adversary is still missing the boat. Kathleen Sullivan, once the dean of Stanford Law School and now the first female name partner of an Am Law 100 firm, takes that tack below. Standing up to the SEC, she represents an executive (Kenneth Goldman) accused of aiding and abetting his company's alleged violation of a securities regulation. Seeking to dismiss the SEC's case, Sullivan cites the SEC's own papers to pivot back to the reasons she was right in the first place:

Kathleen Sullivan, *SEC v. Siebel Systems*

[T]he Commission's papers do not adequately address any of the fundamental—and fatal—flaws in the Complaint:

- **First**, the information that defendant Kenneth Goldman allegedly disclosed was either previously disclosed to the public by the Company in the days leading up to Mr. Goldman's statement or is not material on its face. The Commission acknowledges that this is not a case about revised and selectively-disclosed earnings guidance.... Rather,

---

> according to the SEC's Opposition Brief, it is about noth-
> ing more than purported verb tenses, body language, and
> vague statements of optimism.
>
> - **Second**, the Commission conveniently ignores the U.S.
>   Supreme Court's admonition that a selective disclosure
>   rule—like Regulation FD—must have "explicit" Congres-
>   sional authorization. . . .
> - **Third**, Regulation FD suffers from significant and fatal
>   constitutional issues. It imposes a content-based restrict-
>   ion on. . . .

Notice how Sullivan, rather than retreating into the defensive posture so common in reply briefs, in the very first bullet
turns the SEC's papers into an implied concession while mocking the government's case as a bunch of split hairs and body
language.

Let's move from a boardroom to a football field as I share a similar three-part list from a reply brief for NFL Enterprises signed by
Herbert Wachtell of Wachtell Lipton. The dispute was over which
channels would broadcast a high-stakes Patriots-Giants game during the run-up to the 2008 Super Bowl: the NFL wanted to show
the game on its fledgling TV network, which was available only to
certain subscribers of certain satellite networks. So important was
the game to fans in the New York and New England media markets
that the Senate Judiciary Committee threatened to reconsider the
NFL's antitrust exemption if didn't agree to broadcast the game on
major networks.

The NFL caved. After it did so, EchoStar, the owner of the Dish
satellite network, was livid that it had lost this chance to lure subscribers, so it announced plans to terminate its agreement with the

NFL Network. The NFL sought an injunction to block EchoStar from scuttling the deal:

Herbert Wachtell, *NFL Enterprises v. EchoStar Satellite*

As shown in NFL Enterprises' opening papers, three grounds *independently* compel the conclusion that NFL Enterprises is likely to prevail, any *one* of which is sufficient:

- Even assuming *arguendo* that the simulcast of the Patriots-Giants game would constitute a breach, **the decision here to** *simulcast* **a single game** of a 48-game, six-year Agreement would not under the terms of the contract or as a matter of law rise to the level warranting termination of the parties' Agreement—in whole or in part.
- EchoStar cannot be permitted to **seize upon a claimed breach to cherry-pick and purport to repudiate solely** *selected pieces* of the parties' Agreement—while claiming a right to continue to enjoy the benefit of those portions of the Agreement that it would prefer to remain in force and pay only a fraction of the fees required by the Agreement.
- And in any event, there was no breach of contract of any kind on the part of NFL Enterprises even in the first instance— for **the decision to accede to strong Congressional and public pressure** to make the Patriots-Giants game available on broadcast TV falls squarely within the provisions of the Agreement's *force majeure* clause.

(Two style suggestions: avoid the legalism "even assuming *arguendo*" that you see in the first bullet—and in so many other filings. "Even if" is shorter and more elegant. And don't go crazy with dashes, a punctuation mark that we'll return to in Part Four. For one thing, a dash shouldn't introduce an independent clause, and for another, using a dash in sentence after sentence, as here, defeats the purpose.)

So let me conclude this tour with my own "short list" of reasons to favor lists:

1. Most disputes are won or lost on no more than four main points.
2. Generating those points—60 seconds' worth of talking—is more rewarding and less intimidating than facing a blank screen.
3. Once you settle on those points, your argument section will start to write itself.

In many motions and briefs, a *Short List* of reasons explaining why you're right, preceded—at least in an opening brief—by a *Brass Tacks* passage, is a good recipe for a persuasive introduction or preliminary statement.

Here's an example from David Boies that follows that two-part formula: first *Brass Tacks*, and then *The Short List*. The case involved Hollywood, distribution rights for a movie called *Push* (a winner at the 2009 Sundance Film Festival), and the question of when an e-mail exchange can become an enforceable contract. Boies represented The (Harvey) Weinstein Company (TWC). I've added commentary in brackets and boldfaced Boies's three-item "short list":

David Boies, *Weinstein v. Smokewood Entertainment*

On January 27, 2009 **[when]**, The Harvey Weinstein Company reached an agreement with Smokewood's agents—John Sloss and Bart Walker of Cinetic Media, Inc.—for TWC to acquire the worldwide licensing and distribution rights to the critically acclaimed motion picture *Push: Based on the Novel by Sapphire* **[who and what]**. As is customary in the entertainment industry **[why]**, the deal was negotiated orally and then confirmed in writing via email, with the parties agreeing to memorialize the agreement in a more detailed writing at a later point **[when and how]**. TWC confirmed its agreement with Sloss and Walker in two emails. Each email clearly stated that the parties had reached final agreement and had "concluded this deal." Walker responded to both emails. In his written and signed responses, Walker did not deny that TWC and Smokewood had a deal for the distribution and licensing rights to *Push*. Indeed, Walker promised to provide TWC with a more detailed written agreement within a few hours **[what and when]**.

After midnight on January 28, 2009 **[when]**, Sloss and Walker decided to breach the agreement with TWC and sell *Push* to TWC's competitor, Lions Gate Entertainment Corp. Thus, at 4:42 a.m. on the morning of July 28, 2009, Walker sent an email to TWC claiming that "there has been no agreement reached with The Weinstein Company respecting Push." This was contrary to the previous email exchanges and the first time Walker told TWC that he did not believe TWC and Smokewood had a deal on *Push* **[what]**. A few days later, Smokewood purportedly entered into an agreement with Lionsgate for the exclusive distribution rights to *Push*.

Smokewood's motion to dismiss does not dispute that Sloss, Walker and Cinetic were acting as its agents or that Sloss and Walker had the authority to enter into an agreement with TWC for the rights to *Push*. Smokewood's only argument is that Sloss's and Walker's agreement with TWC is unenforceable because it was not memorialized in a signed writing as required by section 204 of the Copyright Act **[what]**. This argument fails for three independent reasons **[short list]**.

> *First*, TWC's agreement does in fact satisfy the signed writing requirement of the Copyright Act....
>
> *Second*, even assuming... that the emails do not satisfy section 204 of the Copyright Act, it is black letter law that section 204 does not apply to nonexclusive licenses....
>
> *Finally*, wholly independent of any licensing agreement, TWC has stated a claim for breach of its preliminary agreement with Smokewood, which under New York law required Smokewood to negotiate with TWC in good faith and [to] memorialize the agreement in writing.

With no fuss or angst, and despite the difficult facts and law he faces, Boies has crafted a compelling introduction through just these two techniques.

That said, when you want your introduction to be as richly flavored as possible, consider sprinkling in two more ingredients: *Why Should I Care?* and *Flashpoint.*

3

Why Should I Care?: Give the court a reason to want to find for you

The "slippery slope" is one of the great litigator clichés. But although you should avoid the phrase "slippery slope" itself, you do want to explain, as former D.C. Circuit Chief Judge Patricia Wald puts it, "why it is important [for the court] to come out your way, in part by explaining the consequences if we don't."[1]

We'll call that technique *Why Should I Care?* This technique often forces you to lift your head out of the case law and the record so you can draw instead, in the words of Tenth Circuit Judge Stephen Anderson, "on a parade of horribles or ultimate absurdity, unworkability, or untenability to show the fallacy of an opposing argument when carried to its logical extreme."

So how do you make your opponent's position sound "unworkable," if not downright absurd?

You trigger at least one of these three judicial fears:

1. The fear of misconstruing a doctrine or statute.
2. The fear of creating new duties, rules, or defenses.
3. The fear of reaching an unfair result or causing harm.

On the record, all judges are happy to endorse motives 1 and 2: not wanting to apply the wrong law or to create new law. In that respect, they are endorsing the model put forth by Chief Justice John Roberts during his nomination hearing that "a judge is like an umpire calling balls and strikes."

---

1. Patricia M. Wald, *19 Tips from 19 Years on the Appellate Bench*, 1 J. App. Prac. & Process 7, 12 (1999).

But many judges admit off the record to motive 3: trying to reach a fair result or simply "to do the right thing." In practice, says Seventh Circuit Judge Richard Posner, judges are not umpires. According to Posner's book *How Judges Think*, both trial judges and appellate judges are essentially "pragmatists" who care about the effects their decisions may have: "Judges are curious about social reality.... [T]hey want the lawyers to help them dig below the semantic surface."[2]

Experienced advocates appear to sense this intuitively. In my work with law firms and agencies, I have noticed that younger attorneys tend to draft strictly legalistic introductions; senior partners and managers who edit these drafts often add a "common sense" reason for victory. "Judges are concerned about both the institutional and the real-world consequences of the rules they adopt," note appellate superstars Andy Frey and Roy Englert. "[E]ven if favorable precedent is available and you intend to rely heavily on it, write the argument in a way that gives the judges confidence that they *should* follow that precedent."[3]

Let's look at examples of how you can play to each of the three fears, thus enriching your introduction with the *Why Should I Care?* technique.

A. The fear of misconstruing a doctrine or statute

You can always invoke the judge's primal fear: the fear of getting the law wrong.

Playing the *stare decisis* card never hurts, even at the Supreme Court where it matters least of all. In a major case involving racial bias in jury selection, for example, Carter Phillips, one of the most

---

2. RICHARD POSNER, HOW JUDGES THINK 283 (Harv. Univ. Press 2008).

3. Andrew Frey & Roy Englert, Jr., How to Write a Good Appellate Brief, *available at* http://www.appellate.net/articles/gdaplbrf799.asp.

renowned appellate advocates, filed an amicus brief for various former judges and prosecutors, including Attorney General Eric Holder and Beth Wilkinson, who once prosecuted Oklahoma City bomber Timothy McVeigh. Here Phillips cuts to the chase about what will happen if the Supreme Court affirms a lower court decision finding no bias:

Carter Phillips, *Miller-El v. Dretke*

Amici believe that **anything less than a reversal** of the Fifth Circuit's decision would send a highly visible, **detrimental signal that this Court has retreated from** its clear rulings in *Batson* and [earlier in this same proceeding].

To emphasize how undoing a case would do harm, you might also want to remind the court why a case exists in the first place, as Stephen Shapiro does here in a securities case about liability for alleged fraudulent accounting. Note that Shapiro also stresses the real-world consequences of "gutting" that seminal case:

Stephen Shapiro, *Stoneridge Investment Partners v. Scientific Atlantica*

Plaintiff contends that this suit should proceed because [Charter Communications and Scientific Atlantica] engaged in deceptive conduct as part of a "scheme to defraud" [by charging inflated prices for T.V. boxes and then returning the difference as advertising fees]. That expansive theory of liability would **gut *Central Bank*** [*of Denver v. First International Bank of Denver*], **turning product manufacturers who do**

> business with a customer into "primary violators" poten-
> tially liable for unlimited market losses suffered by the cus-
> tomer's investors. **The result here would be** that Motorola
> and Scientific-Atlanta shareholders would have to compen-
> sate Charter shareholders *for a fraud committed by Charter's*
> *own management.*

President Barack Obama once used a similar approach in a brief about the Voting Rights Act, a statute at the heart of his academic focus at the University of Chicago Law School. Along with two other lawyers in a prominent Chicago civil-rights firm, Obama suggests that the Supreme Court needs to correct a misreading of both the statute and the cases construing it:

Barack Obama, *Tyus v. Bosley*

The lower court's holding fundamentally misreads this Court's voting rights jurisprudence, as well as that of other circuits. Moreover, **this holding turns the Voting Rights Act on its head** by immunizing *intentional* racial discrimination as long as the "bottom line" of a single-member district redistricting plan is proportionality.

(As we'll discuss in Part Four, sentences like the second one here often read better as "This holding also turns....")

B. The fear of creating new duties, rules, or defenses

Especially in trial filings, you can also appeal to judges' reluctance to create new law, new claims, or new defenses. For one thing, trial judges don't want to get reversed. More selflessly, they don't want to give plaintiffs more ways to sue—or give defendants more ways to prolong litigation.

Jamie Gorelick, whose career spans from the Clinton White House to BP's public relations, appeals to such motives in her reply brief seeking to dismiss claims against Duke University. Duke got embroiled in this litigation after Duke Lacrosse players were accused of assaulting an exotic dancer and then the state attorney general declared them actually innocent of all charges. In a case in which sympathies lie with the wrongfully accused players and not with the university, she warns against creating new duties for educational institutions that they cannot possibly sustain:

Jamie Gorelick, *Carrington v. Duke University*

The **premise of all these claims is that the University and its administrators had a legal obligation to protect Plaintiffs** from the consequences of a police investigation—by quelling media coverage of the case, preventing campus protests, and even interceding to stop the investigation. **That premise is invalid,** and the Complaint should be dismissed.

Gorelick's pragmatic point strikes a chord: as much as finding for the Duke students would appear to vindicate their rights, imposing new duties on university administrators would encourage them to spend time at the police station rather than interacting with their students. In the end, then, finding for the student-plaintiffs would hurt future students—the very people you think you'd be helping.

For our final example, let's travel to England, where J. K. Rowling lives, or perhaps to Godric's Hollow, where Harry Potter once lived. A former American librarian had the temerity to publish a Harry Potter reference guide. Rowling didn't care for that one bit—and sued. Intellectual-property guru Larry Lessig, whom *National Law Journal* has deemed "one of the lawyers who defined the [2000-2010] decade," came to the librarian's rescue, claiming, among other things, that Rowling is asserting a right that doesn't exist—and shouldn't:

Larry Lessig, *Warner Bros. Entertainment v. RDR Books*

J. K. Rowling, author of the Harry Potter books, asserts that this reference guide infringes both her copyright in the seven Potter novels and her right to publish, at some unidentified point in the future, a reference guide of her own. In support of her position she appears to claim a monopoly on the right to publish literary reference guides, and other non-academic research, relating to her own fiction.

This is a right no court has ever recognized. It has little to recommend it. If accepted, it would **dramatically extend** the reach of copyright protection, and **eliminate an entire genre** of literary supplements: third party reference guides to fiction, which for centuries have helped readers better access, understand and enjoy literary works. By extension, it would **threaten not just reference guides, but encyclopedias**, glossaries, indexes, and other tools that provide useful information about copyrighted works.

C. The fear of reaching an unfair result or causing harm

Now let's turn to the pragmatic concerns that some judges say they ignore. As retired Wisconsin Court of Appeals Chief Judge William Eich once said, judges need advocates "to show them why the result you seek is the soundest of available alternatives, and the one that will bring about a just result for the parties, the public, and the development of the law."[4] In other words, judges want to do the right thing, whether that means treating litigants fairly or creating good incentives—not that all judges will agree on what that "right thing" is.

As an advocate, you shouldn't pat yourself on the back for playing the fairness card when you represent a coal miner burned in a mine blast. Congratulate yourself instead if you can make a judge think "Unfair!" even though your client is an unsympathetic conglomerate—or worse.

Take the Conrad Black case. The fabulously wealthy publisher of such newspapers as *The Daily Telegraph* and the *Chicago Sun-Times*, Black ran into trouble with the SEC and was later convicted of fraud and sentenced to federal prison, though his convictions for two of the counts were eventually overturned.

In the SEC proceedings, Black was represented by Greg Craig, who turns a dispute over a document in the SEC's custody into a question of fundamental fairness—for Black:

Greg Craig, *United States v. Conrad Black*

The Government should not be allowed to cherry-pick one document, withhold it from Mr. Black without any description, and then subject him to intrusive discovery requests from the SEC. Otherwise, he will be forced to make crucial decisions—such as whether to invoke his Fifth Amendment privilege—with **his eyes closed and his hands tied**. This would be both unfair and unconstitutional.

---

4. William Eich, *Writing the Persuasive Brief*, 76 WIS. LAW. 20, 57 (Feb. 2003).

Sometimes it's enough of a challenge to suggest that defeat on the motion would be unfair for your client. But other times, you can go further, suggesting that defeat for your client would be bad for others as well.

In the following example, Bernie Nussbaum represents Judith Kaye and other New York state judges in a suit against the New York State Assembly. The cause—low judicial pay—does not exactly tug at the heartstrings. But Nussbaum manages to turn the issue into something that could harm the entire New York citizenry:

Bernie Nussbaum, *Judith Kaye v. Sheldon Silver*

New York's judges have lost more than a quarter of their salaries to inflation in the last decade, leaving them among the worst-paid judges in the Nation—49th out of the 50 states, to be exact. **Judicial morale is rapidly diminishing, making it difficult to implement initiatives to address growing caseloads** and other problems faced by the judicial system.

Here's yet another way to play to judges' pragmatic concerns: suggest that defeat for your client would cause "grave harm" for the world at large. In this excerpt, Stephen Shapiro is seeking reversal of a sanctions order issued against a bank accused of supporting terrorism—not the most heartwarming of clients. Shapiro catapults over this obstacle with great ease, focusing on the less-than-obvious harm to global order that might arise if the bank doesn't get its way:

Stephen M. Shapiro, *Linde v. Arab Bank, PLC*

Delaying appellate review also would threaten the interests of the jurisdictions whose laws the district court disregarded. As the Palestinian Monetary Authority explained below, a forced

> breach of its privacy laws would lead to the "flight of individual customers from the Palestinian banking system, with the residual impact on the ability of the PMA to regulate that system, **including the identification and interdiction of unauthorized or illegal monetary transactions**." The Kingdom of Jordan told this Court that, unless the Sanctions Order is reversed, the impact on the Bank "could result in **political instability and grave harm to the Jordanian and surrounding regional economies**."

The plight of large banks may not tug at the heartstrings, but no judge is eager to stoke Middle East instability.

Closer to home, in the next example the same lawyer is defending Mayo Collaborative Services against a patent infringement suit brought by Prometheus Laboratories. This important case involved the question of whether two patents were patent-eligible if they mainly relied on "laws of nature" to determine the proper dosage of a drug. Here, too, Shapiro taunts the justices a bit, suggesting that in picking a winning party, they'll also be advancing—or stalling—scientific progress itself:

> ### Stephen M. Shapiro, *Mayo Collaborative Services v. Prometheus Laboratories, Inc.*
>
> The preemptive impact of Prometheus's claims is particularly severe because they are centered on human thought that involves, in any medical context, metabolite ranges that Prometheus observed in patients who took gastrointestinal drugs. Thus, [Mayo Clinic] dermatologist Dr. el-Azhary [whose patients were used in the study] cannot stop thinking about Prometheus's ranges now that she knows of them,

> even if her goal in reviewing a patient's test results is to find entirely different numbers relating only to dermatology. As a result, Prometheus has **obtained a monopoly** in a very **broad field of medical practice**. The preemptive scope of the Prometheus claims is unprecedented. It constitutes an **embargo on research and analysis essential to the development of knowledge and patient care**.

In these few lines, a patent infringement action oozes into a story about a rapacious company threatening our well-being.

Yet perhaps your case is just too far removed from world peace or from the care and feeding of the sick. Don't fret. There's usually still a way to highlight the broader stakes of your case. For instance, Kathleen Sullivan represents a TV network that broadcast the F-word and still manages to raise the specter of a grave threat that would occur if broadcasters could be fined for "fleeting expletives" that Americans would be stuck with lousy television programs.

> **Kathleen Sullivan, *FCC v. Fox***
>
> For many broadcasters, the chilling effect is profound and discourages live programming altogether, with **attendant loss to valuable and vibrant programming** that has long been part of American culture.

In this respect, Sullivan's approach is like Bernie Nussbaum's. To problems of less-than-obvious urgency (Big Brother broadcasters and gloomy state judges), they add problems that are more universal—and frightening: fewer television options and diminished access to the courts.

The sky would also fall, suggested former Solicitor General Ted Olson in an amicus brief, if the Supreme Court upheld the Ninth Circuit's copyright decision in Grokster, the file-sharing case—unless, that is, you want to live in a world with "absurd results," "eviscerated" property rights, "frustrated" creators, "stifled" innovation, and "harmed" artists, not to mention a "thwarted" Copyright Act. Not even the most jaded Justice could ask *Why Should I Care?* after the litany that follows:

Ted Olson, *MGM v. Grokster*

The Ninth Circuit's decision **eviscerates** intellectual property rights. It **frustrates** those who have invested substantial resources in creating an original work, only to see the fruits of their labors snatched away. It **rewards** those, like Respondents, who unjustly profit by designing tools to enable the theft of private property. And it **stifles** innovation by **depriving** citizens of the incentive to create works of art or music or literature that can be enjoyed by people ages hence.

If left uncorrected, the decision below—in the short term—will **deny** creators and artists the financial benefits that are rightfully theirs. But in the long term, the **costs will fall** on society as a whole in the form of songs and movies that are *not* created, precisely because the law (as the Ninth Circuit sees it) will not protect and reward their investments of time and money. The decision below **thwarts** the "basic purpose" and "ultimate aim" of the Copyright Act: to "secure a fair return for an author's creative labor" and "by this incentive, to stimulate artistic creativity for the general public good."

Few cases have such broad implications, of course, but you can try striking the "defeat for me would be bad for them" chord while remaining in the confines of your lawsuit. In Paul Smith's response to the government in a discovery dispute, for example, he suggests that requiring a Native American farmer to track down and then turn over scads of documents would discourage other parties from participating in litigation brought against the United States alleging that thousands Native American ranchers and farmers were deprived of government farm loans:

Paul Smith, *Keepseagle v. Vilsack*

Defendant [USDA] has issued a subpoena to class member and potential witness William Whiting seeking materials, including highly sensitive financial records and tax returns, that have no bearing on Mr. Whiting's potential testimony and are plainly improper at this stage of the litigation.... [I]f Defendant, an agent of the United States government, can compel citizens to disclose their most sensitive financial information as the price to pay to enter the courtroom and testify as witnesses in this case, **defendants will chill participation in this important lawsuit**.

What unifies all these *Why Should I Care?* examples is that the lawyers have expanded beyond the case law and the record, giving the judge a pragmatic reason to want to rule for them—or at least to feel bad about ruling for their opponent. With a bit of creativity and thought, you can rise to that challenge yourself.

4

Flashpoint: Draw a line in the sand

Many legal disputes boil down to a clash between two competing views. By contrasting those two views in your introduction, you can preempt your opponent's attempts to make the case into something it's not.

The *Flashpoint* technique challenges you to draw a line in the sand in that very way.

Take this example from a Ruth Bader Ginsburg amicus brief in *Regents of the University of California v. Bakke*, the pivotal affirmative-action case from the 1970s. The parallel contrast between "compels" and "permits" says it all:

> **Ruth Bader Ginsburg, *Regents of the University of California v. Bakke***
>
> The issue in this case **is not whether** the Constitution **compels** the University to adopt a special admission program for minorities, **but only whether** the Constitution **permits** the University to pursue that course.

The next example is from a much more recent amicus brief penned by Walter Dellinger. The dispute is about the Solomon Amendment, a statute that allows the government to withhold federal funding from law schools that refuse to allow military recruitment, an issue that preoccupied Justice Kagan when she was dean of Harvard Law School and that provided some of the few interesting moments during her confirmation hearing:

Walter Dellinger, *Rumsfeld v. FAIR*

[T]his case is not—and never has been—about whether law schools may "discriminate" against the military or whether they must provide "equal access" to military recruiters. **Instead, the question is** whether the Solomon Amendment confers upon military recruiters the unprecedented entitlement to disregard neutral and generally applicable recruiting rules whenever a school's failure to make a special exception might incidentally hinder or preclude military recruiting. The answer is "no."

In Dellinger's version of the case, the military recruiters, not the law schools, are the ones looking to deviate from "the rules."

Drawing a line in the sand was also important in the following example from Chief Justice Roberts. The case turns on an emotional issue: sex-offender registration. The ACLU and others argued that such registration schemes amounted to an unconstitutional ex post facto punishment.

In the Alaska registration regime, after the sex offenders were released from prison, their names and photos were posted online. Death threats and other attacks often ensued. In these two sentences, Roberts transforms a case about whether the sex offenders were punished after serving the time into a case about whether the

Alaska Legislature *intended* for them to be punished when it passed the statute in the first place:

John Roberts, *Smith v. Doe*

[Alaska's Megan's Law] is a regulatory law **intended to help protect** the public from future harm by collecting truthful information and making it available to those who choose to access it. It is **not a penal law intended to punish** people for past acts.

This technique works just as well in trial settings.

In the variation that follows, patent-litigation guru Morgan Chu ensures that TiVo's version of a dispute over DVRs can be replayed long after the fact:

Morgan Chu, *TiVo v. EchoStar*

EchoStar is correct that this case is being closely watched—but not for the reason it suggests. The case is **not about restricting** the right to design around a patent. **Rather, it tests whether court orders** meant to enforce a patentee's right to exclude impose any real restraint on a large, aggressive, deep-pocketed infringer.

And here, in a summary judgment reply brief, SEC Chair and former Manhattan U.S. Attorney and law-firm partner Mary Jo White invokes a popular defense theme, claiming that Donald Trump sued her book-author client for revenge, not money, after the author allegedly downplayed The Donald's net worth:

Mary Jo White, *Trump v. O'Brien*

This lawsuit **never has been about recovering damages** that Trump allegedly sustained as a result of the Book, **but instead is about Trump attempting to exact revenge** against O'Brien for writing what Trump perceived as a negative book about him and to deter other journalists from doing the same.

(White appears to subscribe to the myth that you can't split a verb phrase, as if you'd have to say "I not yet have begun to fight" rather than "I have not yet begun to fight." "Never" should go right after "has" and before "been": "This lawsuit has never been about recovering damages." The second bolded phrase also includes a grammar mistake called a fused participle: it should be "Trump's attempting," not "Trump attempting." Or better yet, just write "Trump's efforts.")

Similarly, in a Ninth Circuit brief for Microsoft, Nancy Abell, often called the nation's top defense-side employment lawyer, draws a line between isolated lies and what she claims is a more sinister agenda on the plaintiff's part. Here, Microsoft draws out this distinction so it spills into a broader attack on the plaintiff's credibility:

Nancy Abell, *Jackson v. Microsoft*

To sum up: Jackson's misconduct went to the heart of his case. It involved **far more than simply lying** to Microsoft, or lying to the court about a single and wholly peripheral matter. Jackson has proven that, in order to advance his claims, he is

willing to use stolen documents, he is **willing to pay** for stolen data, he is **willing to inveigle** other Microsoft employees into wrongdoing. He has proven that he is **willing to raid** his adversary's attorney-client communications about his case to advance his claims. And he has proven—on multiple occasions—that, if he thinks it will advance his cause, he is **willing to take the stand in a federal court and commit perjury.**

And here, Supreme Court advocate Roy Englert expands on a quotation from the 9/11 Commission to draw a line in the sand between theory and proof when it comes to Saudi Arabia's role in funding terrorist groups:

Roy Englert, *Federal Insurance Company v. Kingdom of Saudi Arabia*

The 9/11 Commission found that Saudi Arabia did not provide financial or material assistance to the September 11 terrorists or their al Qaeda organization: "Saudi Arabia has long been considered the primary source of al Qaeda funding, but we have found no evidence that the Saudi government as an institution or senior Saudi officials individually funded the organization." In keeping with their practice throughout this litigation, **petitioners quote only the first portion of this sentence, as if that were the finding of the 9/11 Commission, while omitting the Commission's actual finding that there was no evidence implicating respondents in the funding of al Qaeda.**

Pulling the techniques together: a preliminary statement dissected

Let's end with a full preliminary statement that incorporates all four techniques. It's from Ted Wells, Scooter Libby's lawyer and the *National Law Journal* Lawyer of the Year in 2006. The example comes from a perfectly structured motion that we will return to later.

The legal issue is common, even mundane. Representing Citigroup, Wells wants to transfer a lawsuit over an auction from New York to England, where many of the events took place. As with the *Push* movie example, I have added commentary in brackets and have highlighted in bold where Wells uses the techniques discussed earlier:

Ted Wells, *Terra Firma v. Citigroup*

This case **belongs in the courts of England**. Plaintiffs are Terra Firma Investments (GP) 2 Limited and Terra Firma Investments (GP) 3 Limited, two **Channel Island investment funds** managed by an English company, with offices in London. Terra Firma asserts that **it was misled** into bidding in an auction conducted in London, under English takeover rules, to purchase the English-listed company EMI Group plc by **London-based bankers** of Citi, which acted both as EMI's financial advisor and as lender to Terra Firma in providing financing for its successful bid. Consistent with the English locus of these transactions, Terra Firma **pledged—in a series of agreements with or for the benefit of Citi—that the courts of England would be the appropriate** and exclusive forum for the resolution of any disputes relating to information that Terra Firma relied upon in bidding for EMI as well as any claim connected to the financing of its bid. **And yet, in contravention of both the terms of the mandatory forum selection clauses** and the principles underlying the doctrine of *forum non conveniens*, Terra Firma filed suit in New York instead of the mandatory and more convenient English forum [*Brass Tacks*: **who, what, when, where, why, how**]. This case should be dismissed on either of two independent grounds [*The Short List*].

First, a series of agreements specifying that the claims asserted by Terra Firma be resolved in the courts of England requires dismissal of this Complaint. Upon entering the bidding process for EMI, Terra Firma executed an agreement relating to the conditions under which information would be supplied to Terra Firma by EMI and its advisors, including Citi....

Second, New York is an inconvenient forum. This case, as pleaded, indisputably arises out of acts that overwhelmingly took place in London....

Although Terra Firma, a stranger to this forum, chose to bring its case in this Court rather than in England, its choice is entitled to little or no weight when the motivation appears to be forum shopping [*Flashpoint*: **plaintiffs are not always entitled to their choice of forum**]. There is no reason to tax the resources of this Court [*Why Should I Care?*] in adjudicating a complex dispute about an English transaction that can and should be resolved by an English court.

With your own mix of these four thematic ingredients in place, let's turn now to the fact section, the argument, and everything else that will come your way.

PART TWO

THE TALE

Part Two will share seven techniques for drafting facts:

Part Two: The Tale

Imagine you're a juror about to hear an opening statement. The plaintiff's lawyer stands up and says the following:

> There are seven important issues in this case. The first issue is whether the stock issued in June 1973 by Mr. Jones was properly registered.

Now imagine a different scenario. This time, the lawyer starts like this:

> The story begins three years ago today. Four men were sitting around a table. One of them is here. One of them is there. The other two wouldn't come to testify. They were discussing a new share of stock. The ownership of the company was at stake.

These dueling examples are courtesy of Fred Bartlit, one of the most in-demand business trial lawyers in the nation and one of the fourteen lawyers profiled in Don Vinson's *America's Top Trial Lawyers: Who They Are and Why They Win.* You'll remember that we saw a prime example of Bartlit's well-paced introductions in Part One.

In his conversations with Vinson, Bartlit relays the preceding two examples as an anecdote about anecdotes. How do you tell an effective story even when your material is dry or complex? "You don't tell [the jurors] what to decide," Bartlit says. "[A]s they hear the story, conclusions emerge in their minds."[1]

Perhaps you think that such a story is easier to pull off when you're speaking before twelve jurors. Not necessarily. Here is how the same lawyer, Fred Bartlit, began a motion he filed in a securities class action. In his writing, you'll hear echoes of his "good" opening statement:

Fred Bartlit, *Stumpf v. Garvey*

In July 2000, during the telecommunications boom, Tyco sold shares to the public in an Initial Public Offering of TyCom, a

---

1. Donald E. Vinson, America's Top Trial Lawyers: Who They Are and Why They Win 262 (Prentice Hall 1994).

telecommunications subsidiary of Tyco engaged in the under-sea cable business. After the TyCom IPO, the telecommunications market sector collapsed. TyCom share prices also dropped, driven by the general market decline.

You can see how Bartlit uses a smooth narrative line to get his point across right away: the Tyco subsidiary is just one of many victims of the telecommunications crash.

Let's dissect this sort of clean, forward-moving, persuasive narrative, breaking it down into seven techniques.

5

Panoramic Shot: Set the stage and sound your theme

Here is a typical opening paragraph in a fact section; I've changed only the dates, names, and details. Imagine you're a judge trying to understand what happened to the injured plaintiff:

> On February 9, 2009, officers of the New York City Police Department caused physical damage to property owned by Plaintiff in the City of New York, New York, during the execution of a search warrant at the property. (Am. Cplt. ¶ 1). Plaintiff made a property damage claim against the City of New York. The New York City Assistant Corporation Counsel ordered Plaintiff to appear in the City of New York for an oral examination in connection with this claim. (Am. Cplt. ¶ 2). Because Plaintiff suffers from a hearing disability, he requested that this examination be by written interrogatories, but this request was denied by the Assistant Corporation Counsel. (Am. Cplt. ¶¶ 3, 4).

Too much, too fast, too soon. As a newspaper editor might put it, the attorneys have buried the lede.

For a better model, imagine a good movie. Sure, some films start with a character in mid-conversation. But more often than not, the camera pans over a grassy meadow or a crowded urban bar. Such images cue you in on what kind of story you're about to hear and arouse your curiosity about what will happen next.

In the brief-writing world, you probably can't start your fact sections with a scene-setting shot that would win you an Oscar. But you can still create a similar bird's-eye-view effect.

Take this opening sentence from the fact section of a Ted Wells motion to dismiss, the same motion that gave us the preliminary statement at the end of Part One. Before delving into the details, Wells lets the court know that it's dealing with a commercial dispute between sophisticated parties, one of which apparently soured on a once-promising deal:

Ted Wells, *Terra Firma v. Citigroup*

This **matter arises out of** Terra Firma's purchase of EMI in May 2007.

That opening sentence raises as many questions as it answers, but that's the whole point: to engage. In some ways, then, a *Panoramic Shot* opener in a fact section is like a good *Brass Tacks* passage in an introduction: both provide the context that readers so crave.

You'll note that Wells's opener has a neutral feel—perhaps he believes that in a complex commercial dispute, too much huffing-and-puffing up front may ring false.

But what if you wanted to climb the rhetorical ladder a rung or two? You wouldn't expect a plaintiffs' lawyer like Joe Jamail, the wiz behind the $10.5 billion verdict that Pennzoil scored against Texaco, to start with a flat opening panorama. Indeed, in a case alleging large-scale fraud on Sunbeam's part, Jamail doesn't hide the ball when he starts his fact section:

Joe Jamail, *In re Sunbeam Securities Litigation*

This **case involves the material misstatement** of Sunbeam Corporation's financial condition during the years 1996–1998.

Nor does "The King of Torts" appear to heed the conventional wisdom that you should strip your fact section of any legal conclusions. And yet I'll give him a pass here, and not just because he's such a flamboyant lawyer that he once called a witness "Fat Boy" during a deposition (see YouTube). After all, wouldn't it seem a little phony to pretend in a securities fraud lawsuit that you didn't think the company had engaged in any fraud?

All the same, you can often find a happy medium between a flat opening line and an obviously slanted one. Why not start with a fact or two that sounds neutral but that just so happens to sound your legal theme? You may remember Fred Bartlit doing that in the Tyco example, connecting the Tyco subsidiary's falling stock price to events outside its control without shoving that link down your throat.

Here's another example. After the Supreme Court allowed the University of Michigan Law School to continue considering race in admissions, Michigan voters passed a referendum measure known as Proposal 2 to stop the practice. Representing a coalition trying to get the referendum measure repealed, Larry Tribe moved for summary judgment to have it declared unconstitutional. By prohibiting consideration based on race, Tribe suggested, the referendum measure made an "impermissible distinction based on race."

So how did Tribe start his fact section? With the referendum process? With its language? With the Supreme Court case that led to it? With the coalition trying to get it repealed? No, not at all:

> **Larry Tribe, *Coalition to Defend Affirmative Action v. Granholm***
>
> **Michigan's public universities have long enjoyed autonomy** over their admissions policies and procedures.

Tribe suggests that the real issue here is academic freedom, not the referendum itself or the rights of the citizens who worked to get it passed.

In starting your own fact sections, then, you want more "it was the best of times, it was the worst of times" and less "it was a dark and stormy night." So how would you have started your fact section if you were recounting the following tale? Alabama doctor Ira Gore bought a new BMW. After discovering that his car had been slightly damaged and then repainted before he bought it, Dr. Gore sued BMW, which had a policy of not disclosing such repairs unless their cost exceeded 3 percent of the new car's value. Dr. Gore won $4,000 for the diminution in value—and $4 million in punitive damages, later cut to $2 million. The case went all the way to the Supreme Court on the question of whether such a high ratio between compensatory damages and punitive damages violated the Due Process Clause. The Court found that it did, in one of the biggest victories ever for the tort-reform set.

Like Tribe in the Michigan referendum case, the lawyers for the winning BMW side had many choices for starting their fact section: the BMW policy, how states besides Alabama regulated similar disclosures, what happened at trial, or how much the punitive damages dwarfed the compensatory ones.

They began with something else entirely:

Andy Frey, *BMW v. Gore*

In their journey from the assembly line to the dealer's showroom, automobiles occasionally experience minor damage requiring repair or refinishing.

In this single sentence, Andy Frey and his crack appellate colleagues at Mayer Brown imbued the entire brief with a winning message. Although the sentence is not in the passive voice, it has a passive feel. BMW—the defendant and their client—is conspicuously absent. When cars cross the Atlantic or travel interstate, Frey suggests, "stuff happens," as Donald Rumsfeld once said about looters in Iraq.

And yet "stuff happens" wasn't the real issue. The Frey opener suggests that Dr. Gore sued because he couldn't stomach a few nicks on his beloved BMW. But Dr. Gore was suing for another reason: because the BMW dealer that sold him the car had a policy of not disclosing the damage. Of course, that's precisely why Frey's first sentence is so clever: it suggests that BMW was more of a hapless victim than an unscrupulous predator.

Here's another example of a great *Panoramic Shot*, this time from a case pitting the rights of the homeless against New York City's quest for order:

Carter Phillips, *Fifth Avenue Presbyterian Church* v. *City of New York*

As part of its **Christian mission** to **care for the poor**, the Church has for many years **ministered** to the homeless by providing limited **sanctuary**. This case arises from the City's **effort to disrupt this religious practice**.

It sounds as though New York City bureaucrats meddled in the church's good works, right?

As usual, things are not so simple. The Rudy Giuliani administration wasn't trying to "disrupt a religious practice." Instead, citing public nuisance laws and other reasons, it was trying to move homeless people from church property into city-provided shelters. When the homeless people and the church didn't comply, the city threatened arrest.

But appellate superstar Carter Phillips didn't start with any of that. Instead, every word of his opening—"Christian mission," "care for the poor," "ministered," "sanctuary," "disrupt this religious practice"—draws your sympathies to the church, and turns this appeal into a case of religious freedom.

Of course, even if you strip your fact section of every hint of law, you can still grab the court's attention through a vigorous personal style. In this twist from Joshua Rosenkranz, who has a gift for witty writing, the *Panoramic Shot* beginning his fact section stages a familiar narrative that likens the founder of Facebook to a struggling entrepreneur:

Joshua Rosenkranz, *Facebook, Inc. v. ConnectU, Inc.*

The plotline of this controversy is **all too familiar**: **Wunderkind entrepreneur conceives** of a transformative business and propels it to a meteoric success, but **failed rivals insist** they thought up the idea first and demand all the profits.

How could you not sympathize with young Mr. Zuckerberg?

Word choice makes all the difference here. In just one sentence, Zuckerberg comes across as a modern-day Benjamin Franklin, while his rivals at ConnectU—"failed rivals" at that—sound like jealous onlookers.

In all these examples, the attorneys have offered a *Panoramic Shot* of their case rather than bombarding the judge with isolated facts, numbers, and details. Once you've done the same, you'll be poised to weave in the rest of your client's story.

6

Show, Not Tell: Let choice details speak for themselves

Read this version of a story about Ivan Boesky, the 1980s insider trading bad boy and the model for the Gordon Gekko character in the movie *Wall Street*:

John Mulheren says that Boesky was always a conspicuous consumer. At his first meeting with Boesky, a dinner at an expensive restaurant in Manhattan, the waiter recited the day's eight specials, and Boesky ordered them all. The waiter wheeled out a table with the dishes on them, Boesky examined each of them, then sent back all but one. Mulheren says he's glad he didn't have to pick up the bill.[1]

Now read another version of the same encounter:

When the Café des Artistes waiter came to take their order, Boesky said he hadn't decided and that the others should make their selections. Then Boesky ordered: "I'll have every entrée." The waiter's pen stopped in midair. "Bring me each one of those entrees...."

1. James B. Stewart, Follow the Story: How to Write Successful Nonfiction 235 (Simon & Schuster 1998).

> When the food arrived, the waiter wheeled a table next to them. On it were the eight featured dishes of the day. Boesky looked over them carefully, circled the table, took one bite of each. He selected one, and sent the rest back.[2]

The second version was penned by James Stewart, a Pulitzer Prize winner and the author of *Den of Thieves*, *Blood Sport*, and other best-sellers. Years after the book with this anecdote appeared, Stewart has said, people still remembered it—not just because Boesky's behavior was so odd, but because his imperiousness and extravagance at the restaurant symbolized an entire decade.

Interestingly enough, Stewart wrote the first version as well and offers it as a teaching tool: "This, unfortunately, is how anecdote is often used in nonfiction writing."[3] So what lesson are we supposed to learn? In the first version, the writer *tells* you that Boesky was a "conspicuous consumer." In the second version, Stewart uses choice details to *show* you what happened at the meal; you draw the same conclusion yourself but in your own meaningful way.

Unfortunately, most litigators subscribe to the "tell 'em he was a conspicuous consumer" school of writing. Fact sections are often riddled with such conclusions as "Plaintiff has engaged in dilatory tactics" and "Defendant has at all times acted with the utmost candor" and "Defendant had a terrible childhood."

Instead, the facts in a brief should read like narrative nonfiction, a bit like something you'd read in *The Atlantic* or *The New Yorker*.

Or perhaps in *A River Runs Through It*. In the following passage, you'll see one of the best bits of fact writing I've seen. Chief Justice Roberts faced a tough task in defending Alaska, which had approved a less-stringent technology for controlling emissions near a mine than

2. *Id.* at 233.

3. *Id.* at 235.

the federal EPA would have liked. Here is Roberts explaining how the
Red Dog Mine got its name:

John Roberts, *Alaska v. EPA*

For generations, Inupiat Eskimos hunting and fishing in the
DeLong Mountains in Northwest Alaska had been aware of
orange- and red-stained creekbeds in which fish could not survive. In the 1960s, a bush pilot and part-time prospector by
the name of Bob Baker noticed **striking discolorations** in the
hills and creekbeds of a wide valley in the western DeLongs.
Unable to land his plane on the rocky tundra to investigate,
Baker alerted the U.S. Geological Survey. Exploration of the
area eventually led to the **discovery of** a wealth of zinc and
lead deposits. Although Baker died before the significance
of his observations became known, **his faithful traveling
companion—an Irish Setter who often flew shotgun**—was
immortalized by a geologist who dubbed the creek Baker had
spotted "Red Dog" Creek.

Why would Roberts mention an Irish Setter? What does a
shotgun-flying dog have to do with the Clean Air Act or with administrative law? Is the passage just a flourish of elegant writing that
wastes everyone's time?

Not at all. In fact, some of the Justices reportedly told their clerks
that Roberts's brief was the best they'd read in decades.

And perhaps the passage isn't as gratuitous as people think. After
all, Roberts is litigating a classic federalism fight between the states
and the federal government. Who knows more about what a mine
means to nearby residents than the local and state officials close to
the ground?

You'll find the same technique elsewhere when Roberts "shows" you why the Red Dog Mine plays a vital economic role in the community without "telling" you what to think:

> **Operating 365 days a year, 24 hours a day,** the Red Dog Mine is the largest private employer in the Northwest Arctic Borough, an area roughly the size of the State of Indiana with a population of about 7,000. The vast majority of the area's residents are Inupiat Eskimos whose **ancestors have inhabited the** region for thousands of years. The region offers only **limited year-round employment opportunities,** particularly in the private sector; in the two years preceding Alaska's permit decision, the borough's unemployment rate was the highest in the State.... Prior to the mine's opening, the average wage in the borough was well below the state average; **a year after** its opening, **the borough's average exceeded** that of the State.

Humanizing a mine is no mean feat. But then again, humanizing saints wouldn't get Ruth Bader Ginsburg to call you the "best" advocate to come before the Supreme Court, as she did when Roberts was nominated to be Chief.

Let me share another example of how to use details to "show" why your client is in the right. In this example, the NAACP accused a Tennessee city council of engaging in environmental racism by poisoning landfills that contaminated the Holt family's water supply and that afflicted several family members with cancer. After the Holt family was poisoned by the landfill, they sued the entity that deposited the industrial waste. According to the Holts' lawyers at the NAACP, that company shifted around its assets to avoid paying the judgment, eventually filing for Chapter 11.

Although John Payton, then the NAACP's legal director, was writing about obscure tenets of bankruptcy law here, he included a series of details that arouse sympathy for this family's plight. The passage feels like something you might read in an epic novel:

> **John Payton and the NAACP, *In re Alper Holdings USA***
>
> The Holt Plaintiffs are twelve family members who belong to **three generations** of an African-American family that have owned the same property on **Eno Road** in Dickson County, Tennessee, for **over one hundred years, going back to the late nineteenth century**.

Perhaps you're feeling cynical, thinking that it's not so hard to humanize a family like the Holts. So let's turn to someone who's less angelic: Robert Stevens. Next to Michael Vick, Mr. Stevens might be the most famous person ever to tangle with the law over dogs. For distributing videos of pit bulls fighting, Stevens was convicted and sent to prison under an animal-cruelty statute designed to squelch "crushing," a thankfully rare fetish that makes men excited to watch videos of women torturing small animals with their bare feet or high heels.

Stevens's case went to the Supreme Court, and the result—in his favor—was one of the most important First Amendment decisions in years.

On the government's side, Justice Elena Kagan, then the solicitor general, stressed how Stevens's videos contained "scenes of savage and bloody dog fights, as well as gruesome footage of pit bulls viciously attacking other animals."

If you're starting to wish that those dogs had attacked Mr. Stevens instead, wait until you read the winning brief that Pattie

Millett filed on his behalf. She turns Stevens into a puppy-loving PETA president:

Pattie Millett, *United States v. Stevens*

Robert Stevens is a sixty-eight-year-old **published author** and documentary producer whose work focuses on the history, **unique traits**, and assets of the breed of dog commonly known as Pit Bulls. Stevens operated a business out of his home in rural southern Virginia called "Dogs of Velvet and Steel," which **sold informational materials** and equipment for the **safe handling** and care of Pit Bulls. His book, *Dogs of Velvet and Steel: Pit Bulldogs: A Manual for Owners* (1983), has been purchased and **marketed by Amazon.com**, Borders, and Barnes & Noble. Stevens has also **published articles** about the beneficial uses of Pit Bulls. Other than the conviction vacated by the Third Circuit, Stevens has no criminal record. Stevens has **long opposed dogfighting**, advocating in his book that "pit fighting should remain illegal." His mission is for "the Pit Bull to be recognized, not as an outlaw, but a respected canine." His work seeks to **educate the public** about the beneficial uses of Pit Bulls for "the legal activities described in this book—obedience, tracking [and hunting], weight-pulling, and the ultimate challenge, Schutzhund [protection]," and about "how to breed, condition, and train this unique animal" for those tasks.

Does Stevens sound to you like the right target for the government's first prosecution under an animal-cruelty statute? I didn't think so.

At least Stevens is a human being. Perhaps the greatest show-not-tell challenge in advocacy is to make an abstract corporation look good, particularly when it's under siege, as General Motors was at the height of its bankruptcy crisis. Given the public's and Congress's hostility at the time, I wouldn't be surprised if the next filing tested the skills of even an advocate as renowned as Harvey Miller, widely considered the best bankruptcy lawyer in the nation.

Miller pulls out every stop here, pleading with the court—and likely the media—to remember General Motors' better days. I don't want to read too much into this excerpt, but does the list of car models invite you to reminisce about owning at least one of these GM products, whether a beat-up old Buick or a sleek silver Saab?

Harvey Miller, *In re General Motors*

Over the past century, General Motors grew into a worldwide leader in products and services related to the development, manufacture, and marketing of cars and trucks under various brands, including: **Buick, Cadillac, Chevrolet, GMC, Daewoo, Holden, HUMMER, Opel, Pontiac, Saab, Saturn, Vauxhall, and Wuling**. The Company has produced nearly **450,000,000 vehicles** globally and operates in virtually every country in the world. The recent severe economic downturn has had an unprecedented impact on the global automotive industry. Nevertheless, particularly in the United States, the **automotive industry** remains a driving force of the economy. It **employs one in ten American workers** and is one of the largest purchasers of **U.S.-manufactured** steel, aluminum, iron, copper, plastics, rubber, and electronic and computer chips. Almost **4% of the United States gross domestic product**, and nearly **10% of U.S. industrial production** by value, are related to the automotive industry.

By playing the nationalism card, Miller manages to make General Motors sound even more essential to the national economy than John Roberts's Red Dog Mine was to Alaska's.

Now I don't mean to suggest that you should use the *Show, Not Tell* technique only to make your client look good. The technique is just as useful for making your opponent look bad. Yet as they say in politics, never interfere when your opponent is destroying himself: let the facts speak for themselves.

If, for example, you believe that your opponent is lying or exaggerating, show it without saying it. Take this example from Attorney General Eric Holder. Do you think he believes that the plaintiff is telling the truth about her chest and back pain?

Eric Holder, *Butler v. MBNA*

Plaintiff alleges that her October 13, 2004 fall "resulted in physical damage to [her] back and chest." **But the only disability certification** submitted by plaintiff's healthcare providers (on October 15) **referred vaguely** to "chest pain" symptoms. **Contradicting this certification were** plaintiff's own reports (on October 13) to an emergency medical technician and to an emergency room physician **that she did not suffer** from current chest pain; **nor did plaintiff submit any further medical documentation** that referred to back pain.

(Just change that semicolon before "nor" to a comma. The only exception to this rule is when the clauses are unusually long and contain many commas. These clauses aren't and don't.)

Now imagine if Holder had been like many defense lawyers in these cases who just can't resist the urge to go for the jugular, adding a line such as "These contradictions cast doubt on the veracity of Plaintiff's claims." Language like that turns your fact sections into a spin job.

Let's end with an example from the ACLU, questioning the police's conduct in a Fourth Amendment knock-and-announce case that wended its way to the Supreme Court.

The ACLU lawyers know that the police are sympathetic, and they appear to take pains here not to impugn the officers' motives. But the drip-drip-drip narrative, though clean and unadorned, makes the officers seem hasty and their actions unfounded:

Steven Shapiro and the ACLU, *Hudson v. Michigan*

On the afternoon of August 27, 1998, approximately seven Detroit police officers arrived at the home of Petitioner Booker T. Hudson, Jr., to execute a search warrant for narcotics. There is **no evidence** in the record that the officers had any reason to believe that anyone in the home would attempt to destroy evidence, escape, or resist the execution of the warrant. Officer Jamal Good, the first member of the raiding party to enter the house, testified that he **did not see or hear any activity** inside the home as the officers approached the door.

Upon arriving at the door to Petitioner's home, some of the officers shouted, "Police, search warrant." The officers **did not knock**, and they **waited only three to five seconds** before opening the door and entering. Officer Good explained that the brief delay between the announcement and his entry was "[a]bout how long it took me to go in the door," and he characterized the entry after the announcement as "[r]eal fast." Officer Good confirmed that the officers **did not wait** to see if anyone would answer the door.

Some lawyers exploit *Show, Not Tell* not just for a party but for an object or even a cause. Imagine that you're defending a monument to the Ten Commandments found on state grounds.

In his amicus brief for the State of Texas, Senator Ted Cruz, then Texas Solicitor General Ted Cruz, takes you on a personal tour of those grounds below, walking you past one memorial after another, some to veterans, some to children, and, yes, one to the Ten Commandments. By playing tour guide himself here, he accomplishes his goal of making you see the monument against the backdrop of secular tributes:

Ted Cruz, *Van Orden v. Perry*

Those wishing to tour the Grounds have access to brochures, laying out a self-guided tour, that the State Preservation Board makes available to Capitol visitors. **The self-guided tour begins** in the southeast portion of the Grounds, where the first monument encountered is a memorial to John B. Hood's Texas Brigade. The tallest monument on the Capitol Grounds (at over forty-four feet in height), it is inscribed with quotes from Jefferson Davis and Robert E. Lee, and is topped by the bronze figure of a **Confederate soldier**. Moving north, the tour continues to the **Texas Peace Officers** memorial and the Disabled Veterans monument.

The tour then crosses over to the Capitol's northwest quadrant, which contains seven of the Grounds' seventeen monuments. This area is the largest grouping of monuments on the Capitol Grounds. Three monuments honor **veterans**—a tribute to veterans of the Korean War (the largest monument in the northwest quadrant), a tribute to veterans of World War I, bearing the inscription "God–Country–Peace," and a monument to Texans who died at Pearl Harbor. And four concern **children**—a replica of the Statue of Liberty in honor of the Boy Scouts of America (at nearly sixteen feet, the tallest monument in the northwest quadrant); a tribute to the Texas

Pioneer Woman, depicting a pioneer mother cradling a baby
in one arm; a tribute to Texas Children, portraying six children
on a visit to the Capitol, one of whom wears a necklace bearing
a small cross; and the Ten Commandments monument at issue
in this litigation, donated by the Fraternal Order of Eagles and
dedicated in 1961 "to the Youth and People of Texas."

(Grammar-nerd alert: In the first sentence, note Cruz's use of
"that" rather than "which" after a comma. "Laying out a self-guided
tour" is just an intervening phrase, so "that the State Preservation
Board makes available" is still restrictive and thus requires "that": it
tells you something essential about the brochures in question.)

Remember, then, to resist the litigator's natural urge to character-
ize the facts and tell the court what they mean. Why burst any illusion
that you're an honest broker trying to give a fair account of the events
in question? Devote your energies instead to combing through the
record in search of facts that are so clear and so strong that they make
your case on their own.

7

Once Upon a Time: Replace dates with phrases that convey a sense of time

Few things are duller than a paragraph stuffed with dates.

"Using an exact date signals to the reader that it is important—that the reader should remember it for future reference," says Judge Mark Painter, a former Ohio appellate judge now a judge on the United Nations Appeals Tribunal. "If that's not your intention, strike it out. You can convey continuity and order by clues like *next* and *later*."[1]

But even when the actual date matters, replacing it with a time signal like "two years later" or "just three days before" can help turn your fact section into the kind of story that people enjoy reading. Even better, such time signals can make your story more persuasive.

Here, for example, Larry Tribe notes that Jennifer Gratz, the plaintiff in the undergraduate version of the University of Michigan affirmative action case, won a partial Supreme Court victory on June 23, 2003. So why not include a date for the next event on the timeline?

Larry Tribe, *Coalition to Defend Affirmative Action v. Granholm*

[Jennifer Gratz] ultimately won a partial success in the Supreme Court of the United States on June 23, 2003.

Within days of the *Gratz* decision, Ms. Gratz approached Ward Connerly (currently Chairman of the American Civil

---

1. Mark P. Painter, The Legal Writer: 40 Rules for the Art of Legal Writing 61–72 (2d ed. Jardyce & Jardyce 2003).

> Rights Institute and formerly a leading proponent of California's Proposition 209), asking him to consider supporting a ballot initiative in Michigan with the purpose of eliminating affirmative action in that state.

That single phrase—"within days of the *Gratz* decision"—doesn't just break up the monotony of a series of dates. It also suggests that Gratz was in a rush to make political hay out of her court victory.

In private practice, Attorney General Holder did something similar below with the phrase "one day after." Sure, he could have just written that the plaintiff allegedly "fell down" on October 13 and that she had an approved leave from August 23 to October 11. Although Holder would probably take the Fifth if we asked him, I bet he was happy to point out that the plaintiff's alleged injury occurred just "one day after" she returned from a 50-day leave:

Eric Holder, *Butler v. MBNA*

Plaintiff's current claim arises from an incident where she allegedly "fell down" during an October 13, 2004 meeting with MBNA Human Resources Personnel. This incident occurred **one day after plaintiff returned to active employment** (on October 12) following a **50-day period** (from August 23 to October 11) of approved [Short Term Disability] leave for a vision problem.

Sometimes, of course, you want to show that the events happened slower, not faster, than the court might expect. Take how long the state waited in the California gay marriage case to argue that the presiding judge should have recused himself:

David Boies and Ted Olson, *Perry v. Brown*

Not until April 25, 2011—**almost two years after initially intervening** in this case, **more than one year after an adverse ruling** at trial, and **four months after arguing their appeal** before this Court—did Proponents move to vacate the district court's judgment, raising the argument they had previously (and publicly) foresworn: that Judge Walker should have recused himself because he is "gay and in a committed same-sex relationship."

Finally, this technique can also be used not to show that something happened faster or slower than expected, but to complain that it happened at all:

Morgan Chu, *eBay v. IDT*

On November 26, 2008, **the day before Thanksgiving**, Defendants served a subpoena on Irell & Manella, which had at one time represented Mr. Gordon and the previous assignee of the '350 patent.

8

Headliners: Use headings to break up your fact section and to add persuasive effect

Nearly all the top advocates break up their fact sections through headings.

You can format such headings the way you would format headings in your argument:

> **The Loan Terms**
>
> The debt was securitized by Debtor's primary residence....

Or you can run your headings into your paragraphs, boldfacing or italicizing them for emphasis:

> *The Loan Terms.* The debt was securitized by Debtor's primary residence....

Either way, strive for a novelistic effect. I have yet to see anything better in that regard than the government's fact section headings in its response to Martha Stewart's appeal:

> **Department of Justice, *United States v. Stewart***
>
> 1. "Get Martha on the Phone"
> 2. "Peter Bacanovic Thinks ImClone is Going to Start Trading Downward"

3. Stewart **Sells** Her ImClone Stock
4. "Something is Going on With ImClone and Martha Stewart Wants to Know What"
5. Stewart's Conversation With Mariana Pasternak
6. The Investigations Begin
7. The Tax Loss Selling Cover Story
8. January 3, 2002: Faneuil **Lies** to Investigators
9. Bacanovic **Changes** the Cover Story
10. January 7, 2002: Bacanovic **Lies** to Investigators
11. Stewart Alters Bacanovic's Telephone Message
12. February 4, 2002: Stewart **Lies** to Investigators
13. February 13, 2002: Bacanovic **Lies** in Sworn Testimony
14. March 7, 2002: Faneuil **Lies** to Investigators Again
15. April 10, 2002: Stewart **Lies** to Investigators Again
16. Stewart's False Public Statements
17. Faneuil **Reveals the Truth**
18. Bacanovic's Defense Case
19. Stewart's Defense Case
20. The Government's Rebuttal Case
21. Judgment of Acquittal on Count Nine
22. The Verdict

Here we see the *Show, Not Tell* technique transposed to headings. No heading claims that "Stewart Associated With Many Liars" or "Stewart's Associates Have a Problem With Truth-Telling." Instead, the government's headings *show* facts, however unpleasant those facts may be. Notice something else in the Martha Stewart example: The verbs are all in the present tense—another way to give your headings a conversational feel.

Such techniques are not just for celebrity trials. If anything, they are even handier when your subject matter is dry.

In the following fact section headings from Seth Waxman, for example, the present tense gives this soulless bankruptcy tale an almost breathless feel:

Seth Waxman, *In re Winstar Communications*

A. The Parties **Begin** a Strategic Relationship Intended for Mutual Benefit
B. The Parties **Execute** the "Subcontract" and Thereafter **Engage** in "Pass-Through" Transactions To Finance the Build-Out of Winstar's Network
C. Winstar **Assists** Lucent In Meeting Revenue Targets; Lucent **Provides** Winstar Reciprocal Benefits
D. At The Height of the Telecom Boom, Winstar **Obtains** More Favorable Financing Terms
E. The Lucent and Winstar Relationship Further **Deteriorates**

Very similar are these five fact-section headings in Steve Susman's motion for judgment as a matter of law below. The present tense dominates here, too:

Steve Susman, *Capitol Justice LLC v. Wachovia Bank, N.A.*

A. Wachovia and AAJ **Enter** into a Rate Lock Agreement That Wachovia **Represents** Will "Eliminate []" AAJ's Interest Rate Risk
B. Wachovia and AAJ **Enter** Into a Loan Commitment Agreement With a Material Adverse Change Clause that Wachovia **Represents** Was Limited to a "9/11–Type" Event
C. Six Weeks After Executing the LCA[,] Wachovia **Tries** to "Reprice" the Loan

. . . .

   D. Staubach **Rejects** Wachovia's Attempt to Reprice the AAJ Loan As Inconsistent with the RLA and Wachovia's Prior Statements About the Operation of the MAC Clause

   E. Wachovia **Invokes** the MAC Clause Based on Events It Knew About Before Executing the LCA

Susman's fourth and fifth headings are great examples of neutral-sounding headings that still pack a persuasive punch. And splicing in the short quotations helps buttress the headings as well.

If you prefer phrase-like headings that are shorter than Waxman's and Susman's, consider this model from Fred Bartlit, yet another fan of present-tense headings and the slyly persuasive neutral "fact":

Fred Bartlit, *Stumpf v. Garvey*

   I. The Growth of the Fiber Optic Cable Industry

  II. July 26, 2000: The TyCom IPO and Prospectus

  III. 2001: **The Collapse** of the Telecommunications Industry

  IV. December 2001: Tyco **Buys Back** All TyCom Stock

  V. 2002: **The Revelation** of **Unrelated** Management Misconduct at Tyco

  VI. **This Litigation**

(The colons after the dates make them less dry and more dramatic.)

9

Back to Life: Center technical matter on people or entities

It's not too hard to write a clear fact section when your case involves sex, crimes, or even slip-and-falls. It's far harder when you're writing about failed securitizations or infringing semiconductor chips.

"Hard" doesn't mean "impossible," but it does mean that you'll need every technical writing technique you can muster.

Here is a typical example of the way many lawyers handle technical material in their briefs. As you read it, think about how the "electronic market" described would work:

> [T]he '265 patent, in general terms, describes an "electronic market" for the sale of goods. In a market such as this, merchandise can be put on display through the posting of pictures, product descriptions, and prices on a network of computers (e.g., the Internet). The subsequently displayed products can be viewed by potential buyers through a connection to the network in which such product data resides. Following the selection of an item or product, a purchase can be completed electronically. This hypothetical transaction is mediated by an "electronic market" that assists in the facilitation of payment and fulfillment. In addition to this mediation, enforcement by a central authority can ensure that the obligations and performance of all parties are fulfilled. Therefore, trust among participants is promoted.

Confused? Now read Seth Waxman's explanation of that same "electronic market," also known as eBay:

Seth Waxman, *MercExchange v. eBay*

[T]he '265 patent, in general terms, describes an "electronic market" for the sale of goods. In such a market, **sellers** can display their wares by posting pictures, descriptions, and prices of goods on a computer network, such as the Internet. **A prospective buyer** can electronically browse the goods on sale by connecting to the network. After selecting an item, **the buyer** can complete the purchase electronically, with the "electronic market" mediating the transaction, including payment, on the buyer's behalf. **The seller** is then notified that the buyer has paid for the item and that the transaction is final. **A central authority** within the market can police the obligations and performance of sellers and buyers over time, thereby promoting trust among participants.

Do you notice the main difference in the writing?

In the first example, the first sentence describes the patent, and then the following sentences shift from one abstract subject to the next: merchandise, products, selection, transaction, enforcement, trust. In Waxman's version, the second example, every sentence after the first is about someone doing something, whether that "someone" is a buyer, a seller, or a central authority.

If your material is so abstract—banking or technology, for example—that you're desperate for a whiff of humanity, you can always attribute the concepts to a "user," as Carter Phillips does in explaining how Microsoft Outlook's calendar works:

Carter Phillips, *Lucent Technologies v. Gateway*

Entry of the date using the date-picker tool is the only use of Outlook alleged to infringe. By clicking on a "down arrow," **the user can** bring up the date-picker. The date-picker displays a monthly calendar page, with a month and year on top and an array of the dates in that month below. **The user selects** a particular date by clicking on it with the mouse. **If the user** seeks a date in a different month, she uses arrows or a drop-down list to navigate to the desired month and then clicks on a specific date in that month. Technically, the software creates the month display, fills it in with dates (shown as falling on the correct day of the week), and tracks the correct order of dates and times by calculating the number of minutes elapsed between January 1, 1601 and the date and time in question. **When the user selects** a particular date in a particular month with the mouse, **she is thus selecting** a particular number of minutes since January 1, 1601.

Interlude: Gauging your brief's readability

If you enjoy competing with yourself, go to Options under the File tab, select Proofing, and then check "Show readability statistics." The next time you spell-check, you'll also get all sorts of metrics about your document that you can use to make your writing more readable.

Aim for these numbers and your writing will approach that of some of the profession's top technical writers:

- Fewer than 27 average words per sentence
- "Flesch reading ease" score above 30
- Less than 20% of your sentences are passive

For comparison purposes, the introduction to this book has eighteen words per sentence on average and a reading ease score of 60. And in case you're wondering, both Waxman and Phillips pass all three tests as well.

10

Poker Face: Concede bad facts, but put them in context

"The facts give the fix," says former D.C. Circuit Chief Judge Patricia Wald. "[S]pend time amassing them in a compelling way for your side but do not omit the ones that go the other way. Tackle these uncooperative facts and put them in perspective."[1]

As Judge Wald suggests, rare is the dispute in which every fact favors only one side. If anything, most judges are leery of a fact section that reduces "life in all its fullness" to a simplistic morality tale.

And it's better to spin that sometimes awkward "fullness" yourself than to let your opponent do it for you. In the copyright case below, for example, Larry Lessig is defending a filmmaker who used protected footage of the fighter Count Dante in a trailer for his own documentary on the man. Lessig's use of such passive constructions as "it is not disputed that" and "it can be inferred that" reminds me of when politicians say "mistakes were made": you know someone messed up. But Lessig does his best to dilute the impact, pooh-poohing the "borrowed" footage's length, importance, and visibility:

Larry Lessig, *Aguiar v. Webb*

It is not disputed that Defendant Webb used a portion of the Footage in one of the trailers for his biographical documentary about Count Dante. That trailer, as well as a still image of the portion of the trailer containing the Footage, is already

---

1. Patricia M. Wald, *19 Tips from 19 Years on the Appellate Bench*, 1 J. App. Prac. & Process 7, 11 (1999).

before the Court. In the trailer, the Footage runs for approximately **fifteen seconds** as **part of a collage** of images. The Footage appears **in the background**, with a photograph of Count Dante in the foreground. The Footage is also **obscured** in part by the text of a quotation by Count Dante. Although perhaps it can be inferred that one of the fighters is Count Dante, the other fighter is **not mentioned** or identified explicitly or by inference. The faces of both fighters are **washed out** and **barely visible**.

Lessig backed into his bad facts with a strategic use of the passive voice. Ted Olson, for his part, uses another classic bad-fact strategy in his winning brief in *Citizens United*: starting a sentence with "although" to subordinate the bad fact to its more favorable context:

Ted Olson, *Citizens United v. United States*

In mid-2007, Citizens United began production of *Hillary: The Movie*, a biographical documentary about Senator Hillary Clinton, who was then a candidate to become the Democratic Party's nominee for President. **Although Senator Clinton's candidacy was the backdrop** for the 90-minute documentary, **neither the movie's narrator nor any of the individuals interviewed** during the movie **expressly advocated her election or defeat** as President. The movie instead presents a critical assessment of Senator Clinton's record as a U.S. Senator and as First Lady in order to educate viewers about her political background.

You can feel for Olson as he walks a fine line: the film was distributed during Hillary Clinton's 2008 campaign for president, it was about her very candidacy, it offered what Olson poignantly calls "a critical assessment," but it didn't "expressly advocate" her defeat. Oh, the beauty of American election law!

And the beauty of subordinating unpleasant facts: follow Olson's lead by including an "Although" sentence the next time you're walking a tightrope in your own fact section.

Now that we've touched on politics, let's move to another conversational taboo: money. Here, ex-U.S. attorney and current SEC chair Mary Jo White seeks summary judgment by trotting out the old "I am not a lawyer" defense. In doing so, she's trying to explain why her sophisticated client Ken Lewis, the Bank of America CEO and graduate of the Stanford Executive Program, didn't disclose "interim and forecasted losses" at Merrill Lynch before acquiring the foundering company:

Mary Jo White, *In re Bank of America Corporation Securities, Derivative and ERISA Litigation*

[T]he undisputed facts unique to Mr. Lewis show that he **did precisely what the CEO of a large enterprise should have done when faced with the prospect of large interim and forecasted losses at Merrill:** he engaged on the question of disclosure with [Bank of America's] CFO and received reports from BAC's CFO that the question of disclosure had been **vetted proactively with expert counsel on two occasions** and that counsel had concluded that disclosure was not warranted. Mr. Lewis, who, like most CEOs, **is a non-lawyer not steeped in the securities laws**, did not overrule that determination and had absolutely no basis for doing so.

In her own savvy way, White turns a damaging fact—Lewis's less-than-ideal due diligence—into a credible story about deference to expert advice.

When you really need to make lemonade out of lemons, consider how Miguel Estrada puts a positive spin on the conviction of Conrad Black. After all, Estrada suggests, look at all the things Black *wasn't* convicted of.

Miguel Estrada, *Black v. United States*

After a four-month trial, however, the jury **acquitted petitioners on nearly all counts**, including the most serious. The jury **convicted on just three counts** of mail fraud and, **as to Black alone, a single count** of obstruction of justice based on instructions expressly referencing the criminal investigation and trial.

Perhaps you're thinking "OK, but my client didn't just steal footage or cause financial losses; my client's crime was downright gruesome."

What would you do if, say, your client put poison on her husband's mistress's mailbox to burn her in revenge? You would humanize her motives while sanitizing her actions, as appellate superstar Paul Clement does here:

Paul Clement, *United States v. Bond*

[Bond's] federal sentence stems from a domestic dispute that occurred when Bond learned that her **once closest friend,** Myrlinda Haynes, was pregnant and that **Bond's husband was**

the child's father. In the wake of that **upsetting discovery**, Bond tried to injure Haynes by placing certain toxic chemicals on Haynes's mailbox, car door handles, and other areas likely to be touched. Her plan "succeeded" to the extent of a **minor** chemical burn on Haynes's thumb, which Haynes **treated by rinsing with water**...The undisputed evidence establishes that **Bond had no intent to kill** Haynes.

11

End with a Bang: Leave the court with a final image or thought

T. S. Eliot said that the world ends not with a bang but a whimper.

Don't let your fact sections do the same. According to James Stewart, the author of the Ivan Boesky anecdote discussed earlier, "after the lead, the ending is the most important part of a story."[1]

In that spirit, I will close this chapter with two fact-section endings that help rile up the court in the way the attorneys would have liked.

In the first example, Brendan Sullivan represents the beleaguered former CEO of Freddie Mac, Leland Brendsel, in a case against the government. Because the agency regulating Freddie Mac (now part of the Federal Housing Finance Agency) believed that Brendsel had engaged in improper conduct, it insisted that he be fired for cause and cut his $54 million compensation package. The case settled in 2005.

In a successful motion for a preliminary injunction to get Brendsel his money back, Sullivan ends with the idea that this case is not about accounting, or fraud, or corporate governance, or even the limits of the regulatory state. Instead, it's about property rights:

Brendan Sullivan, *Brendsel v. Office of Federal Housing Enterprise Oversight*

The hold on that compensation is particularly damaging because Mr. Brendsel's right to exercise the previously-

---

1. STEWART, *supra* note 2, at 272.

> restricted options lapses twenty four months after his resignation. Thus, Defendant's hold **could deprive Mr. Brendsel of that property permanently** and he would be **unable to vindicate his right** to that property through the enforcement proceedings.

And here's a final example of ending loud and clear. You may remember from Part One the dispute over the movie *Push*, a film that Harvey Weinstein saw at the 2009 Sundance festival and wanted to distribute. He approached agents for Smokewood Entertainment. A flurry of e-mails followed, but the Weinstein Company lost out. Smokewood offered the rights to Lionsgate instead—and the Weinstein Company sued.

Representing Weinstein in an opposition to a motion to dismiss, David Boies ends his fact section with what journalists call "tick tock," a blow-by-blow account:

> **David Boies, *Weinstein v. Smokewood Entertainment***
>
> Instead of providing The Weinstein Company with the promised documentation memorializing the agreement, [Smokewood's agent] went **behind TWC's back** and negotiated a **conflicting deal** with Lionsgate for the rights to distribute *Push* that had already been granted to TWC **at 4:42 a.m.** on July 28, 2009.
>
> Smokewood, through [one of those agents], **repudiated** its agreement with TWC in an email claiming that "there has been no agreement reached with The Weinstein Company respecting Push." **A few days later, Cinetic and Smokewood announced that Lionsgate had obtained the exclusive rights to distribute *Push*.**

Boies thus ends the section by portraying Harvey Weinstein the way Brendan Sullivan portrays the Freddie Mac CEO: as someone stripped of his right to something he deserves.

This Hollywood example is perhaps a fitting end for a list of techniques that started with a *Panoramic Shot*. Use these techniques to link your fact section to your themes, and then carry that spirit to the argument section, the challenge we'll tackle next.

PART THREE

THE MEAT

Part Three will share twenty techniques for crafting arguments:

Part Three: The Meat

Why do some argument sections work better than others? Did the writers find better facts or case law than what other lawyers would have found? Probably not. You write a brief with the record and law you have, not the ones you might wish to have. So do these standout lawyers simply know more about the doctrines they discuss? Not necessarily. Many specialists write poorly organized arguments.

The standout writers usually start with the same law, facts, and knowledge that other lawyers do. But they treat those data points like pieces in a jigsaw puzzle. The picture on the puzzle box is always the same: a way to make a judge feel comfortable finding for them and not for their opponent. The pieces inside the box are the headings, subheadings, paragraph openers, case law, and facts, along with the transitions that snap the other pieces together. Each of those pieces is a key part of the puzzle, and it's the writer's job to figure out how each one boosts the client's prospects.

As Chief Justice William Rehnquist once said, the challenge is to make order out of chaos: "The brief writer must immerse himself in this chaos of detail and bring order to it by organizing—and I cannot stress that term enough—by organizing, organizing, and organizing, so that the brief is a coherent presentation of the arguments in favor of the writer's clients."[1]

Let's discuss twenty ways to put that puzzle together.

Using Headings

Strong headings are like a good headline for a newspaper article: they give you the gist of what you need to know, draw you into text you might otherwise skip, and even allow you a splash of creativity and flair.

The old test is still the best. Could a judge skim your headings and subheadings and know why you win? In the words of Federal Circuit Judge Dan Friedman, the right headings "explain where the brief is going and provide signposts along the way."[2]

A good way to provide such "signposts" is to make your headings complete thoughts that, if true, would push you toward the finish line.

This practice dates back decades. Consider this example from Thurgood Marshall's brief for the NAACP in *Sweatt v. Painter*. The 1950 case arose when an African-American man was refused admission to the University of Texas Law School because the Texas State Constitution prohibited integrated education.

1. William H. Rehnquist, *From Webster to Word Processing: The Ascendance of the Appellate Brief*, 1 J. APP. PRAC. & PROCESS 1 (1999).

2. Daniel M. Friedman, *Winning on Appeal*, 9 LITIG. 15, 17 (Spring 1983).

The numbered subheadings offer four takes on the main point in the section's heading. The first two are rooted in policy, the third ties those policy reasons to a legal basis, and the fourth offers three key *Why Should I Care?* factors:

> ### Thurgood Marshall, *Sweatt v. Painter*
>
> A. In making admission to the University of Texas School of Law dependent upon an applicant's race or color, Texas has adopted a classification **wholly lacking in any rational foundation**. Therefore, it is **invalid under the equal protection clause**.
>
> 1. There is no valid basis for the justification of racial segregation in the field of education. Enforced racial segregation **aborts and frustrates the basic purposes and objectives of public education** in a democratic society.
> 2. Racial segregation **cannot be justified as essential to the preservation of peace** and good order.
> 3. There is **no rational basis** for a legislative assumption that different races have different intellectual potentialities and should therefore be educated in separate schools.
> 4. State ordained segregation is a **particularly invidious policy which needlessly penalizes Negroes, demoralizes whites and tends to disrupt our democratic institutions**.

As much as I love these headings, in today's world of short attention spans and bloated dockets, a two-sentence heading is probably one sentence too long. The top advocates of our own era cap their headings at the length of a normal sentence.

Headings are typically organized in one of four ways:

1. **Set order.** According to statutory or common law factors, in order: *Plaintiff has established (1) duty, (2) breach, (3) causation, and (4) damages.*
2. **Set points.** According to statutory or common law factors, with the dispositive one first: *The Court should dismiss this action because (1) Plaintiff has not alleged damages.*
3. **"Even if."** Arguing in the alternative, with procedural arguments often before substantive ones: *(1) The claim was filed too late, (2) Even if the claim had been timely filed, Defendant had no duty.*
4. **Independent.** Self-generated points with the strongest one first: *The misstatement was "material" for three reasons. First, it caused a 7% drop in share price the very next day. Second, it reflected the company's first-quarter profits for one of its main products. Third, it exaggerated those profits by 17%.*

How does this work in practice? Let's revisit the motion to dismiss for Citigroup discussed in Part One. As you may recall, in his preliminary statement, Ted Wells listed two main reasons to dismiss Terra Firma's complaint and transfer the lawsuit to England. First, he said, Terra Firma had agreed to an English forum. And second, New York was an inconvenient venue because most of the events happened in England. In other words, Citi's preliminary statement falls into the fourth category above: two independent points with the stronger one—the existence of a binding agreement—listed first.

As we walk through how to organize your argument—first the headings, and then the order and structure of the paragraphs in each section—I'll show you how Wells took this two-item "short list," broke it into pieces, and then, in the argument itself, arranged those pieces into a perfectly structured puzzle that favors his client's position.

12

Russian Doll: Nest your headings and subheadings

You have probably seen one of those Russian nesting dolls. As you open each wooden figure, you find a smaller version of the same doll inside.

Great advocates create a similar effect in their headings and subheadings. As the various levels get "smaller" and more detailed, they build back toward their larger and broader siblings.

To see such nesting in action, let's return to the first reason for dismissing Terra Firma's complaint that Wells listed in Citi's preliminary statement:

Ted Wells, *Terra Firma v. Citigroup*

First, a series of agreements specifying that the claims asserted by Terra Firma be resolved in the courts of England requires dismissal of this Complaint.

Look how much Citi's first heading below tracks its first reason above. Wells then breaks down that first heading into subheadings A and B, each about one of the lawsuit's claims:

I. This action should be dismissed pursuant to the forum selection clauses governing Terra Firma's claims.

   A. Terra Firma's claims relating to **alleged misrepresentations made during the auction** must be litigated in England.

> B. Terra Firma's claim regarding **Citi's performance under the finance agreements** must also be litigated in England.

There's some perfect nesting at work, but consider drafting Heading I in the active voice and change "pursuant to" to "under": "The Court should dismiss this action under the forum-selection clauses governing Terra Firma's claims."

In our next example, Kathleen Sullivan embellishes a legal conclusion—her nuclear-power-plant client will suffer irreparable harm without an injunction—through four fact-specific subheadings, all presented in parallel form for easy reference. The injunction sought to stop the state of Vermont from shutting down the plant:

> **Kathleen Sullivan, *Entergy Nuclear Vermont Yankee,***
> **LLC v. Shumlin**
>
> II. Plaintiffs will suffer **irreparable harm** absent a preliminary injunction.
> > A. **Irreparable harm** from loss of the Vermont Yankee Station's Skilled Workforce.
> > B. **Irreparable harm** from preparation for the fall 2011 refueling outage.
> > C. **Irreparable monetary losses** from a "temporary" shutdown that may be irreversible.
> > D. **Irreparable harm** from loss of long-term power contracts.

(You'll note that Sullivan's subheadings A, B, C, and D are technically sentence fragments, not complete sentences, but the main point is that they are factual and specific, not circular or topical.)

Not that you have to limit yourself to two levels of headings. Here, for instance, ABA President (2009–2010) Carolyn Lamm nests three levels to explain why a parent company should be subject to personal jurisdiction in Virginia based on both its business activities and its relationship to one of its subsidiaries:

Carolyn Lamm, *Inversiones & Servicios, S.A. de C.V. v. Barceló Hospitality USA*

I. Barceló GH is subject to **personal jurisdiction** in Virginia.
   A. Barceló GH conducts **business in Virginia**.
   B. Barceló GH is subject to jurisdiction in Virginia **through its wholly-owned subsidiary and alter ego** Barceló USA.
      1. The **tribunal's finding** that Barceló GH is indistinguishable from Barceló USA should be given preclusive effect.
      2. Barceló GH's **corporate merger activities** in Virginia are further evidence that it is indistinguishable from Barceló USA.
      3. **Overlapping corporate officers and directors** underscore that Barceló USA is an alter ego of Barceló GH.

More nesting: A and B prove I, while 1, 2, and 3 prove B. If only the American Bar Association could run that smoothly!

Our next example has even more layers. In supporting the merger of Sirius and XM Radio, Dick Wiley nests four levels of reasons that the fate of the radio-listening world rests in the anti-trust authorities' hands:

Richard Wiley, *In re XM-Sirius Merger*

II. The record demonstrates that the transaction will produce many merger-specific **benefits for consumers** and is unquestionably in the public interest.

    A. The merger will facilitate **greater choice** and convenience for consumers, at lower prices.

        1. The combined company will provide **a la carte programming** and a variety of other program packages.

        2. This increased choice in programming and prices will **benefit consumers**.

            a. The combined company will be able to provide **increased opportunities** for a wider variety of content providers.

            b. The merger will facilitate the commercial **availability** of interoperable radios.

            c. The combined company will be able to offer **new, advanced services**.

            d. The transaction will produce significant **efficiencies** and will **safeguard** the future of satellite radio.

Each level answers "why" with increasing specificity. *Why* should I approve this merger? *Why* will it benefit consumers? *Why* will it offer more choices? *Why* is increased programming a benefit?

As an added benefit, once you fit your moving parts together logically, the argument starts to write itself. To show you how, I'll end with a final example of sterling headings and subheadings on appeal—a set that tells a compelling story about the lower court's alleged lack of fairness toward attorney Steven Donziger:

Larry Robbins, *Chevron Corp. v. Donziger*

D. In this action, Judge Kaplan **refuses** to hear Donziger before besmirching his character and reputation and enjoining him from a broad range of enforcement activities.

1. Chevron **spends "thousands of hours"** on its injunction papers and then arranges for the case to come before Judge Kaplan.

2. Judge Kaplan effectively **shuts Donziger out** of the preliminary-injunction proceedings.

3. The district court's preliminary-injunction order focuses on Chevron's allegation that Donziger subverted the Ecuadorian court, while largely **ignoring** that court's decision.

   a. The district court's irreparable-harm finding was founded on **minimal evidence** that Chevron submitted on reply—too late for the defendants to respond to it.

   b. After **refusing** to hear Donziger, the district court authored an opinion placing him at the center of an alleged plot to subvert justice in Ecuador.

   c. The district court's opinion **deals only cursorily** with the substance of the Ecuadorian court's ruling, and assumes unfairly that it must have been the product of fraud.

   d. The district court **uncritically accepts** Chevron's misleading quotations from the Crude outtakes as evidence of Donziger's wrongdoing.

> e. The district court furnishes **no adequate justification** for rushing to judgment without Donziger's input.
>
> E. Judge Kaplan continues to push Chevron's suit forward, while **blessing** procedural maneuvers that will exclude Donziger and his counsel from participating in the most critical aspect of the suit.
>
> F. This Court calls the prospect of a final, enforceable Ecuadorian judgment "purely hypothetical" and **rejects** Chevron's attempts to evade its commitment to be sued in Ecuador.

(Also note how Robbins puts his headings in the present tense, a bit like what we saw with some of the fact-section headings in Part 2.)

13

Heads I Win, Tails You Lose: Argue in the alternative

As we saw in Part One, sometimes your "short list" works better as an argument in the alternative: "Even if Plaintiff had standing, the case still fails on the merits." "Even if the statute applied, Plaintiff can still prosecute these claims."

"No matter what," you suggest, "I can't lose."

Headings can work the same way. Take these two headings in a trial motion that Attorney General Eric Holder filed in the Chiquita Banana case we visited in Part One. This is as classic arguing-in-the-alternative as you'll ever see. The statute does not apply, Holder says. Even if it did, it does not allow equitable tolling. And even if it did, plaintiffs have not alleged enough to invoke the doctrine.

Eric Holder, *In re Chiquita Banana*

1. The [Antiterrorism Act] statutory tolling **provision does not apply**.
2. There is **no equitable tolling** under the ATA.
3. **Even if equitable tolling were available** under the ATA, plaintiffs do not and cannot allege the "extraordinary circumstances" necessary to invoke the doctrine.

Let's head north from Colombia to Alaska, the home of the *Exxon Valdez* oil spill. At the Supreme Court, Walter Dellinger, who once served as Bill Clinton's Acting Solicitor General, was trying to chip away at a $2.5 billion punitive-damage award against Exxon. The Clean Water

Act's provisions should govern, Dellinger insisted. But even if they don't, Dellinger pleaded, you should slash those punitives all the same:

Walter Dellinger, *Exxon v. Baker*

A. **The Clean Water Act establishes** federal maritime policy concerning punishment and deterrence of unauthorized discharges and displaces judicial regulation of the same subject.

B. **Even if the CWA leaves room** for judicial lawmaking concerning punishment and deterrence of maritime oil spills, **the Court should not choose to authorize punitive damages**.

Dellinger was smart to cover all bases here: He persuaded the Court to slash the punitive damages to $500 million, saving Exxon two billion bucks. Too bad the captain of the *Exxon Valdez* wasn't so careful.

Interlude: Love "because"

Consider adding the word *because* to your headings to help you reach the sweet spot of specificity.

Imagine the following headings without the "because" clause, and you'll see how much the word can improve your headings and subheadings:

Fred Bartlit, *Micron v. Rambus*

Rambus's attorney-client privilege and work-product claims should be pierced **because** Micron has shown prima facie that Rambus obtained legal advice in furtherance of a crime or fraud.

> **John Payton and the NAACP,** *Greater New Orleans Fair Housing Action Center v. HUD*
>
> This Court has subject-matter jurisdiction over Plaintiffs' claims against Rainwater **because** they are claims against a state officer for prospective relief from unlawful acts.

> **John Payton and the NAACP,** *Greater New Orleans Fair Housing Action Center v. HUD*
>
> Ex parte *Young* applies **because** Plaintiffs seek no funds from the state treasury.

The heading below also uses "because" effectively, but be careful. After a negative word like "not," the word "because" can create confusion.

> **Andy Frey,** *BlackRock Financial Management Inc. v. Ambac Assurance Corp.*
>
> This case was not removable as a "mass action" **because** [Plaintiff's] claim does not seek "monetary relief" and **because** Walnut is not a "defendant."

Is the point about the claim why the case is *not* removable, or is it why the case *would be* removable?

(You can avoid any ambiguity with "because" after a negative phrase by simply setting off the "because" with a comma, as some grammarians advise and as, say, Chief Justice Roberts does in his own writing.)

Organizing the Sections

Now that you have nesting headings, use similar techniques to organize the paragraphs in each section. In fact, making the paragraphs work in a section is much like making the headings work in an argument. Remember the puzzle metaphor. The headings are puzzle pieces that form the "picture" of why you win. And under each of those headings, the paragraph openers are the puzzle pieces that form the "picture" of why the heading is true.

Let's walk through this step by step.

14

Sneak Preview: Include an umbrella paragraph before your headings and subheadings

Many lawyers swoop too fast from "Argument" to their headings. First show the court a trailer, as Roy Englert does here in a brief about Indianapolis's refusal to refund tax payments:

Roy Englert, *Armour v. Indianapolis*

Argument

Other than the court below, every state supreme court to address the issue has held that the Equal Protection Clause prohibits tax-forgiveness measures that favor taxpayers who delayed full payment over those who promptly paid their tax assessments in full. Those decisions rest on the proposition—equally applicable here—that a taxing authority acts arbitrarily when it "prefer[s] those who do not pay their taxes promptly over those who do." That proposition is firmly grounded in this Court's precedents, and this Court should reverse the contrary decision of the Indiana Supreme Court.

I. The City's discriminatory taxation scheme denies the "rough equality of tax treatment" required by the Equal Protection Clause.

(Incidentally, I'm not a big fan of the law-school word "road-map." What passes for a roadmap in many briefs is a guide to topics, not to substance. So rather than doing what Englert does above, many lawyers would have simply introduced the argument with something like "Numerous other courts have already addressed this issue, as explained below." Englert's version, by contrast, has enough heft to stand alone; it helps the Court understand how the discriminatory-tax-scheme piece fits into his broader argument.)

Consider doing something similar after each heading as well. Here, for example, patent-litigation guru Morgan Chu wants to spare his client, Mr. Gordon, from another deposition. Heading III tells you why Gordon should be spared, but then Chu includes an umbrella passage that sets the stage for the two subheadings that follow:

Morgan Chu, *eBay v. IDT*

III. Defendants' motive is an improper re-deposition of Mr. Gordon.

Defendants' true motive in bringing this motion is clear. They are unhappy with their former counsel's questioning at Mr. Gordon's first deposition, and hence wish to re-depose Mr. Gordon on the same issues and documents about which they questioned, or could have questioned, Mr. Gordon in December 2008.

A. Defendants seek to re-depose Mr. Gordon on topics they have already covered in Mr. Gordon's first deposition.

. . . .

B. Defendants rejected Mr. Gordon's good faith compromise.

In our next example, defense attorneys Alan Dershowitz and Greg Craig set up their jurisdictional arguments even more methodically, previewing the headings with a pithy numbered unit that's easy to follow and to understand:

Alan Dershowitz and Greg Craig, *Mamani v. Bustamante*

I. Under traditional separation-of-powers and comity principles, this court lacks jurisdiction.

A number of traditional separation of powers and comity principles deprive this Court of subject matter jurisdiction. **First**, the [Amended Complaint] poses political questions that this Court does not have jurisdiction to consider. **Second**, under the act-of-state doctrine, this Court should not judge the Lozada government's official response to an uprising. **Third**, the doctrine of head-of-state immunity immunizes [Bolivian] President Lozada from suit here, and the [Foreign Sovereign Immunities Act] similarly immunizes Minister Berzaín. Each doctrine independently bars suit.

A. The [Amended Complaint] presents a political question appropriately left to the Executive.

B. Under the Act-of-State Doctrine, the Court should not judge the actions of foreign governments.

C. The defendants are each immune from suit in the United States.

(Note the smooth use of "under" rather than "pursuant to" here. Also note the hyphenation of the phrasal adjectives "act-of-state" and "head-of-state." I'll address the hyphen issue in an Interlude in Part 4.)

With umbrella in hand, you're now ready to write the paragraphs in each section.

The best advocates organize those paragraphs in two main ways:

1. *With You in Spirit*: Start each paragraph by answering a question that you expect the court to have.
2. *Sound Off*: Start the paragraphs with numbered reasons.

15

With You in Spirit: Start each paragraph by answering a question that you expect the court to have

Let me start by showing you what happens in the sections of most motions and briefs, even when the attorneys know the law and the facts cold.

I've reproduced the beginnings of the six paragraphs in a summary judgment opposition that Paula Jones filed in her famous case against President Bill Clinton. Read these six paragraph openers in a row and then try to explain why the court should allow Jones's claim to go to a jury.

Jones v. Clinton: Original

	Paragraph opener
1	Even as to the "sexual harassment" form of gender-based discrimination, "tangible job detriment" is *not* an essential element of proof in an action under Section 1983 for denial of equal protection rights.
2	In *Bohen v. City of East Chicago*, 799 F.2d 1180 (7th Cir. 1986), the court contrasted a claim of sexual harassment under the equal protection clause with a claim of sexual harassment under Title VII.
3	Correct application of these principles is illustrated in *Ascolese v. Southeastern Pennsylvania Transportation Authority*, 925 F. Supp. 351 (E.D. Pa. 1996).
4	The same principles apply here.

| 5 | As supposed authority for the proposition that Plaintiff absolutely cannot recover under Section 1983 unless she proves every element of "sexual harassment" within the meaning of Title VII, Mr. Clinton's counsel cites two Seventh Circuit cases (and no Eighth Circuit cases), *Trautvetter v. Quick* and *King v. Board of Regents of the University of Wisconsin System*. |
| 6 | Based as it is on a misreading of the two Seventh Circuit cases, the second premise of Mr. Clinton's argument is false. |

As you can see, it's hard to understand exactly why the court should deny summary judgment. Now here is my attempt to revise Jones's motion so that each paragraph opens strong:

Jones v. Clinton: Revision

	Paragraph opener
1	Under Jones's Section 1983 equal protection action, she must prove intentional discrimination but not "tangible job detriment."
2	The federal courts have long distinguished Section 1983 claims such as Jones's from Title VII claims.
3	Because of this distinction, when public officials such as the president have cited the Title VII standard in seeking summary judgment in Section 1983 sexual harassment cases, courts have denied the motion.
4	Here, then, the "relevant context" is what the president did to Jones, not, as the president suggests, Jones's "entire work experience."
5	Even if some cases suggest that Title VII sexual harassment claims and Section 1983 sexual harassment actions "generally follow the same contours," that hardly means that the two actions share the same elements.
6	For all these reasons, the president cannot obtain summary judgment here by forcing Jones's Section 1983 claim into Title VII.

The way to capture this linear effect is to imagine a dialogue with the judge:

> Q. **So you want me to deny summary judgment. But President Clinton says Jones hasn't proved that she suffered on the job.**
>
> A. Under Jones's Section 1983 equal protection action, she must prove intentional discrimination but not "tangible job detriment."
>
> Q. **But where do you get the authority to draw that line?**
>
> A. The federal courts have long distinguished Section 1983 claims such as Jones's from Title VII claims.
>
> Q. **Can you assure me that I won't be reversed if I believe you?**
>
> A. Because of this distinction, when public officials such as the president have cited the Title VII standard in seeking summary judgment in Section 1983 sexual-harassment cases, courts have denied the motion.
>
> Q. **If you're right, what evidence should I be looking at?**
>
> A. Here, then, the "relevant context" is what the president did to Jones, not, as the president suggests, Jones's "entire work experience."
>
> Q. **One last thing: aren't these statutes essentially the same, as President Clinton's lawyers suggest?**
>
> A. Even if some cases suggest that Title VII sexual harassment claims and Section 1983 sexual harassment actions "generally follow the same contours," that hardly means that the two actions share the same elements.
>
> Q. **So what's the bottom line?**
>
> A. For all these reasons, the president cannot obtain summary judgment here by forcing Jones's Section 1983 claim into Title VII.

If you apply this *With You in Spirit* dialoguing technique, each paragraph opener will give the court a reason the heading is right, answer a question on the court's mind, and flow from the previous paragraph opener and into the next.

It is thus no surprise that the briefs of yesteryear had better structure than the briefs of today. Copying and pasting and typing on a computer all day are not a good recipe for linear structure and flow.

So let's reach back in time, unpacking a key section from the brief that Thurgood Marshall wrote in *Brown v. Board of Education*. Notice how Marshall provides the Justices with a five-part linear pathway to his heading. I've bolded the first sentence in each paragraph:

Thurgood Marshall, *Brown v. Board of Education*

Heading: The state of Kansas in affording opportunities for elementary education to its citizens has no power under the Constitution of the United States to impose racial restrictions and distinctions.

	Paragraph Opener
1	**While the State of Kansas has undoubted power to confer benefits or impose disabilities upon selected groups of citizens in the normal execution of governmental functions, it must conform to constitutional standards in the exercise of this authority.** These standards may be generally characterized as a requirement that the state's action be reasonable. Reasonableness in a constitutional sense is determined by examining the action of the state to discover whether the distinctions or restrictions in issue are in fact based upon real differences pertinent to a lawful legislative objective.

2	**When the distinctions imposed are based upon race and color alone, the state's action is patently the epitome of that arbitrariness and capriciousness constitutionally impermissive under our system of government.** A racial criterion is a constitutional irrelevance, and is not saved from condemnation even though dictated by a sincere desire to avoid the possibility of violence or race friction. Only because it was a war measure designed to cope with a grave national emergency was the federal government permitted to level restrictions against persons of enemy descent. This action, "odious" and "suspect," even in times of national peril, must cease as soon as that peril is past.
3	**This Court has found violation of the equal protection clause in racial distinctions and restrictions imposed by the states in selection for jury service; ownership and occupancy of real property; gainful employment; and graduate and professional education.** The commerce clause in proscribing the imposition of racial distinctions and restrictions in the field of interstate travel is a further limitation of state power in this regard.
4	**Since 1940, in an unbroken line of decisions, this Court has clearly enunciated the doctrine that the state may not validly impose distinctions and restrictions among its citizens based upon race or color alone in each field of governmental activity where question has been raised.** On the other hand, when the state has sought to protect its citizenry against racial discrimination and prejudice, its action has been consistently upheld, even though taken in the field of foreign commerce.
5	**It follows, therefore, that under this doctrine, the State of Kansas which by statutory sanctions seeks to subject appellants, in their pursuit of elementary education, to distinctions based upon race or color alone, is here attempting to exceed the constitutional limits to its authority.** For that racial distinction which has been held arbitrary in so many other areas of governmental activity is no more appropriate and can be no more reasonable in public education.

You can see the puzzle metaphor at work here: Marshall has broken his heading into five pieces and then put the heading back together in five linear steps, each building on the one before.

Don't despair, though: some of our contemporaries manage to live up to this lofty standard.

Take former Solicitor General Seth Waxman's motion for a permanent injunction against eBay in *MercExchange v. eBay*, a dispute over eBay's "Buy It Now" technology.

Here is one of Waxman's headings:

Seth Waxman, *MercExchange v. eBay*

Heading: Depriving MercExchange of the right to choose to whom it licenses its patented technology is a harm that cannot be remedied with money damages.

Now look at how Waxman starts the five paragraphs in the section that follows.

On the left, I include the questions I would expect most judges to ask after reading Waxman's heading. On the right, I include Waxman's paragraph openers. It's almost as if he's predicting and then answering the judges' questions before they even have a chance to raise them.

Imagined questions	"Answers" in the five paragraph openers
Under what standard is there a "harm" here?	. . . . [A forced license] is "**antithetical to a basic tenet of the patent system** . . . that the decision whether to license is one that should be left to the patentee. . . ."

Imagined questions	"Answers" in the five paragraph openers
But even if you're right, why is that harm irreparable?	Forcing MercExchange to license its patent to someone not of its choosing is an **irreparable** harm—once lost it cannot be retroactively restored nor remedied with money. That is true **whether MercExchange uses** its patented invention itself in a commercial enterprise, **licenses** that invention, **or even refuses to license** or make any other use at all of the patent....
And why is the harm so bad that it warrants an injunction?	But the harm to MercExchange is particularly severe here. MercExchange, and MercExchange's licensees or potential licensees, are (or aspire to be) **competitors of eBay**—an entity that commands 90% of the relevant market....
But what about eBay's point that money damages like royalties could remedy any such harm?	And as the court explained in *Odetics*, the argument that future royalty payments ameliorate such harm to a patent holder is **untenable**....In addition, a compulsory license **denies the inventor** the opportunity to take an active role in the exploitation of his invention.
So what's the bottom line?	Permitting eBay to continue using MercExchange's technology without authorization is antithetical to the patent law and **irreparably harmful** to MercExchange.

I don't know where former Solicitor General Waxman learned to write the way he does, but as you'll see below in a brief filed by one of his GOP counterparts, the government takes a back seat to no one when it comes to logical progression in briefs. Here, for example, in a case from the Clinton years, Ted Olson is defending the federal government for declining to turn over autopsy photos of the White House Counsel Vince Foster. The government was trying to stave off a FOIA request from a man named Alan Favish who claimed that Hillary Clinton might have had Foster murdered to cover up some Whitewater shenanigans:

Ted Olson, *Office of Independent Counsel v. Favish*

[T]here is **no broadly recognized tradition** in the United States of public access to autopsy or crime-scene photographs or similar depictions of individuals immediately prior to or in the throes of their death....

Those cases and laws grow out of **long-established cultural traditions** acknowledging familial control over the body and image of the deceased....

The **need for such privacy protection** is crucial in modern times....

[B]ecause withholding cannot be predicated on the identity of the requester, it is the **privacy interest of surviving family members that allows** the government to deny requests by child molesters, rapists, murderers, and other violent felons for photographs and other records of their deceased victims....

Established tradition and **judicial practice thus demonstrate** that, like the rap sheets at issue in Reporters Committee, death-scene photographs and other images of the deceased and dying in the possession of the government are "not freely available to the public" and, instead, are "intended for or restricted to the use of a particular person or group or class of persons," giving affected family members a FOIA-protected privacy interest in restricting "the degree of dissemination."

Thus, the Foster family's privacy interest in these photographs is compelling....

In the end, then, the best advocates appear to sense that judges have predictable questions when reading a section:

1. What's the standard?
2. How does it apply in cases like this one?
3. Which courts have done what you're asking us to do—and why?
4. What about the other side's points?
5. What's the bottom line?

For our final example, let's return to the motion to dismiss in the Terra Firma case that Ted Wells & Co. wanted to ship to England.

Here you have the outline of a complete section. I've numbered the beginnings of Wells's six paragraphs:

Ted Wells, *Terra Firma v. Citigroup*

Heading: Terra Firma's claim regarding Citi's performance under the finance agreements must also be litigated in England.

1. Terra Firma is similarly required to litigate in England Count IV of its Complaint, which is connected to Citi's conduct **under the Finance Agreements**.
2. It is clear that the alleged misconduct occurred **"in connection with"** the Finance Agreements.
3. The allegations of the Complaint are **consistent with Citi's experience** throughout the auction, negotiation of the transaction financing and administering of the credit.
4. The same conclusion is **compelled under U.S. law**.
5. The **Second Circuit has also held** that non-parties may be bound to a forum selection clause: "the fact a party is a non-signatory to an agreement is insufficient, standing alone, to preclude enforcement of a forum selection clause."

---

6. Thus, **under either English or Second Circuit law**, the forum selection clauses contained in the Finance Agreements cover both the claim and the parties, and thus require Terra Firma to bring Count IV in England.

This Wells section brings us full circle in the structure realm: from preliminary statement to headings, and from headings to paragraph openers. You're simply putting together one puzzle after another by imagining and then recording a conversation with the court.

16

Sound Off: Start the paragraphs with numbered reasons

Some sections are more of a monologue than a dialogue. You're not trying to simulate a Socratic dialogue with a judge that addresses all possible concerns and counterarguments, as you would with the *With You in Spirit* technique. Instead, you need to *Sound Off*: "We're right, and here's why."

In another section of the Ted Wells motion to dismiss, for example, he starts with this heading:

> **Ted Wells, *Terra Firma v. Citigroup***
>
> **Terra Firma's Choice of Forum Is Entitled to Little or No Deference**

And then with this single sentence repeating the heading:

> Terra Firma's choice of forum is entitled to little or no deference.

And then with these three paragraphs, each starting with one of these numbered reasons:

> *First*, as a foreign plaintiff with no connection to the forum, Terra Firma is entitled to less deference than a U.S. plaintiff....

> **Second**, Terra Firma is not entitled to deference because the Project Mulberry Agreement and the Finance Agreements contain mandatory forum selection clauses requiring this dispute to be litigated in England. . . .
>
> **Third**, the events giving rise to this lawsuit do not have the required "bona fide" connection to this forum. . . .

Point made, indeed—and three times at that.

I cannot discuss lists without including an example from Maureen Mahoney, who, as I suggested in Part One, is one of brief writing's best list-makers.

Mahoney once had occasion to represent Arthur Andersen, the accounting firm convicted of corporate crimes after its client Enron, a former $100 billion energy-trading company, went bankrupt. Andersen was accused of overstating Enron's numbers and then shredding documents to cover it up. The conviction essentially put Andersen out of business.

A little too late for Andersen's employees, Mahoney persuaded the Supreme Court to reverse the company's conviction. Here, as part of her attack on the jury instructions used in the case, she devotes a section to listing four reasons that the intent to impede governmental fact-finding is not inherently corrupt. Here are the beginnings of her paragraphs:

> **Maureen Mahoney, *Arthur Andersen v. United States***
>
> **First**, it makes little sense to conclude that destruction of any potentially relevant documents prior to the pendency of a proceeding is inherently corrupt when Congress chose not to criminalize that conduct for the century preceding [lead Arthur Andersen partner] David Duncan's meeting with his managers. . . .

Second, this Court has rejected the view that any intentional effort to impede fact finding is inherently corrupt, even when a proceeding is pending....

Third, any presumption that an intent to impede fact finding is inherently corrupt cannot reasonably be extended beyond the context of judicial proceedings....

Finally, the interpretation of "corruptly" adopted by the Fifth Circuit would criminalize a wide variety of common conduct that is intended to impede official fact-finding within the bounds of the law....

Also from the criminal-law world, uber-defense lawyer and death-penalty opponent Judy Clarke argues below that prison officials violated Tucson, Arizona, shooting suspect Jared Loughner's due process rights when they medicated him against his will. Clarke also objects that because the medication matter was decided during administrative hearings rather than during an adversarial court hearing in front of a judge, her client had no opportunity to cross-examine witnesses:

Judy Clarke, *United States v. Loughner*

The district court's commitment order violated the *Williams/Hernandez-Vasquez/Evans* specificity rule in three ways. **First,** the district court deprived the defense of any "meaningful ability to challenge the propriety of the proposed treatment" by preventing defense counsel from cross examining the government's witnesses on the issue.

Second, the district court altogether failed to consider the medical appropriateness of the involuntary medication whose administration was necessary to fulfillment of its commitment order.

> **Third**, the substantial probability finding was made without reference to any specific course of future treatment....

(Quick formatting note: when you do use one of these enumerated lists, start a new paragraph for the first reason so it doesn't get buried in the introductory paragraph.)

Analogizing

Now that you've organized your overall paragraph progression, let's turn to ways to develop your opening sentences through case law and other authorities.

But first a general point: your success with these authorities depends on how much you use your own words and thoughts when you write about why those authorities support your client's position—or at least why they don't support your adversary's.

Yet most lawyers are too quick to announce that a given case is "on point" or "illustrative" or "easily distinguishable"—and then to summarize a bunch of facts from that case before appending a long block quote from the holding. That all-too-common approach can drive judges crazy. As Third Circuit Judge Leonard Garth once put it, "There is nothing more frustrating than a brief that spends 15 pages discussing every detail of every case tangentially related to the real question at issue."[1]

Here is a typical example of what Judge Garth means. First the attorneys say that they seek summary judgment on an employment claim. Fair enough. Then the attorneys cite a case called *Elrod* in support. But how long must you read about *Elrod* before learning why it

---

1. Leonard I. Garth, *How to Appeal to an Appellate Judge*, 21 Litig. 20, 24–66 (Fall 1994).

means that the judge should grant summary judgment here and now, in your case?

To survive summary judgment Plaintiff is required to produce evidence suggesting the existence of a genuine issue of material fact.

In *Elrod v. Sears Roebuck & Co.*, 939 F.2d 1466 (11th Cir. 1989), the plaintiff claimed he was terminated from employment because of his age. The defendant claimed it terminated the plaintiff based upon receipt of allegations of sexual harassment and the resulting investigation of those claims. **[Are you still reading?]** At trial, the evidence focused on whether the plaintiff actually engaged in the conduct with which he was accused. After the jury found in the plaintiff's favor, the Eleventh Circuit held the focus of the inquiry should not have been whether the plaintiff engaged in sexual harassment, but whether the defendant established a legitimate non-discriminatory reason for its actions—i.e., did the employer honestly believe the plaintiff had engaged in sexual harassment, and if so, whether that belief was the reason for the discharge. *Elrod* at 1470. Accordingly, the court assumed that "the complaining employees were lying through their teeth," but noted nevertheless that:

Federal courts do not sit as a super-personnel department that reexamines an entity's business decisions. No matter how medieval a firm's practices, no matter how highhanded its decisional process, no matter how mistaken the firm's managers, the ADEA does not interfere. Rather our inquiry is limited to whether the employer gave an honest explanation for its behavior.

Elrod at 1470. If the employer provides an honest explanation for its behavior, the remaining inquiry is whether the plaintiff has produced evidence of pretext or, put another way, has the plaintiff produced evidence that the employer's justification for its actions is "unworthy of credence." *Elrod* at 1470. Holding that no such evidence was presented to the court, the Eleventh Circuit held that the defendant was entitled to judgment as a matter of law.

In this example, and in millions just like it, the attorneys' discussion of a case has become an end in itself. It's as if the attorneys were saying to the court, "Go read what one judge once said about a dispute between strangers—and then figure out on your own how all those details from the past relate to the present." After a while, a lawyer who treats cases that way starts to come across as a summarizer and scribe, not as a true writer.

So make your discussions of authorities just a means to an end—and that end is a reason you win, or at least don't lose. Or in the words of the great Supreme Court advocate John Davis, as quoted by Justice Ruth Bader Ginsburg, a first-rate brief "uses citations to fortify the argument, not to certify the lawyer's diligence."

Let's consider seven ways to follow their advice.

17

Long in the Tooth: Say "me too"

One of the most persuasive points you can make as an advocate is that courts have long done what you want—or have never done what your opponent wants.

In the following example, former Solicitor General Greg Garre argues that doctors can diagnose a disability based on a patient's self-reported medical history:

Greg Garre, *Weber v. Infinity Broadcasting*

Courts have recognized this principle where, as here, the disability concerns a reaction to chemicals, including **perfume-related products**. *See Whillock v. Delta Air Lines, Inc.*, 926 F. Supp. 1555, 1562–63 (N.D. Ga. 1995) (rejecting…defendant's attacks on the medical opinions offered by plaintiff's doctors—based primarily on plaintiff's own recitation of her medical history—and finding a triable issue regarding whether sensitivity to smell of alcohol and perfume constituted a disability).

And in an antitrust case, David Boies similarly claims that *no* court has found what his adversary suggests about the functional availability doctrine, which is a judge-created defense to a price-discrimination antitrust claim. What is especially helpful here is how Boies presents these three distinct cases. Note the parallel structure: the court did such and such, "even though" the plaintiff faced one difficulty or another. Boies also gives you just enough facts about the "difficulty" to understand why the case helps prove the opening sentence true. We learn, for example, that in the first case the company had "inventory problems," but we don't need to know where its warehouse was or what kind of widgets it sold. Boies knows exactly why he's citing each case—and we get no more and no less:

David Boies, *Smith Wholesale v. Phillip Morris*

No decision applying the functional availability doctrine has turned upon the claimed difficulty or reasonableness of the choice. In *Bouldis*, **functional availability was found even though** the plaintiff had "cash flow and inventory problems that prevented him" from receiving the discount. In *Capitol Ford*, **summary judgment was granted even though** the plaintiff's focus on small customers made it "impossible" to meet the seller's conditions. In *Krist Oil Co., Inc.*, **the claims were dismissed even though** the plaintiffs "needed" to make business decisions that made qualifying impossible under the defendant's pricing structure.

Obama Solicitor General Don Verrilli sounded *Long in the Tooth* himself in arguing to the Supreme Court below that federal law preempts Arizona's controversial immigration statute:

Don Verrilli, *Arizona v. United States*

Arizona's contention is well wide of the mark. That the State purports to regulate the same conduct as federal law is the beginning of the inquiry, not the end. A scheme that depends on national uniformity cannot co-exist with a patchwork of different state regimes, whether that patchwork involves 50 different decision-makers, 50 different remedies, or 50

> different substantive rules. **Indeed, this Court has repeatedly held that in areas committed to the National Government, the States may not second-guess Congress's choice of how to carry out its aims, or though whom—even if the States profess to share the same aims as Congress.**

(Note Verilli's repetition of "50." Also note that he writes the possessive form of "Congress" as "Congress's," not "Congress'." That's in keeping with the practices of the Solicitor General's Office, with the federal government's own style manual, and with major contemporary usage authorities, most of which mandate an apostrophe *s* for a singular noun made possessive unless it's a biblical, classical, or mythological name like Jesus or Achilles.)

On the private-practice side, Sri Srinivasan (now a D.C. Circuit judge) and Deanne Maynard similarly touted Supreme Court precedent to bolster their argument that the Federal Arbitration Act is, well, pro-arbitration:

Sri Srinivasan and Deanne Maynard,
CompuCredit Corp. v. Greenwood

This **Court has repeatedly emphasized** that the Federal Arbitration Act "embodies the national policy favoring arbitration."

You can use a variation on this technique when you want a decision upheld on appeal—or when you don't want the Supreme Court to review it at all. Employment-defense lawyer Nancy Abell had such a goal in mind in a cert petition for Coca-Cola in a case about whether alcoholism is a per se disability:

Nancy Abell, *Burch v. Coca-Cola*

The Fifth Circuit in this case **applied well-established law to reach a predictable disposition**: An employee who failed to prove that he was substantially limited in any major life activity at the time of his alcohol-induced misconduct or consequent termination is not entitled to recover under the Americans with Disabilities Act.

For good measure, you might even highlight how people have relied on the precedent, as Seventh Circuit Chief Judge Frank Easterbrook did here while representing the United States as deputy solicitor general:

Frank Easterbrook, *United States v. Crittenden*

In 1827, when this Court decided *Rankin v. Scott*, a case involving the relative priority of two private judgment liens, the first in time rule was already a settled principle of law. As Mr. Chief Justice Marshall observed, "[t]he principle is believed to be universal that a prior [valid] lien gives a prior claim, which is entitled to prior satisfaction out of the subject it binds." The rule has been followed, at common law, ever since. . . .

The rule has been followed for so long that expectations— indeed, entire systems of lending—have been built on it.

18

Peas in a Pod: Link your party with the party in the cited case

One of the bad habits lawyers-to-be pick up in law school (and often keep for decades) is mentioning that a case is "on point," only to rehash all the facts of that case in an endless paragraph stuffed with citations and quotations. Then, in a new paragraph, the attorney starts with "that case is just like the present case," only to rehash all the facts from the current dispute.

The best advocates spare the court all that tedium: They link the parties, old and new alike, as soon as they can.

Here's a prime example from former Solicitor General Seth Waxman, who was defending Lucent in a bankruptcy proceeding appealed to the District Court of Delaware. One of the issues was whether Lucent was an "insider" because it was a "person in control" over Winstar Communications, the debtor. Note how quickly Waxman inserts "like Lucent here" and "like the Trustee here," joining old and new. And when he does refer to this so-called leading case, he uses "defendant bank" and "debtor" rather than the parties' real names. Why muddy up the discussion?

> **Seth Waxman, *In re Winstar Communications***
>
> The leading case of *In re Badger Freightways, Inc.* exemplifies the correct analysis of "person in control," and throws into stark relief the errors made by the bankruptcy court here. In that case, **the defendant bank, like Lucent here,** contended that the debtor "must allege facts demonstrating that [the alleged insider] had management control over [the debtor]." In

> contrast, **the debtor, like the Trustee here,** claimed that "[a]ll it must allege are facts demonstrating that [the debtor] and the [defendant bank] representative were sufficiently close that the restructuring was not negotiated on an arms-length basis...."

Here's a final example by Herbert Wachtell, who cites the notorious Ponzi schemer Bernie Madoff as part of his effort to fight against a related class-action lawsuit:

Herbert Wachtell, *Barron v. Igolnikov*

Here, Madoff **engaged in precisely the type of conduct** described in *SEC v. Zandford*: he told investors he would purchase and sell securities but never did.

19

Mince Their Words: Merge pithy quoted phrases into a sentence about your own case

I'll discuss later what to do about long block quotes, but here's a preview: Too many attorneys quote too much and too often. Yes, of course you sometimes need the court's actual language. But if you push that idea too far, your brief can become a "promiscuous uttering of citations," as former Third Circuit Chief Judge Ruggero Aldisert has called it.[1]

Mince Their Words offers a compromise. First write a sentence about your own case, and only then intersperse snippets from the authorities you cite.

Here, for example, Ted Olson and David Boies are fighting Proposition 8, the California gay-marriage ban. They include some apt words and phrases from *Romer v. Evans*, an earlier gay-rights case, but the sentence is still mostly theirs:

> **Ted Olson and David Boies, *Perry v. Schwarzenegger***
>
> Indeed, the implausible justifications proffered by Proposed Intervenors merely reinforce the **"inevitable inference that the disadvantage imposed"** on gay and lesbian individuals by Prop. 8 **"is born of"** nothing more than naked **"animosity."**

---

1. RUGGERO J. ALDISERT, OPINION WRITING 141 (2nd ed. 2009).

Let's move from California to the East Coast. You may remember when NBA executive Anucha Browne sued the New York Knicks' Isaiah Thomas and Madison Square Garden. On the defense side, Miguel Estrada "minces" a case's "words" in similar fashion here:

Miguel Estrada, *Sanders v. Madison Square Garden*

Nor is there the slightest evidence that [Sanders] was a **"financially vulnerable"** **"target"** of **"economic injury"** inflicted by Madison Square Garden.

Likewise, Sri Srinivasan and Deanne Maynard weave in the Supreme Court's words from a 1987 opinion to remind the Court that it has historically ruled in favor of arbitration:

Sri Srinivasan and Deanne Maynard,
CompuCredit Corp. v. Greenwood

While the [Federal Arbitration Act's] strong federal policy **"may be overridden by a congressional command,"** this Court's precedents require Congress to speak clearly when issuing any such **"command."**

(Try to reserve "While" for time, as in "While the case was on appeal, the parties settled." For subordination, as here, prefer "Although" or "Even though.")

20

One Up: Claim that the case you're citing applies even more to your own dispute

Though it's not for the faint of heart, another technique can deepen your persuasive voice: suggest that the holding in the case you're citing applies to your own case even better than it applies to the original. Just make sure that you're not setting the bar higher than need be.

In this example, Larry Tribe is litigating a Supreme Court case about whether schools and churches can ban alcohol permits to establishments within 500 feet. Tribe claims that the statute authorizing such bans is even worse than a law that the Court had already struck down in an old 1912 case called *Eubank*. In that case, the challenged ordinance allowed two-thirds of the residents of a district to set back another resident's property line:

Larry Tribe, *Larkin v. Grendel's Den*

One of the vices noted by this Court in its review of the *Eubank* ordinance was its lack of uniformity: one side of a street might have a set-back line while the other did not; houses might be staggered back and forth on successive blocks; set-back lines might be set at greatly different distances. **Yet, for all that, the *Eubank* ordinance at least had the virtue of being consistent** for the group of property owners who compelled a set-back line's establishment and were thereby reciprocally

---

> bound, along with their neighbors, by the results of their action....
>
> Section 16C is in this sense **far** *more* **offensive**, because it allows a church to target and veto particular license applicants on an ad hoc, non-uniform, and wholly non-reciprocal basis.

(After an abstract verb like "compelled," the reader is searching for the object. So "compelled the establishment of a set-back line" would have been a little longer than "compelled a set-back line's establishment," but it also might have been clearer.)

Greg Garre used this same technique to suggest that the damages his country-music-DJ client has obtained are much smaller than the damages the Michigan courts have upheld before:

> **Greg Garre, *Weber v. Infinity Broadcasting***
>
> Defendants suggest that the award of non-economic damages is not in line with other awards in other cases and therefore must reflect passion, prejudice, or bias. But the most analogous case from Michigan compels the opposite conclusion. In *Olsen v. Toyota Technical Center*, **the court upheld an award** of mental distress damages in a discrimination case **two and a half times greater than the award here**.

Here is a similar *One Up* example from the Affordable Care Act wars, this one penned by Paul Clement, who claims that the Act's

Medicaid provisions are more "coercive" than those that the Supreme Court has previously struck down:

Paul Clement, *Florida v. Dep't of Health & Human Services*

Here, as in *New York [v. United States]*, "Congress has crossed the line distinguishing encouragement from coercion." **If anything, the coerciveness is even more profound in the [Affordable Care Act]** because States are, for practical purposes, *incapable* of assuming that financial burden so long as Congress continues to collect billions of tax dollars from their residents to fund a massive spending program for which they will no longer be eligible.

For our final example, let's turn to Jamie Gorelick as she tries to dismiss claims against Duke University arising out of the Duke Lacrosse scandal. In confronting the lacrosse players' claims that the university owed them contractual duties based on its student handbook, she *One Ups* a line of cases about employee handbooks, stressing not their facts but their reasoning:

Jamie Gorelick, *Carrington v. Duke University*

The reason that the courts have declined to recognize an employee handbook as part of a contract between an employer and an employee—avoiding excessive interference in an employer's internal affairs—**appl[ies] with even greater force to the university setting**, where anti-harassment policies must be balanced against principles of academic freedom, including the right of professors and students to speak out on issues of public concern, and the right of the university to insist that its students and employees observe standards of behavior.

(Kudos to Gorelick for using "even greater force" rather than the pretentious "*a fortiori!*" But try to keep like parts of the sentence together. Many lawyers write sentences like "Plaintiff's contention that ... is erroneous." Here's the problem: by the time you get to "erroneous," you've forgotten what the "contention" is all about. Better to write "Plaintiff is incorrect in claiming X." "Reason" is so far away from "applies" that the sentence is hard to follow. How about two sentences: "Courts have declined to recognize employee handbooks as binding contracts, because courts want to avoid meddling in employers' internal affairs. That motive applies with even more force to the university setting, where ....")

21

Interception: Claim that a case your opponent cites helps you alone

Still not feeling faint of heart? Here's a technique requiring even more courage: you "intercept" a holding your opponent cites, not by saying that it applies to you even more, but by saying that it applies to you and you alone.

On Martha Stewart's behalf, Walter Dellinger intercepts a case that the Justice Department itself paraded to the Court:

Walter Dellinger, *United States v. Stewart*

Finally, the Fifth Circuit's decision in *United States v. Robinson* **supports Stewart, not the Government**. In explaining why [the Confrontation Clause case *Crawford v. Washington*] permitted admission of a co-conspirator's threat to kill a witness who had "snitched," the court stressed that the threat "was made during the course of the conspiracy and *is non-testimonial in nature*." If the Government's reading of *Crawford* were correct, the italicized language would have been entirely unnecessary. Under Stewart's, however, it makes perfect sense. Because *Crawford* leaves *Roberts* intact as to non-testimonial statements, a conclusion that the threat fell within some valid hearsay exception (or was otherwise "reliable") was necessary, but not sufficient.

(Hats off to Dellinger for using the subjunctive mood here: it's "If the reading *were* correct," not "*was* correct," because he's assuming something that to his mind isn't true. It's just like "If I *were* a rich man.")

22

Rebound: "Re-analogize" after the other side tries to distinguish

Still more "Games Lawyers Play": First you cite a case. Then the other side distinguishes it. But then you get the last word: it's analogous after all. These examples speak for themselves; the attorneys acknowledge the other side's claimed grounds for distinguishing their case, but note that the court's decision hinged on something else entirely.

> **Andy Frey, *Elbit Systems v. Credit Suisse Group***
>
> Plaintiff argues that this case law is irrelevant because the releases in the cases Credit Suisse Group cited were broader than the release at issue here. **But the outcome in those cases did not hinge on how broadly the release was drafted.** "New York law does not construe a general release to bar claims for injuries unknown at the time the release was executed, *even when the release contains broad language*."

> **Virginia Seitz, *Williams v. Mohawk Industries***
>
> Plaintiffs simply have not and cannot distinguish *Baker*. Plaintiffs purport to distinguish it on the ground that the *Baker* employees were "unionized." ***Baker*, however, is not based on the unionized status of employees**. To the contrary, the Baker court expressly held that amending the complaint to "cure" the flaws resulting from the allegation that the employees were

> unionized would be futile because plaintiffs failed to state a
> sufficient claim under RICO § 1962(c).

(Note that "have not" doesn't work here, because it would require "distinguished" not "distinguish." Better yet, just cut the "have not" altogether and stick with "cannot distinguish." If they can't distinguish it, who cares if they tried to?)

In this final twist, Federal Circuit Judge (and one-time Supreme Court advocate) Richard Taranto rebounds by parroting back the government's own claimed basis for distinguishing a major First Amendment case:

Richard Taranto, *Holder v. Humanitarian Law Project*

The government's attempt to distinguish *Gentile v. State Bar of Nevada* [is] unpersuasive. **If *Gentile* involved "classic political speech," so does this case**: teaching people to advocate for peace and human rights is at least as "political" as commenting on a criminal case.

As we have seen through all these examples, in analogizing authorities, you should sound like an informed commentator, not like a news anchor reading from a prompter. You can't just say that a case is important, only to summarize its facts and copy its language. You have to work with the case, shaping it and molding it until you find your own way of describing how it fits into your logical puzzle.

The same skill set applies to our next challenge: distinguishing unfavorable authorities.

Distinguishing

Never panic when your opponent cites a case that goes against you. As with analogizing, just avoid reciting a barrage of facts or a slew of quotations from the decision.

Use these four techniques instead.

23

Not Here, Not Now: Lead with the key difference between your opponent's case and your own

One simple but underused technique for distinguishing a case is the mirror image of *Peas in a Pod*: home in on the point of distinction immediately before reciting any other facts.

After author Tim O'Brien claimed in a book that Donald Trump was worth between $150 million and $250 million, Trump sued him for defamation, insisting that the number was way off. "I am a billionaire, many times over, on a conservative basis," said The Donald in a deposition. Mary Jo White came to O'Brien's rescue and helped get the case dismissed.

Note White's perfectly parallel contrasts here. Say someone libels you in an article and you publish your own rebuttal article in response. You can count those "corrective advertising expenses" as mitigation damages if the ads run right away and concede that the original article was false—but not if they run one year later and don't mention the libelous words at all:

Mary Jo White, *Trump v. O'Brien*

[To recover mitigation damages, Trump] must be able to demonstrate some clear connection between alleged injuries flowing from the defamatory statement and the advertising. In *Den Norske*, for example, the court granted corrective advertising expenses as mitigation damages because the advertisements **ran "promptly"** following the alleged defamatory

---

> statements and **explicitly denied** "the truthfulness of the
> allegations contained in the libelous article." **By contrast,**
> here the [advertisement that Trump ran on his behalf] **ran
> one year** after the alleged defamatory statements, and the
> advertisement was general in nature and **did not even men-
> tion** Trump's net worth—the subject of the allegedly defam-
> atory statements.

Let's shift from books to music. In one of the great copyright
disputes of all time, former Solicitor General Ted Olson similarly
distinguishes *Sony v. Universal City Studios*, a 1984 Supreme Court
decision involving VCRs, of all things. Olson focuses on a key difference between one set of defendants and his opponent, Grokster, the
now-defunct Napster-like file-sharing company:

Ted Olson, *MGM Studios v. Grokster*

Unlike the defendants in *Sony*, **[Grokster has] done far
more than simply release** into the stream of commerce a
product that can be used to infringe. Rather, [Grokster has]
launched a scheme with the primary purpose of assisting
infringement; any lawful use of their services is an incidental byproduct.

For the next example, we shift to yet another mode of entertainment: video games. This excerpt comes from Paul Smith's winning brief against California's law restricting the sale of violent video
games to minors. When Smith distinguishes a case that the other side
relied on, he doesn't start by recounting the case's facts, as so many

other lawyers would. Instead, he targets the main point of distinction: homes are not schools.

Paul Smith, *Brown v. Entertainment Merchants Association*

For example, California relies on *Bethel School District Number
403 v. Fraser*, which upheld regulation of lewd comments at
school. **But the world is not a schoolhouse**, and this Court
recently emphasized that *Fraser* would have come out differently had the comments been made outside of school.

Sometimes, you may have more than one reason a case is *Not
Here, Not Now*. Take this example from Attorney General Eric Holder
in an ERISA dispute involving race-discrimination claims. He swipes
at a case called *Teamsters* in two sentences, the first distinction rooted
in fact, and the second in law:

Eric Holder, *Barham v. UBS*

[Plaintiff] Spradley cites *Teamsters v. United States*, for the
proposition that a plaintiff is excused from proving that he
applied for a particular position if he can prove that an application would have been futile. **Spradley, however, has not
offered any evidence of futility.** Moreover, **even in cases
where futility is established, a plaintiff nevertheless must
identify** particular positions and demonstrate that he would
have applied for them were it not for the defendant's discriminatory practices.

(The "moreover" in the second sentence drags down the prose,
as do "in cases where" and "nevertheless." How about just "And even

when futility is established, a plaintiff must still identify particular positions"?)

You might remember that Mattel and rival toymaker MGA went head-to-head over the Bratz dolls. MGA had infringed on Mattel's copyrights, and Mattel wanted the dolls recalled (an injunction to that effect was granted and then reversed, and MGA ultimately won the dispute in 2011). Representing plaintiff Mattel, John Quinn, like Holder, lists two reasons that a case cited by MGA does not apply:

John Quinn, *Mattel v. MGA Entertainment*

MGA's reading of the case—that "a recall order is only appropriate in [the Ninth] Circuit when the party seeking the recall can establish *both* factors necessary to obtain an ordinary prohibitory injunction *and* has prevailed with respect to three additional factors"—**doubly misstates** the holding. **Ordering a recall** of an allegedly infringing product **at the outset** of a case on a motion for a preliminary injunction is obviously **far different than ordering one after years** of litigation and months of trial, with the benefit of the "fully developed record" the *Marlyn* court emphasized it lacked. Moreover, even at the preliminary injunction stage, the *Marlyn* **court merely** "requir[ed] the district court to *consider* [specified] factors before granting...."

(More style tips: When you're comparing like things like ordering, "different" takes "from," not "than." And after a line like "doubly misstates the holding," numbering *First* and *Second* can help the court follow your reasoning.)

Even if you have three or more bases for distinction, you can still list them in a single sentence, as Richard Taranto does here. Note that he doesn't beat you over the head with the obvious—that the current case, unlike *Pierce*, *does* present a vagueness challenge, *does* involve a criminal statute, and so forth:

Richard Taranto, *Holder v. Humanitarian Law Project*

The government also contends that . . . the distinction between "general knowledge" and "specific skills" has a "settled usage." But the best the government can cite for support is *Pierce v. Underwood*, 487 U.S. 552 (1988), which **(a) presented no vagueness challenge, (b) involved a non-criminal statute**, the Equal Access to Justice Act, that does not use the terms "general knowledge" or "specific skills," and **(c) actually underscores the terms' ambiguity** here.

(Taranto really knows his *which vs. that* rules. The "that" after "Justice Act," is correct. As I mentioned earlier while discussing a Ted Cruz excerpt, it's simply not true that after a comma you always need "which," especially when there's an intervening phrase like "the Equal Justice Act." One tip, though: as with the Larry Tribe example above, rather than "underscores the terms' ambiguity" here, consider putting the object after the verb "underscores" and losing the apostrophe: "underscores the ambiguity of these terms.")

24

One Fell Swoop: Distinguish a line of cases all at once

Few things are more tedious to read than the announcement that "The cases that Defendant cites are all distinguishable" followed by endless paragraphs summarizing the facts of each.

Turn that common habit on its head: can you dismiss a line of cases up front in *One Fell Swoop*, focusing on the one thing that makes all those cases irrelevant here and now?

Consider how Maureen Mahoney disposes of cases cited by her opponent, the proposed intervenors in a dispute over lead regulations:

Maureen Mahoney, *Toy Industry Association v. City and County of San Francisco*

The decisions upon which Proposed Intervenors rely are inapposite. **In each case, there was a clear divergence between** the government's duty to protect the public, broadly defined, and the applicant's narrow or parochial interests in the litigation.

Now see how Larry Lessig defends the author of a Harry Potter lexicon against J. K. Rowling, who had sued him for copyright infringement. After mentioning the cases Rowling cites, Lessig neutralizes them all—in one fell swoop:

Larry Lessig, *Warner Bros. Entertainment v. RDR Books*

None of the works at issue in those cases served a purpose comparable to the Lexicon's; each was essentially

---

an abridgement that retold the original story in its original sequence, albeit in shortened form. Each was therefore a plausible substitute for the original work.

Let's end with three virtuoso versions of *One Fell Swoop*.

Below, two WilmerHale veterans—the NAACP's Payton and former Solicitor General Waxman—obliterate two lines of cases in a pre-*Shelby* Voting Rights Act dispute over whether state electoral-law changes must receive preclearance from the federal government:

> **John Payton and Seth Waxman, *Northwest Austin Utility District Number One v. Gonzales***
>
> The authorities cited by the City offer no support for the City's expansive reading of Section 435. Neither *People v. Westchester County* nor *People v. Lieberman* concerns Section 435, and in any event, **neither addresses a situation as here, where the owner's consent to public use of its property is limited in scope.** Likewise, although *People v. Garland* and *Fieldston Property Owners' Ass'n v. Bianchi* address the scope of Section 435, their **failure to address the status of private properties whose permitted public use is limited** render them equally inapplicable:

(I'm happy to see the singular verb "addresses" after "neither." But there's one nit: Payton and Waxman mean "addresses a situation like the one here," not "addresses a situation as here": they are comparing like things. John Quinn gets this like-as distinction right below.)

Speaking of John Quinn, who defended Mattel in the Bratz dispute, in just one quick paragraph below, he distinguishes two cases that JPMorgan had asserted against his client:

John Quinn, *Lehman Brothers Holding Inc. v. JPMorgan Chase Bank, N.A.*

JPMorgan's cited cases do not address Plaintiff's argument. In both *In re Bernstein* and *Banks v. Siegel*, a secured loan was made in reliance on a financial statement that was partially false. In each case, the court held that the fact that the loans were secured did not "necessarily negat[e]" the creditor's reliance on the false statement. These cases are thus **only relevant to the straw-man argument** JPMorgan constructs about whether secured creditors can ever reasonably rely on fraudulent misrepresentations. **Neither case addresses a situation like this one, where the creditor continued to operate under the assumption that the alleged misrepresentation was incorrect after the misrepresentation was made.**

For a final example of *One Fell Swoop*, let's turn to a reply brief filed by Patrick Fitzgerald, the former corrupt-politician-busting U.S. Attorney for Chicago. In this example, Fitzgerald was prosecuting an ex-cop for obstructing justice during an investigation into alleged torture of suspects:

Patrick Fitzgerald, *United States v. Burge*

Defendant does not cite a single case to support his argument that perjury and obstruction of justice do not exist if someone else committed perjury or obstruction of justice first. Nor does defendant cite a single case to support his argument that someone is free to commit perjury or obstruction of justice if he decides that he is facing a meritless lawsuit.

Each of the cases the defendant does cite **stand for the same proposition—that false statements designed to influence the criminal justice system, especially those of law enforcement officers, are abhorrent to the pursuit of justice and should not be countenanced.**

(Avoid "exist" and "do not exist." Maybe "Defendant does not cite a single case to support his argument that a defendant cannot be charged with perjury and obstruction of justice if someone else committed those offenses first." And a grammar tip: "Each" is singular, not plural, so each of those cases "stands," not "stand.")

25

Not So Fast: Show that the case does not apply as broadly as your opponent suggests

Sometimes, your opponent cites a case that just doesn't apply. That's when you want *Not Here, Not Now*. Other times, the case your opponent cites applies in theory, but not in practice. Your best bet in that situation is to scream *Not So Fast*, swatting at the case until it becomes more of an annoying fly than a poisonous snake.

Sometimes you can use a court's opinion in one case to undercut the same court's proclamation in another. Defending the New York Knicks below, for example, Miguel Estrada concedes that punitive damages can be many multiples of compensatory damages—just not too many:

Miguel Estrada, *Sanders v. Madison Square Garden*

To be sure, the Supreme Court has also made clear that "low awards of compensatory damages may properly support a higher ratio than high compensatory awards if, for example, a particularly egregious act has resulted in only a *small amount* of economic damages." Similarly, the Second Circuit has held that "the use of a multiplier to assess punitive damages is not the best tool" where a Plaintiff is awarded only nominal damages. **But neither court has ever suggested** that an award of *zero* actual damages may properly support a punitive damages award in the hundreds of thousands of dollars, much less an award of $6,000,000.

Here, too, Seth Waxman concedes that a doctrine exists, but he insists that it goes only so far:

Seth Waxman, *In re Winstar Communications*

Certainly, some courts have begun the insider discussion by reference to dealing at "arm's length." For example, the Second Circuit has stated that an insider is one who has "a sufficiently close relationship with the debtor that his conduct is made subject to closer scrutiny than those dealing at arm's length with the debtor." **But even those courts have made clear** that such general observations cannot replace the requirement that an insider have actual managerial control.

You can also claim, as David Boies does, that an isolated sentence has been cited "out of context":

David Boies, *American Express Travel Related Services Company v. Visa*

The Association Defendants simply ignore this black letter law. Instead, they repeatedly cite, **out of context**, a single sentence in *Johnson v. Nyack Hosp.*, 86 F.3d 8, 11 (2d Cir. 1996)— "An antitrust cause of action accrues as soon as there is injury to competition"—to suggest that that alone is sufficient to start a particular plaintiff's statute of limitations. **The decision does not remotely stand for this proposition....** [T]he question of when the plaintiff's claim initially accrued **was not even at issue** because it was undisputed that the plaintiff was injured when the challenged action first occurred (through the revocation of plaintiff's hospital privileges).

Similarly, you can stress that the language your opponent cites just doesn't have the persuasive force your opponent suggests, as Roy Englert does here:

> **Roy Englert, *Federal Insurance Company v. Kingdom of Saudi Arabia***
>
> **Petitioners highlight (and characterize as a "holding")** a single sentence from the background section of *Price v. Socialist People's Libyan Arab Jamahiriya* in which the court stated that, "[u]nder the original FSIA,...terrorism, torture, and hostage taking committed abroad were immunized forms of state activity." **Petitioners infer** from that statement that the FSIA's terrorism exception—which they say was intended to provide a remedy for acts of terrorism where none previously existed—is confined to terrorist acts occurring outside U.S. borders, while terrorism committed inside U.S. borders is and always has been covered by the torts exception. **But the D.C. Circuit held no such thing**, and for good reason.

Sri Srinivasan and Deanne Maynard effectively use this technique in a reply brief below. Note how they start off broadly—arguing why the case *generally* does not support what respondents suggest it does—before delving into the specifics:

> **Sri Srinivasan and Deanne Maynard, *CompuCredit Corp. v. Greenwood***
>
> In contending that the Court should resolve this case without regard to the FAA's strong policy favoring arbitration, respondents rely on a footnote in this Court's opinion in *14 Penn Plaza LLC v. Pyett*, 129 S. Ct. 1456, 1470 n.9 (2009). *Pyett,*

> **however, affords no basis for departing from the estab-**
> **lished rule** "that questions of arbitrability must be addressed
> with a healthy regard for the federal policy favoring arbitra-
> tion." To the contrary, *Pyett* strongly reaffirms *Gilmer* and
> its requirement that the Court will read a statute to preclude
> arbitration only if Congress makes any such intention unmis-
> takably clear. *Pyett* addressed the enforceability of a term in a
> collective bargaining agreement...

(Put "however" after a complete unit of thought that contrasts
with the sentence before. You're not contrasting *Pyett* with itself.
You're contrasting what *Pyett* does and doesn't stand for. So "*Pyett*
affords no basis, however, for departing from the established
rule.")

In the examples above, the advocates focus on just one or two reasons that their opponents shouldn't pop the cork quite yet. If you're
lucky, though, you might be able to keep the count going. To that end,
representing pharmaceutical sales reps in an overtime fight against
the company now known as GlaxoSmithKline, SCOTUSblog founder Tom Goldstein included in a Supreme Court reply brief not one
but four reasons that a key case doesn't go as far as the respondent
suggests:

> **Tom Goldstein, *Christopher v. SmithKline Beecham***
>
> Contrary to respondent's insinuations, *Auer [v. Robbins]* def-
> erence [to the Department of Labor's interpretation of over-
> time regulations] is not *carte blanche* for agencies. **First,** if an
> agency position is plainly erroneous or inconsistent with the
> relevant regulations, then deference is not warranted. **Sec-**
> **ond,** *Auer* does not authorize deference when a regulation

merely parrots the statute. **Third**, courts need not defer when "faced with a post-hoc rationalization...of agency action that is under judicial review," or if there is "other reason to suspect that the interpretation does not reflect the agency's fair and considered judgment on the matter in question." *Talk Am., Inc.*, 131 S. Ct. at 2263. **Fourth**, before the agency can interpret its regulations, it must enact them....

Authority Problems: Suggest that the case deserves little respect

What should you do when the case is just bad? You can always attack its reasoning and hope for the best. But you also have a few other tricks at your disposal.

Consider this example, again from Deanne Maynard. This former Assistant to the Solicitor General doesn't hide her scorn for the contrary authorities here: They just aren't high enough on the judicial totem pole to warrant the High Court's attention:

> **Deanne Maynard, *KFC Corporation v. Iowa Department of Revenue***
>
> Thus, no decision of this Court ever has sustained a state tax imposed on an out-of-state business that has no in-state presence in the taxing State. **It is only the state court below— and the rulings of 12 other state courts—that have reached a contrary result.**

Or try another tack. Don't call the court "wrong," call it "old." In this example, Paul Smith mocks California's reliance on two fusty cases from more than a century ago. For good measure, though, he distinguishes them on the merits as well:

> **Paul Smith, *Brown v. Entertainment Merchants Association***
>
> This Court has unambiguously held that obscenity is limited to "works which depict or describe sexual conduct."

California's citation to **two 19th-century** obscenity statutes referring to "vulgar" or "indecent" materials **hardly suffices to demonstrate that depictions of violence alone can ever be obscene.** And the fact that some depictions of sexual obscenity may involve violence does not mean that violence, standing alone, is obscene.

In rare cases, you can also accuse a court of being just plain wrong, even when the case is controlling. Bob Bennett doesn't shirk from such a claim as part of his defense of Judy Miller, the *New York Times* reporter jailed for refusing to testify to a grand jury investigating the outing of CIA agent Valerie Plame during the George W. Bush years:

Bob Bennett, *Miller v. United States*

The Ninth Circuit and now the D.C. Circuit have recognized a privilege for reporters subpoenaed in criminal cases but not those subpoenaed by a grand jury. Like the Special Counsel, neither court even attempted to provide any rationale for such a distinction except to observe that *Branzburg* arose in the grand jury context. **Ultimately, the criminal trial/grand jury distinction is not only unpersuasive but is irreconcilable with *Branzburg* itself, which used the phrases "criminal trial" and "grand jury" interchangeably.**

(Style tips: great writers often repeat prepositions for clarity, so consider "but not **for** those subpoenaed by a grand jury." And make sure your "not only…but" constructions have parallel structure. So try "is not only unpersuasive but irreconcilable.")

One obvious time to use this strategy is when you want a decision reversed on appeal. Direct your hostility toward the decision, though, and not toward the judge or court. Otherwise your anger may backfire, as Ninth Circuit Chief Judge Alex Kozinski has cautioned: "Chances are I'll be seeing that district judge soon at one of those secret conferences where judges go off together to gossip about the lawyers."[1]

Another Chief Judge, Seventh Circuit Chief Judge Frank Easterbrook, got the tone right as a lawyer in a case involving Henry Kissinger. As deputy solicitor general, he stressed the *Why Should I Care?* factor below, criticizing the trial and appellate decisions without attacking the judges themselves:

Frank Easterbrook, *Kissinger v. Reporters Committee for Freedom of the Press*

The remarkable thing about the district court's opinion (which was adopted by the court of appeals) is that it awarded extraordinary equitable relief under the FOIA without ever finding that a violation of the FOIA had occurred. The court apparently found that the Federal Records Act of 1950 (or State Department regulations) had been violated by an improper removal of the notes. It then invoked its equitable jurisdiction under the FOIA to restore the notes to the agency for disclosure under FOIA. **This holding necessarily means that anyone may sue an agency and compel it to retrieve records removed in violation of the agency's records-management rules; it supplies, in effect if not in design, a private right of action to enforce the Records Act.**

Of course, sometimes you may want to soft-pedal your critique, especially when you need to attack the court you're before. In this

---

1. Alex Kozinski, *The Wrong Stuff*, 325 B.Y.U. L. Rev. (1992).

final example, Alan Dershowitz and Greg Craig need to tip-toe around an Eleventh Circuit case, hoping that the same court will be swayed by an intervening Supreme Court decision:

Alan Dershowitz and Greg Craig, *Mamani v. Bustamante*

Defendants recognize that this Circuit's ruling in *Cabello v. Fernandez-Larios* upheld a jury verdict, *inter alia*, on the basis that the jury could have found the defendant in that case liable for aiding-and-abetting a violation of customary international law. **We respectfully suggest that *Cabello* would be decided differently today.** The *Cabello* trial took place prior to the Supreme Court's decision in *Sosa*, and the Eleventh Circuit did not even mention *Sosa* in its decision.

Using Parentheticals

I am often asked about case parentheticals, as if they were newfangled or controversial.

Newfangled? As far back as the 1940s, John Davis, who argued 140 cases before the Supreme Court, said that a great brief "furnishes parenthetical explanations to show the relevance of the citation."

Controversial? Under my empirical approach—looking at what the most respected advocates do—any controversy is overblown. Nearly all the top advocates use parentheticals, as do the Justices of the Supreme Court. Other judges are equally enthusiastic: "The single, easiest way to make a good brief better is by the judicious use of parentheticals following case citations," says Third Circuit Judge Leonard Garth.[2]

---

2. Leonard I. Garth, *How to Appeal to an Appellate Judge*, 21 LITIG. 20, 24–66 (Fall 1994).

His one-time colleague Ruggero Aldisert is just as effusive, and even gives some choice examples:

Former Third Circuit Chief Judge Ruggero Aldisert

In recent years, the parenthetical has become very popular, and I **strongly recommend** its use. If a case is cited **to show resemblances or differences in the facts**, a parenthetical disclosing the material facts of the cited case will be very effective: *Fisher & Sons v. Gilardi*, 345 F.4th 666, 678 (9th Cir. 2012) (holding that the reuse of burial caskets differs from the reuse of funereal urns under the statute).

The parenthetical can also be used **to state the reasons that supported the conclusion** of the cited case: *Gandolfini v. HBO, Inc.*, 543 F.4th 123, 126 (2d Cir. 2004). ("Where a party has not performed to a substantial extent of the contract, the other party is entitled to damages for the missing degree of performance.")

The parenthetical also may be used **to state the legal rule that constitutes the holding**: *Upton Sinclair Muckraking Indus. v. Jimmy Dean Co.* ("Where the parties agreed to sell and purchase a specific number of dressed hogs as promised, there was not substantial performance of the contract, and the purchaser is entitled to damages for the missing degree of performance.")

Accompanying a citation with a parenthetical serves **three important purposes**—(1) it tells the brief reader **why you are citing** the case, (2) it shows **where the case fits into the theme** or focus of your brief, and (3) it **achieves the objective of concise brief writing**.[3]

---

3. Ruggero J. Aldisert, Winning on Appeal: Better Briefs and Oral Advocacy 263–264 (2d ed. NITA 2003).

Aldisert is such a fan of parentheticals that he quotes Justice Stephen Breyer using them:

> An example of an excellent use of parentheticals by the United States Supreme Court appears in Justice Stephen Breyer's opinion in *Meyer v. Holley*.[4]
>
> [T]he Court has assumed that, when Congress creates a tort action, it legislates against a legal background of ordinary tort-related vicarious liability rules and consequently intends its legislation to incorporate those rules. *Monterey v. Del Monte Dunes at Monterery, Ltd.*, 526 U.S. 687, 709 (1999) (listing this Court's precedents that interpret Rev. Stat. § 1979, 42 U.S.C. § 1983, in which Congress created "a species of tort liability," "in light of the background of tort liability" (internal quotation marks omitted)). *Cf. Astoria Fed. Sav. & Loan Assn. v. Solimino*, 501 U.S. 104, 108 (1991) ("Congress is understood to legislate against a background of common-law...principles."); *United States v. Texas*, 507 U.S. 529, 534 (1993). ("In order to abrogate a common-law principle, the statute must 'speak directly' to the question addressed by the common law.")

I reproduced the Breyer quote for my own purposes, too. As we'll discuss later, and as you've just seen, the best parentheticals (1) start with a present participle—an *-ing* word relating to something courts do, like "holding"; (2) consist of a single-sentence quotation (as do the last two parentheticals); or (3) alternate between the two (as the entire Breyer example does).

But before we tackle those three techniques, I want to show you what to avoid so you can see why parentheticals sometimes get a bad rap.

---

4. *Meyer v. Holley*, 123 S. Ct. 824, 828–829 (2003).

Can you see why judges don't care for case parentheticals like this one?

> There is nothing in the settlement agreement or any order issued by the district court to indicate that the settlement agreement, or orders pertaining thereto, were made in favor of Smith or that non-parties could seek enforcement of the settlement agreement. *Cf. Floyd v. Ortiz*, 300 F.3d 1223, 1225–27 (10th Cir. 2002) **(a non-party could seek enforcement of a consent decree because, at the time of settlement, the parties had reached a consensus that the decree would benefit and be enforceable by all inmates, provided those inmates employed the grievance procedure specified in the agreement).**

Long parentheticals that start mid-thought—"a non-party could seek"—can seem more like notes-to-self than a way to explain case law concisely. Parentheticals are one of the rare areas in brief writing where creativity gets you nowhere.

Case in point: the federal government's parentheticals below, taken from a motion opposing bail for the villainous Bernie Madoff, don't follow the format I recommend and are thus difficult to follow and parse:

> ### *United States v. Madoff*
>
> The legislative history of the Bail Reform Act of 1984 makes clear that Congress intended that the "safety of the community" language in Section 3142 was expected to be given a broad construction.... Courts have, therefore, appropriately construed the statute to find that the protection of the community from economic harm is a valid objective of bail conditions. *See*

United States v. Schenberger, 498 F. Supp. 2d 738, 742 (D.N.J. 2007) (**holding that** "[a] danger to the community does not only include physical harm or violent behavior" and citing the Senate Committee Report language reproduced above); *United States v. Persaud*, 2007 WL 1074906, at *1 (N.D.N.Y. Apr. 5, 2007) (**concurring with** the Magistrate Judge that "economic harm qualifies as a danger within the contemplation of the Bail Reform Act"); *United States v. LeClercq*, 2007 WL 4365601, at *4 (S.D. Fla. Dec. 13, 2007) (**finding that** a large bond was necessary to, among other things, "protect the community from additional economic harm"); *United States v. Gentry*, 455 F. Supp. 2d 1018, 1032 (D. Ariz. 2006) (**in a fraud and money** laundering case, in determining whether pretrial detention was appropriate, the court held that danger to the community under Section 3142(g) "may be assessed in terms other than the use of force or violence... including economic danger to the community"); *see also United States v. Reynolds*, 956 F.2d 192, 193 (9th Cir. 1992) (**post-conviction for mail fraud** and witness tampering, the Court held that "danger may, at least in some cases, encompass pecuniary or economic harm."); *United States v. Provenzano*, 605 F.2d 85, 95 (3rd Cir. 1979) (**in a pre-1984 Bail Reform Act case**, post-conviction, the Court rejected an application for bail finding that "danger in the community" is not limited to harms involving violence).

We'll solve this problem below.

Ping Me: Introduce your parentheticals with parallel participles

The classic technique is still the best: start with an *-ing* word that describes something courts do (admitting, reversing, listing, excluding, affirming, granting, finding, holding, and so on). Add a reason the court did what it did. And presto, your parentheticals are concise, parallel, and easy to follow.

Patent litigation guru Morgan Chu, a writer of textbook legal prose, uses this old-school technique to good effect:

Morgan Chu, *eBay v. IDT*

Defendants should not be heard to complain that they did not have Alpha Holdings' documents prior to Mr. Gordon's deposition when Defendants did not even subpoena Alpha Holdings for documents until *after* Mr. Gordon's deposition. *See E.E.O.C. v. Honda of America Mfg., Inc.*, 2008 WL 440437 at *6–7 (S.D. Ohio February 13, 2008) (**refusing** to permit the re-deposition of a witness **because** the deposing party failed to pursue obvious avenues for discovering documents before taking the deposition).

Critics accuse former Whitewater Special Counsel Ken Starr of being outside the mainstream, but he, too, favors playbook parentheticals, as you can see in this excerpt from his brief for the school system in a blockbuster case about whether a school could punish a student for wearing a "Bong Hits for Jesus" t-shirt at an off-campus event:

Ken Starr, *Morse v. Frederick*

In the context of regulating pro-drug messages in schools, courts have wrestled with the *Tinker-Fraser-Kuhlmeier* trilogy. Yet, the courts had reached a bottom-line consensus—at least prior to *Frederick*. Applying *Fraser*, several courts recognized that prohibitions on pro-drug messages are constitutional because such expression is offensive and inconsistent with the mission of schools to promote healthy lifestyles (including by seeking at every turn to combat substance abuse). *See, e.g., Boroff*, 220 F.3d at 471 (**upholding** ban on Marilyn Manson t-shirts because singer promoted drug use)...

Sometimes you can depart from the *-ing* format when you're simply providing various examples of the same thing, as the ACLU does with jury pool categories here:

Steven Shapiro and the ACLU, *Mary Berghuis v. Diapolis Smith*

Discrete groups in our society often have been excluded from jury pools. *See, e.g., Taylor*, 419 U.S. 522 (1975) (**women**); *Thiel*, 328 U.S. at 219 (**daily wage earners**); *Hernandez v. Texas*, 347 U.S. 475 (1954) (**Mexican Americans**); *Smith*, 311 U.S. 128 (**African Americans**); *Norris v. Alabama*, 294 U.S. 587 (1935) (**same**).

And as Virginia Seitz does with professional athletes here:

> ### Virginia Seitz, *C.B.C. Distribution and Marketing v. MLB Advanced Media*
>
> [P]rofessional athletes and other prominent persons have the celebrity status which the right of publicity is intended to protect. *See, e.g., Palmer v. Schonhorn Enterprises*, 96 N.J. Super. 72, 232 A.2d 458 (1967) **(professional golfer)**; *Motschenbacher, supra* **(race car driver)**; *Ali, supra* **(boxer)**; *Uhlaender, supra* **(baseball player)**; *Abdul-Jabbar, supra* **(basketball player)**; *Grant v. Esquire, Inc.*, 367 F. Supp. 876 (S.D.N.Y. 1973) **(actor)**.

28

Speak for Yourself: Include a single-sentence quotation

Another way to use parentheticals is for a single-sentence quotation that speaks for itself. Former Solicitor General Paul Clement uses that technique below, addressing a line of cases about one state's ability to punish conduct in another state:

Paul Clement, *Jimenez v. DaimlerChrysler*

More fundamentally, however, [*BMW v. Gore*] reaffirms the broader principle that a state's regulatory interests are properly limited by its borders. "[N]o single State" may promulgate regulatory policies for the nation, "or may even impose its own policy choice on neighboring states." *See also Bonaparte v. Tax Court*, 104 U.S. 592, 594 (1881) ("**No State can legislate except with reference to its own jurisdiction…**") (quoted with approval in BMW); *accord Johansen v. Combustion Engineering, Inc.*, 170 F.3d 1320, 1333 (11th Cir. 1999) ("**The Supreme Court has instructed that punitive damages must be based upon conduct in a single state—the state where the tortious conduct occurred—and reflect a legitimate state interest in punishing and deterring that conduct.**").

Walter Dellinger includes a similar series in his appellate brief for Martha Stewart, and note how he truncates the second quoted sentence to make for even less work for the court:

Walter Dellinger, *United States v. Stewart*

To have "waived" a *Crawford* claim, Stewart would have to have foreseen the most significant Confrontation Clause ruling in the last half-century, but nevertheless deliberately (and irrationally) decided to ignore core constitutional violations that substantially prejudiced her. Not only is there no evidence to support such a supposition, this Court has emphasized how unrealistic it is. *See Bruno*, 383 F.3d at 78 ("[O]nly a soothsayer could have known with any certainty that [Crawford] would change the legal landscape."); *United States v. Viola*, 35 F.3d 37, 42 (2d Cir. 1994) ("[P]enaliz[ing] defendants for failing to challenge entrenched precedent...would...insis[t] upon an omniscience...about the course of the law we do not have as judges.").

29

Hybrid Model: Combine participles and quotations

I know I said there's little room for creativity when it comes to parenthetical form, but I don't want to be too rigid here. You could, for example, live on the edge a bit, mixing the preceding two techniques while quoting select language in an *-ing* parenthetical.

On the *Forbes* list of the richest Americans is Dr. Henry T. Nicholas, III, the founder of Broadcom. Although Nicholas was once accused of various drug and securities offenses, all charges were dropped. I can't promise that Greg Craig's excellent parentheticals played a role, but they are admirable all the same. To the classic *-ing* participle opener, Craig's second and third parentheticals add quoted key phrases:

Greg Craig, *United States v. Henry T. Nicholas, III*

Because the false statement itself is the "very core of criminality," *see Russell*, 369 U.S. at 764, the indictment must identify the false statement with sufficient particularity. *See United States v. Cuevas*, No. 07-50230, 2008 WL 2787525, at *1 (9th Cir. June 11, 2008) ("Because the indictment on this charge completely fails to identify what the alleged false statement was, it failed to apprise Cuevas sufficiently of what she must be prepared to meet at trial."); *United States v. Fried*, 450 F. Supp. 90, 93 (S.D.N.Y. 1978) (**dismissing** charges that failed **"to state precisely what in the allegedly felonious paper is**

> claimed to have been false"); *United States v. Devine's Milk Labs., Inc.*, 179 F. Supp. 799, 801 (D. Mass. 1960) (**dismissing** indictment that did not "**indicate what specific false statements or claims were to be made or presented**").

Nor can I resist sharing this provocative example from Kathleen Sullivan, if only because I had no idea that Wal-Mart's critics printed t-shirts touting the words "Walocaust" and "Wal-Qaeda":

> ### Kathleen Sullivan, *Adidas v. Payless*
>
> Courts have rejected such consumer survey shortcuts in other trademark cases, reasoning that a finding of likelihood of confusion with respect to one product provides no basis for a similar finding with respect to another product of different design. Courts have done so even where, unlike here, a survey tested the defendant's own unrelated product as a stimulus. *See, e.g., Smith v. Wal-Mart Stores, Inc.*, 537 F. Supp. 2d 1302, 1322 (N.D. Ga. 2008) (**concluding** that "**test results from one Walocaust or Wal-Qaeda t-shirt provide no data upon which to estimate consumer confusion regarding another Walocaust or Wal-Qaeda t-shirt**").

(In the text before the parenthetical, the two "with respect to" constructions are cumbersome. Both times the phrase could have been cut to just the word "for." In fact, changing "with respect to" or "with regard to" to "on," "for," or "about" is one of the best quick style edits you can make.)

Introducing Block Quotations

I suggested earlier that the controversy over parentheticals is over-blown. Nearly all judges endorse them, and nearly all top advocates include them.

Block quotes—the long, indented kind—are another story. In a way, they remind me of the hullabaloo over the *and/or* construction.

Let me explain. It's fashionable for judges to say how much they hate *and/or*, with one Wisconsin judge calling it "a Janus-faced verbal monstrosity" and "the child of the brain of someone too lazy or too dull to express his precise meaning." And yet nearly every English-language agreement contains at least one *and/or*, and sometimes dozens.

So, too, with block quotations. Both on the record and off, judges claim to hate them—and even skip them:

- Judge Alex Kozinski: "**Whenever I see a block quote I figure the lawyer had to go to the bathroom** and forgot to turn off the merge/store function on his computer. Let's face it, if the block quote really had something useful in it, the lawyer would have given me a pithy paraphrase."[1]
- Judge Ruggero Aldisert: "**Don't use long quotations.** It is a strong judge who can resist the temptation to skip all or a part of a long, unindented quotation."[2]
- Justice Ruth Bader Ginsburg: "[A first-rate brief] **skips long quotations**, but doesn't unfairly crop the occasional quotations used to highlight key points."[3]
- Judge Morey Sear: "My preferred practice is for brief writers simply to cite the case and its holding, with **brief references to**

---

1. Alex Kozinski, *The Wrong Stuff*, 325, 329 B.Y.U. L. Rev. (1992).

2. Ruggero J. Aldisert, Winning on Appeal: Better Briefs and Oral Advocacy 266 (2d ed. NITA 2003).

3. Ruth Bader Ginsburg, *Remarks on Appellate Advocacy*, 50 S.C. L. Rev. 567, 568 (1999).

key quoted language, rather than reprint lengthy excerpts verbatim from cited decisions."[4]

- Judge Roger Miner: "I have seen page after page of quoted materials in some briefs and have thought: 'What a waste of precious space!' **Excessive quotation leaves little space for persuasion. Paraphrase!**"[5]

Yet all this hostility aside, rare is the motion or brief that doesn't contain at least one block quotation, and yes, sometimes dozens.

We attorneys have our reasons. For one thing, you simply cannot paraphrase, say, a statute or a regulation, nor can you paraphrase what a deponent said at a deposition. For another thing, sometimes a court says something so crisply and elegantly—and aptly—that you want to leave the original language intact.

That's why in this section on quotations, I've saved my favorite quotation on quotations for last.

Federal Circuit Judge Dan Friedman, who once did a tour writing briefs in the Solicitor General's Office, starts by attacking lazy block quoting: "Quotations from cases are effective only if used sparingly. Quoting at length from opinion after opinion is a lazy way of writing a brief, and the finished product is likely to be unconvincing. Long before the brief approaches its end, the reader has begun to skip over the quotations."[6] But then Judge Friedman concedes an exception to his own rule: "If used with discretion, however, pertinent quotations from judicial opinions give a brief force and emphasis."[7]

Our sole technique in this section reflects how the better advocates exercise such "discretion" when they need to quote at length.

---

4. Morey L. Sear, *Briefing in the United States District Court for the Eastern District of Louisiana*, 70 TUL. L. REV. 207, 218 (1995), *available at* http://heinonline.org/HOL/LandingPage?collection=journals&handle=hein.journals/tulr70&div=16&id=&page=.

5. Roger J. Miner, *"Do's" for Appellate Brief Writers*, 3 SCRIBES J. LEGAL WRITING 19, 23 (1992).

6. Daniel M. Friedman, *Winning on Appeal*, 9 LITIG. 15, 17 (Spring 1983).

7. *Id.*

30

Lead 'Em On: Introduce block quotations by explaining how they support your argument

Avoid introducing block quotes with such throw-away lines as "The court held the following" or "The witness testified as follows." If you use flat, bland language like that, you're acknowledging what many judges already suspect: that you're taking the lazy way out by plopping in copied language that forces the judge to figure out how the quoted language relates to why you should win and the other side should lose. "Here are some more puzzle pieces, Your Honor. Enjoy!"

Introduce the quotation instead with language that ties it to the client's cause. In other words, the block quote is just an insurance policy; it's there to back up your point, not to make it for you.

Let's start with an example of what must be one of the few times the ACLU has quoted Justice Clarence Thomas as an authority:

> **Steven Shapiro and the ACLU,**
> *Mary Berghuis v. Diapolis Smith*
>
> Securing impartiality presents challenges. For example, Justice Thomas has noted the persistent difficulty of reaching fair verdicts when defendants encounter racially homogeneous juries that do not fully reflect the community's demographics:
> [T]he racial composition of a jury may affect the outcome of a criminal case. We explained [in *Strauder*]: "It is well known that prejudices often exist against particular classes in the community, which sway the judgment of jurors, and which,

> therefore, operate in some cases to deny to persons of those classes the full enjoyment of that protection which others enjoy." ... [S]ecuring representation of the defendant's race on the jury may help to overcome racial bias and provide the defendant with a better chance of having a fair trial. I do not think that this basic premise of *Strauder* has become obsolete [citing *Georgia v. McCollum*].

Walter Dellinger is another lawyer who has navigated those waters well, this time in a dispute over punitive damages in the *Exxon Valdez* oil-spill case. Watch how he introduces the quoted language about punitive damages under maritime law:

Walter Dellinger, *Exxon v. Baker*

Speaking through Justice Story, its leading maritime-law scholar, the Court affirmed the Circuit Court's ruling that **the owners' liability for the officers' wanton acts did not extend to punitive damages:**

> [T]his must be pronounced a case of gross and wanton outrage, without any just provocation or excuse.... [The owners] are bound to repair all the real injuiries and personal wrongs sustained by the libellants, but they are not bound to the extent of vindictive damages.

In this Dellinger example, you might have wondered whether the Supreme Court's own words would be so interesting to the current Justices that writing "As the Supreme Court so aptly stated" would be enough.

The best advocates don't give in to such temptation. Here, for example, two top appellate advocates appear to think that even the words of our first president need a strong lead-in, quoting him in an amicus brief for the military in the University of Michigan affirmative action case:

Carter Phillips and Virginia Seitz, *Grutter v. Bollinger*

President George Washington eloquently underscored **the vital importance of direct association among diverse individuals in education and in the profession of arms:**

[T]he Juvenal period of life, when friendships are formed, & habits established that will stick by one; the Youth, or young men from different parts of the United States would be assembled together, & would by degrees discover that there was not that cause for those jealousies & prejudices which one part of the Union had imbibed against another part.... What, but the mixing of people from different parts of the United States during the War rubbed off these impressions? A century in the ordinary intercourse, would not have accomplished what the Seven years association in Arms did.

Similarly, Judy Clarke block-quoted from a state-appointed psychiatrist's deposition testimony to reinforce her argument that Tucson, Arizona, shooting suspect Jared Loughner was improperly medicated against his will:

Judy Clarke, *United States v. Loughner*

At this hearing, [Dr.] Pietz testified that Mr. Loughner suffers from both schizophrenia and depression but that **it is depression, not schizophrenia, which gives rise to his agitation, pacing, and suicidality:**

The agitation [Dr. Sarrazin and I have] talked about that. And we believe that his pacing is ruminating, it's anxiety, and it's depression he's being consumed with constantly thinking about events.

Using Footnotes

In theory, footnotes are about as popular with judges as block quotations are. Some judges have even quoted Noel Coward on the subject: "Having to read a footnote resembles having to go downstairs to answer the door while in the midst of making love."

In practice, though, many great lawyers do use footnotes, just not in the same way other lawyers do. As Justice Antonin Scalia has noted, "The Solicitor General of the United States, after all, is a highly skilled and experienced advocate, and the briefs of that office almost always contain substantive footnotes."[1]

So where to draw the line?

To begin with, I suggest that you avoid using footnotes for any of these three reasons:

- **To stay within word or page limits**. Judge Roger Miner: "We are well aware of the efforts to increase the number of words in the brief by extensive footnoting. We deplore such efforts.... The small print of footnotes doesn't fool anyone."[2]
- **To avoid seeing your research go to waste**. Judge Dan Friedman: avoid using footnotes for "[d]emonstrations by the author of the research he has done (which, unfortunately, has proven unnecessary) or his erudition."[3]
- **To take a potshot at the other side**. Judge Ruggero Aldisert: "I strongly discourage the use of footnotes for the making of remarks and asides, in the manner of a character in a play sharing a private joke with the audience. These marginal comments, often piddling objections to minor points in the

1. GARNER & SCALIA, MAKING YOUR CASE: THE ART OF PERSUADING JUDGES 129 (Thomson West 2008).

2. Roger J. Miner, *"Do's" for Appellate Brief Writers*, 3 SCRIBES J. LEGAL WRITING 19, 23 (1992).

3. Daniel M. Friedman, *Winning on Appeal*, 9 LITIG. 15, 20 (Spring 1983).

opponent's brief or the lower court's opinion, add little to and subtract much from the impact of your brief."

That said, feel free to use footnotes to list binding or nonbinding authorities, to preempt likely arguments, or to rebut distracting but unimportant side points.

Remember, though, as former Ohio Judge Mark Painter once said, "If you make your document look like a law review article, it will be just as unreadable!"[4]

Interlude: Citations in footnotes

Attorneys often ask me about a landmine in footnote-land: putting citations in the footnotes. Writing expert Bryan Garner has famously proposed such a reform, one that has gained traction with some advocates and judges. Yet most judges still want citations the old-fashioned way—in the text—and nearly all the top advocates in this book still put them there.

Even so, just because you put your citations in the text doesn't mean that you should stick them in the middle of your sentences.

So not this:

> Likewise, in *Roy v. Volkswagen of America, Inc.*, 896 F.2d 1174 (9th Cir. 1990), *cert. denied*, 500 U.S. 928 (1991), the Ninth Circuit reinstated a $3,000,000 verdict in favor of a family injured in 1982 when their van rolled over.

---

4. Judge Mark P. Painter, 30 Suggestions to Improve Readability 13, *available at* http://www.plainlanguagenetwork.org/Legal/legalwriting.pdf.

But this:

> The Ninth Circuit has reinstated a $3 million jury award for a family injured in a rollover. *Roy v. Volkswagen of America, Inc.*, 896 F.2d 1174 (9th Cir. 1990), *cert. denied*, 500 U.S. 928 (1991).

31

Race to the Bottom: Use footnotes only in moderation to address related side points and to add support

Experienced advocates use footnotes in four main situations:

1. To show widespread adoption of a principle
2. To buttress a point in the text
3. To distinguish authorities not deemed worthy of discussing in the text
4. To preempt a counterargument

One classic way to use a footnote is to add support by showing that many states or circuits have done what you say. Here, Andy Frey uses such a list to strengthen his argument for the plaintiff:

Andy Frey, *Catskill Litigation Trust v. Park Place Entertainment*

Courts in other States agree. *See, e.g., CSY Liquidating Corp. v. Harris Trust & Savings Bank*, 162 F.3d 929, 932–33 (7th Cir. 1998) (Posner, J.) (Illinois law); *In re Burzynski*, 989 F. 2d 733, 738 (5th Cir. 1993) (Texas law); *Phillips USA, Inc. v. Allflex USA, Inc.*, 1993 WL 19161, *1 (D. Kan. 1993) (Kansas law); *Eden United, Inc. v. Short*, 573 N.E.2d 920, 925 & n.2 (Ind. App. 1991) (Indiana law).

Another uncontroversial use of a footnote is to provide more support for a related point, as the ACLU does in a Supreme Court case about a media "ride along" with the police:

Steven Shapiro and the ACLU, *Wilson v. Layne*

We are also aware of two cases where juries returned verdicts against police officers for unreasonable searches due to the presence of the media during the search. *See* Rogers & Callender, *Jurors Award Couple $25,000 in Privacy Lawsuit*, The Capital Times (Madison, Wis.), Jan. 10, 1987, at 3 (reporting that a state court jury found detectives liable "as co-trespassers and that their search was unreasonable in light of the presence of the TV crew"); Umhoefer, *Ripon Police, Newspaper Lose Lawsuit Over Search of Home*, Milwaukee J., Nov. 26, 1986, at 6B (reporting that a federal court jury found that the search constituted "an unreasonable invasion of privacy under Wisconsin law, and a violation of the family's constitutional rights.").

If you are convinced that the other side's cases or points aren't serious enough to address in the text, consider challenging them in a footnote. That appears to be Mary Jo White's mindset as she relegates to footnote-land some cases that Donald Trump cites in his defamation suit against White's client, that book author whose estimates of Trump's net worth were far lower than The Donald's own:

Mary Jo White, *Trump v. O'Brien*

The cases Trump cites in support of his claimed recovery of attorneys' fees as mitigation damages provide no support. For example, in *Dobies v. Brefka*, the only New York state case plaintiff cites, it appears that the court awarded attorney's fees to plaintiff for costs he incurred during a custody dispute resulting from the false allegations that he had abused his daughter. In *Houston v. New York Post Co.*, the court simply allowed a plaintiff leave to replead expenses incurred in mitigating the impact of the defamatory statements, noting that it was difficult to tell whether plaintiff was claiming attorneys' fees, to which he would likely not be entitled, or mitigation damages. Finally, in *Metropolitan Opera Ass'n v. Local 100*, the court found that attorneys' fees were recoverable as mitigation damages where the party had to seek a temporary restraining order to stop the conduct alleged to be wrongful.

(White lowercases "plaintiff" both when she's talking about the plaintiff in her own case, aka Donald Trump, and when she's talking about the plaintiff in a case she's citing. Traditonally, though, you capitalize words like "Plaintiff" when they're the party in your own case.)

You can also use a footnote to preempt counterargument, as Ted Olson does here in a global warming case. Olson is talking about CARB, the California agency that sets vehicle emissions standards:

Ted Olson, *California v. GM*

The Attorney General may argue that CARB certifications do not provide a defense under section 3482 because carbon dioxide is not one of the vehicular emissions currently regulated by CARB. Not only is this claim unavailing—the point is that the *sale* of defendants' vehicles was expressly authorized—but it underscores the preemption arguments advanced in Section IV. California cannot seek to regulate through the guise of a common-law tort suit that which it cannot regulate through appropriate administrative channels.

Finally, although a footnote is not a place to take potshots at your opponent, if you want to use your opponent's words as a weapon, and the point relates to your argument, in rare instances such a "potshot" might work. Here, for example, Richard Taranto was no doubt delighted to throw Justice Kagan's words as an academic right back at her when she was defending a federal statute as solicitor general (now that he's a Federal Circuit judge, let's hope that none of his opinions come before her):

Richard Taranto, _Holder v. Humanitarian Law Project_

At times, the government seems to deny that the statute penalizes speech at all: it maintains that the statute "does not target expression at all"; that "Sections 2339A and 2339B say nothing about speech"; and that the statute does not regulate "speakers attempting to reach particular audiences." This is false both on its face and as applied. Prohibitions on "advice" and "training" are nothing if not a regulation of speech. And as applied here, the government concedes the provisions criminalize such core speech as lobbying Congress or writing amicus briefs, as well as teaching or advising "particular audiences." **As the Solicitor General wrote when an academic, this conflation of speech and conduct renders the doctrine incoherent: "For a court to ... classify an explicit speech-directed action as 'incidental' whenever it can be conceptualized as a component of a broader, non-speech prohibition would subvert the very basis of the doctrine [of incidental restraints]."** Elena Kagan, _When a Speech Code Is a Speech Code: The Stanford Policy and the Theory of Incidental Restraints_, 29 U.C. Davis L. Rev. 957, 961–62 (1996).

We've now covered the toughest tasks in brief writing: the "theme of the case," the fact section, and the argument from headings to footnotes. Now it's time for some fun with style, and for that we turn to Part Four.

PART FOUR

THE WORDS

Part Four will share seventeen techniques for improving your style:

Part Four: The Words

*When it comes to plain talk, lawyers are the worst. Most speak
and write as if they live in a repository for dead bodies. When
they write briefs that some poor trapped judge must read, they
fill them with heavy, gray, lifeless, disgustingly boring word
gravel—piles of it, tons of it. When I read most briefs I want
to scream. I want to throw the brief out the window and jump.
If I could find the author and had the power, I would make the
villain eat the thing a page at a time without salt or catsup.[1]*

—Gerry Spence

"Heavy, gray, lifeless, disgustingly boring word gravel"? What does
Gerry Spence *really* think about the style of most briefs?

Many judges would agree with him, as it turns out. "If neither you
nor anyone you know would ever utter a sentence like the one you have
written, head back to the drawing board," says former Colorado Court
of Appeals Judge Robert Kapelke. Lawyers lose appeals by using "con-
voluted sentences" and by avoiding "periods like the plague," huffs
Ninth Circuit Chief Judge Alex Kozinski. And most harshly of all,
warns former Wisconsin Court of Appeals Chief Judge William Eich,
"Good legal writing does not sound like it was written by a lawyer."

---

1. GERRY SPENCE, HOW TO ARGUE AND WIN EVERY TIME 104–105 (St. Martin's
Press 1995).

Why are these critics so harsh? I can think of four reasons:

- The law is dense and dry.
- Many lawyers cultivate a haughty style in an effort to impress.
- Most style advice in law firms and agencies is too general to help: "Be clear" and "Be concise."
- The rest of the style advice you hear is too negative to inspire: "Avoid long sentences" and "Avoid the passive voice" and "Avoid split infinitives."

No wonder writing is such a pain for so many lawyers—and no wonder reading is such a pain for so many judges.

It doesn't have to be that way. I'd even suggest that for most of the lawyers in this book, writing is a pleasure.

But don't some of these lawyers write better than others? And don't they all have different styles? Yes and yes. But the lawyers in this book are also united on two fronts.

First, even if some of these lawyers aren't the greatest prose stylists, their prose reflects passion for the law, their client's cause, or both. And second, they all do something—anything—to add interest, variety, and elegance to their words, sentences, and transitions.

Let me share seventeen ways for you to follow their lead.

Zingers: Colorful words

Many lawyers lament that legal writing squelches their creativity. It doesn't need to. Take the first sentence of this paragraph. In my first draft, I wrote, "Many lawyers tell me that legal writing leaves no room for them to be creative." Luckily, I objected to my own wilted prose, replacing "tell me that" with "lament that" and replacing "leaves no room for them to be creative" with "squelches their creativity." That sort of word play is "creative" legal writing at work.

Even as a lawyer beholden to forms and terms of art, you have many options on the wording front. Take verb–adverb combinations. Lawyers often write things like "In response to the press release, the stock price **fell precipitously**." Not crack trial lawyer Joe Jamail. Here's what he wrote in the Sunbeam/Al Dunlap securities litigation: "In response to the press release, the stock price **plunged**."

You can also trim stock phrases into vivid verbs. Not "take into consideration" but "**heed**." Not "take out of context" but "**pluck**." Not "cause harm to" but "**slash**."

Vivid verbs can also shape how judges see you and your adversary. Great writers also hunt for vivid nouns, adjectives, gerunds, and so on: the perfect word can sharpen almost any idea.

Take the jeans dispute between Calvin Klein and Linda Wachner that we've discussed before.

What if Brendan Sullivan and his team had written these two versions of the same sentence? What impression do you have of each?

Version I:	"Calvin Klein partnered with Wal-Mart."
Version II:	"Calvin Klein exploitatively profited from Wal-Mart's business."

Version I makes no impression. You wouldn't even know which side Sullivan's team was on.

Version II makes too much of an impression. The forced adverb "exploitatively," added to try to save the weak verb "profited," makes the sentence awkward and self-serving.

Now let's see what Brendan Sullivan & Co. actually wrote:

> **Brendan Sullivan, Greg Craig, and Nicole Seligman,**
> *Calvin Klein Trademark Trust v. Wachner*
>
> Indeed, [Calvin Klein International] was **delighted to enjoy** the business of Wal-Mart, the biggest discounter of them all....

In a first draft, of course, "delighted" would roll off few lawyers' fingertips. But there's a prize for winning this word-search game: "Delighted" transforms a benign transaction—two large companies partnering for mutual benefit—into a symbol of hypocrisy.

If Brendan Sullivan is one of the country's greatest trial lawyers, his knack for the perfect cutting verb might be one reason. Watch how these other excerpts from the brief color your view of Calvin Klein International and its eponymous executive:

> **Brendan Sullivan, Greg Craig, and Nicole Seligman,**
> *Calvin Klein Trademark Trust v. Wachner*
>
> Until after Mr. Klein began **searching** for a lawyer, [Calvin Klein International] was only too happy to **pocket** the expanding royalties from sales to "discounters and mass-market retailers" and warehouse clubs, of which it now complains.... Plaintiffs also have attempted to **clone** their ordinary breach-of-contract allegations into four trademark claims....
>
> [P]laintiffs here are asking to **recover for being made rich.**

As these Sullivan-Craig-Seligman sentences suggest, choice verbs can zing your adversary. Can you think of catchy alternative for these boldfaced yawners: "**mislead** Wall Street" "**manufactured** a term," "**dividing** a class of married persons," "the State Department's **delaying**," and "**transforming** exculpatory evidence into inculpatory evidence"? Now see below.

Joe Jamail, *In re Sunbeam Securities Litigation*

Sunbeam intentionally played fast and loose with its accounting numbers to **hoodwink** Wall Street.

David Boies, *In re Vitamins Antitrust Litigation*

Defendant, not plaintiffs, **coined** the term "persons with decision making authority" to define the files to be searched.

Paul Smith, *Gill v. Office of Personnel Management*

This **sundering** of the class of married people violates the Equal Protection guarantee of the Fifth Amendment.

Alan Dershowitz, *In re People's Mojahedin Organization of Iran*

Indeed, *amici* submit that the State Department's **foot-dragging** and failure to timely comply with this Court's mandate is itself powerful evidence that the continued designation of PMOI as a foreign terrorist organization cannot be justified.

Larry Robbins, *United States v. Bayly*

It is not hard, however, to understand the government's abrupt change in position. For one thing, the new theory, if accepted by this Court, would **alchemize** *exculpatory* evidence (that a third-party purchase, such as by LJM2, was assured) into *inculpatory* evidence (that an Enron buyback was guaranteed.)

Ruth Bader Ginsburg, *Craig v. Boren*

Oklahoma's sex/age classification to determine qualification for association with 3.2 beer **pigeonholes** impermissibly on the basis of gender in violation of the fourteenth amendment's equal protection principle....

Paul Clement, *Department of Health and Human Services v. Florida*

The power to compel individuals to enter commerce, by contrast, **smacks of** the police power, which the framers reserved to the states.

Walter Dellinger, *Bank of America v. Cleveland*

Bank of America's crucial allegation—that Cleveland is attempting to curb Bank of America's lending activities by **bludgeoning** its parent company—provides the requisite case or controversy....

Morgan Chu, *TiVo v. EchoStar*

So far, of course, EchoStar has managed to **thwart** that goal.

Larry Lessig and Kathleen Sullivan, *Eldred v. Ashcroft*

This **mocks** intermediate review.

Bernie Nussbaum, *Crest v. Wal-Mart Stores*

Dr. Howard suggests, without any support, that any below-cost pricing of "sensitive items" **dupes** customers and creates "halos."

Roy Englert, *District Attorney for the Office for the Third Judicial District v. Osborne*

Osborne's § 1983 complaint essentially asked the federal court to **superintend** discovery in the state court.

Tom Goldstein, *Moncrieffe v. Holder*

But the Government's attempt to **teleport** the criminal burden of proof to the very different context of removal proceedings would have dramatically different consequences in immigration cases.

Choice verbs can add interest throughout a brief or motion, as Joshua Rosenkranz shows here in his brief defending MGA against the owners of "princess Barbie":

Joshua Rosenkranz, *MGA Entertainment, Inc. v. Mattel, Inc.*

After brash Bratz **dethroned** princess Barbie, Mattel responded with a strategy to "litigate MGA to death."

After zinging his opponents in his introduction, Rosenkranz keeps the hits coming in the fact section:

As Bratz thrived, Mattel panicked. By 2003, the head of Mattel's Girls Division **sounded the alarm** that Barbie was a "Brand in Crisis." By the next year, with Barbie's sales **taking a nosedive**, an internal report **screamed**, "The House is on Fire."

And also in his argument section:

Short of **chiseling** its objections on the judge's bench, there was nothing more MGA could have done to preserve.

At a certain point, of course, nosedives and screaming can get to be a bit much. But even when your adversary is a court, such zingers can work if used in good taste:

Deanne Maynard and Joshua Rosenkranz,
TiVo Inc. v. EchoStar Corporation

Affirming a finding of contempt on the facts of this case would **bleed** *[KSM v. Jones]* of all meaning.

Ken Starr and Eric Holder, *McDonald v. United States*

The Ninth Circuit's **blinking** at these racial gerrymandering tactics deepens a divide among the lower courts regarding the balance between due process rights and prosecutorial discretion.

Larry Robbins, *Chevron Corp. v. Donziger*

After preliminarily enjoining Donziger, the district court **blessed** a series of procedural maneuvers that effectively will deny him and his counsel any opportunity to participate in the upcoming trial concerning the enforceability of the Ecuadorian judgment—a trial that inevitably will focus on Donziger's conduct.

(In the previous two examples, consider changing "regarding" and "concerning" to "over.")

You can also use a choice verb like "echoes"—or play on a familiar verb phrase like "mince words"—in your own favor:

John Payton and the NAACP, *Greater New Orleans Fair Housing Action Center v. HUD*

But *Barton* simply **echoes** the point highlighted above . . . : the Eleventh Amendment acts as a bar when the relief sought constitutes a raid on the state's general revenues.

> **Bob Bennett, *United States v. Miller***
>
> This is not mere **word mincing**. It is of little comfort to Ms. Judith Miller, the 42 news organizations and reporters' groups [that] submitted briefs, amici curiae, to this Court and to the many other reporters who cover sensitive issues of national importance on a daily basis that a future panel of the court of appeals is left with the "maneuverability" to decide whether and to what extent a journalist has any right not to reveal her confidential sources when the government demands that she do so.

Interlude: 50 zinger verbs

Here's a list of vivid verbs to spice up your advocacy writing:

Afflict	Etch
Besiege	Evoke
Bleed	Falter
Blink	Feign
Block	Flinch
Bludgeon	Flout
Burst	Hoodwink
Chisel	Leap
Clamor	Mark
Clone	Marry
Coin	Mask
Dodge	Meander
Duck	Mimic
Dupe	Mince
Echo	Mint
Eclipse	Mock
Erode	Morph

Pluck
Plunge
Pocket
Rehash
Savor
Search
Seek
Skate

Skirt
Slash
Smack of
Strike
Stymie
Sunder
Thwart
Wring

33

What a Breeze: Confident tone

When I work with attorneys in law firms, I often ask the associates if they think the partners' final drafts are better than their own. They generally do. If I ask them why, I nearly always hear the word *punchy* in response.

The associates may be on to something: As a group, senior partners write "punchier" motions and briefs than junior lawyers do. And the most renowned advocates of all write "punchier" motions and briefs than most of those senior partners do.

One reason is that experience begets confidence, confidence begets joy, and joy begets fresh, conversational language.

So if you want your next brief to scream "I'm experienced," sit back, smile, and exhale when you turn on your computer. As former D.C. Circuit Chief Judge Patricia Wald once said, don't be "afraid to show strong feelings" when you write, as long as you direct those feelings at the law and not at your adversary.

One way to do that is to lighten your prose with breezy language. If Larry Tribe and Ruth Bader Ginsburg and Paul Clement can do so before the Supreme Court, so can you:

Larry Tribe, *Larkin v. Grendel's Den*

Unless such claims are being made **in jest**, the premise they reflect is a profoundly dangerous one. Not even Section 16C honors a supposed wish on the part of school or church leaders always to have their way, **no questions asked**, on threat of taking the law into their own hands.

(Tribe avoided splitting an infinitive but wound up with the awkward-sounding phrase "always to have their way." It might have been better to replace "always to have their way" with a stronger verb like "to get their way." Otherwise, the breeziness of "in jest" and "no questions asked" evaporates.)

Ruth Bader Ginsburg, *Craig v. Boren*

Goesaert is a decision overdue for **formal burial**.

Paul Clement, *Department of Health and Human Services v. Florida*

The power to force individuals to engage in commercial transactions against their will was the kind of police power that they reserved to state governments more directly accountable to the people **(or "applicable individuals," as the [Affordable Care Act] would have it).**

You see how Paul Clement uses gentle mocking humor to enliven his prose by taking a potshot at such routine statutory language as "applicable individuals." In the next example from the same brief, Clement twice throws in a colloquial "really" to convey another hint of exasperation.

If Congress really had this remarkable authority, it would not have waited 220 years to exercise it. **If this power really existed,** both our Constitution and our constitutional history would look fundamentally different.

(Of course, anything stronger than this "hint" would have been overkill.)

In these next five examples, other lawyers use similarly breezy language to goad their targets, whether they be federal legislation, a beloved author, a corporation, a plaintiff, or a governmental agency:

Pattie Millett, *United States v. Stevens*

More broadly, the real test of a "compelling interest" is not whether all 50 States have laws against the conduct—**there are lots of laws against lots of conduct**—but the government's allegiance to that interest when confronted with powerful countervailing interests.

Larry Lessig, *Warner Bros. Entertainment v. RDR Books*

While the Copyright Act reserves certain exclusive rights to Ms. Rowling, it does not give her complete **control over all things Harry Potter.**

Herbert Wachtell, *NFL Enterprises v. EchoStar Satellite*

EchoStar (a multi-billion-dollar-company) also argues that the loss of NFL Network to millions as a result of its improper conduct is **no big deal**, because they could just pay $12 more a month to obtain the second tier—which is "the price of a movie ticket." Of course, **if it were so simple** for people to just pay $12 extra for the second tier, **one can only wonder** why 3.2 million do not already do so.

> **Nancy Abell,** *Jackson v. Microsoft*
>
> The district court did not abuse its discretion in finally saying, **enough is enough.**

> **Richard Wiley,** *Comsat v. FCC*
>
> Instead, the [FCC] adheres to its mantra that the Satellite Act is "silent on the precise question of Comsat's exclusivity" and that, therefore, **anything goes.**

Using some Yiddish may work, at least when the parties are in New York:

> **Brendan Sullivan, Greg Craig, and Nicole Seligman,** *Calvin Klein Trademark Trust v. Wachner*
>
> It is one thing to fail to make discovery. It requires real *chutzpah* for [Calvin Klein International] and Mr. Klein to go further, and ask for summary judgment based on the state of the mind of someone whose corporeal existence they will not identify.

A final way to mimic conversational language is through a burst of short words. Here, for example, Morgan Chu creates a sentence of single syllables—one of the legal profession's most endangered species:

> **Morgan Chu,** *Brunskill Associates v. Rapid Payroll*
>
> This is not the first case like this to be tried.

34

Manner of Speaking: Figures of speech

Certain clichés have drenched so many briefs that you should, well, "avoid them like the plague." How many times have you heard these well-worn expressions?

- Defendant's expert is "eminently qualified"
- Plaintiff engages in a series of "bald accusations" and "conclusory assertions"
- Defendant wants a "second bite at the apple"
- Causation is "inextricably linked" with damages

But that doesn't mean that you should avoid all folkloric language. Even if you pledge to avoid these five clichés, you still have many fresh ways to exploit figures of speech.

In this example from trial guru Joe Jamail, for instance, "cooking the books" hits home much more than "material fraud" would:

> **Joe Jamail, *In re Sunbeam Securities Litigation***
>
> After turn-around-artist Al Dunlap took the helm at Sunbeam, he engaged in a scheme of **cooking the books** to make his turnaround look real.

Another way to drive home your themes is by implanting folkloric sayings that will likely resonate with the judge. David Boies takes this approach twice, both times for plaintiffs in class actions, both times while opposing defense motions to compel, and both times in the first sentence of his argument:

David Boies, *Renton v. Kaiser*

Kaiser's motion to compel exemplifies **the old adage "the best defense is a good offense."**

("Exemplifies" might be a bit pretentious for this homespun sentence, though. How about "brings to mind"?)

David Boies, *In re Vitamins Antitrust Litigation*

Defendants' motion to compel is an excellent example of **the axiom that "no good deed goes unpunished."**

Paul Clement, for his part, doggedly pursues a canine figure of speech in his Supreme Court brief attacking "Obamacare's" individual mandate:

Paul Clement, *Department of Health and Human Services v. Florida*

The statute the federal government defends under the tax power is not the statute that Congress enacted. In that statute, **the penalty provision is merely the tail and the mandate is the proverbial dog,** not vice-versa.

Clement's adversary both there and in the Arizona immigration case below, Solicitor General Don Verrilli, calls Clement's dog metaphor and raises him a stopped clock:

Don Verrilli, *Arizona v. United States*

Section 2 [of the Arizona immigration law] has no valid applications because it always precludes officers from taking [the federal government's] priorities and discretion into account in the first place. **A stopped clock may be right twice a day, but it is still a facially invalid method of timekeeping.**

Few lawyers would think to combine a stopped clock with the phrase "facially invalid." And few would ever juxtapose "transitive reading" and "train wreck," as Maureen Mahoney did on Arthur Andersen's behalf below:

Maureen Mahoney, *Arthur Andersen v. United States*

A **transitive reading** of "corruptly" avoids this interpretive **train wreck** entirely.

(Note Mahoney's knack for alliteration as well: lots of *t* sounds and *r* sounds here.)

Would you even go so far as to join "patent portfolio" with "sweet spot"?

Morgan Chu, *Tessera v. United Test and Assembly Center*

The truth, which UTAC would prefer the jury not learn, is far different: the parties' contract provides a definition that is closely related to the **sweet spot of Tessera's patent portfolio.**

And yes, in Chu's example we have alliteration twice over as well. It's not quite Winston Churchill's "we shall not fail or falter," but it's close enough.

Let's end with one last way to use figures of speech: by "pushing the envelope," so to speak.

In this first example from the Sunbeam/Al Dunlap litigation, Joe Jamail's witness—Sunbeam's internal auditor—does the heavy lifting for him, milking the "robbing Peter to pay Paul" line for all it's worth:

Joe Jamail, *In re Sunbeam Securities Litigation*

As Deidra DenDanto, Sunbeam's internal auditor, told her auditing supervisor about two months before Texas Plaintiffs commenced their large-scaled purchases of Sunbeam stock:
  "[W]e're no longer robbing Peter to pay Paul, we are actually raping and beating him and pillaging his village."

Could a plaintiff's lawyer dream of a better quotation than this? And guess where Jamail put it: at the very beginning of his introduction.

In the next example, Jamail couldn't resist "going for the kill." The same internal auditor "threw him a bone"—the bathe-with-muddy-water image—and Jamail "took the bait and ran":

Joe Jamail, *In re Sunbeam Securities Litigation*

[The internal auditor] poignantly told Bob Gluck:
"If you bathe with **muddy water** long enough, you inevitably get dirty, and I don't want to be part of the company any longer."
The accumulated evidence shows that Sunbeam under the Dunlap regime was a **mud puddle.**

But here's a word of warning: Your opponent can also turn your own figures of speech against you.

After the Calvin Klein plaintiffs trotted out a common horse metaphor, for example, the Brendan Sullivan team saddled them with it:

Brendan Sullivan, Greg Craig, and Nicole Seligman,
Calvin Klein Trademark Trust v. Wachner

Plaintiffs promised that "We'll choose which horses we ride as the case moves forward towards trial."

Instead of riding them, the time has come to put both these frail animals out to pasture.

To use a final figure of speech, "What goes around comes around."

35

That Reminds Me: Examples and analogies

Another way to animate your prose is through evocative examples and analogies that crystallize an abstract principle, stoke your reader's emotion, or both.

Some lawyers risk their entire case on an analogy. Look how David Boies and Joshua Rosenkranz began their appellate brief in a dispute between Oracle and Google over the Droid smartphone. In the very first words of their introduction, the lawyers create a mythical figure named Ann Droid who steals from *Harry Potter* in a way that's similar to what these lawyers claim Google has done to their own client:

David Boies and Joshua Rosenkranz, *Oracle America v. Google*

Ann Droid wants to publish a bestseller. So she sits down with an advance copy of Harry Potter and the Order of the Phoenix—the fifth book—and proceeds to transcribe. She verbatim copies all the chapter titles—from Chapter 1 ("Dudley Demented") to Chapter 38 ("The Second War Begins"). She copies verbatim the topic sentences of each paragraph, starting from the first (highly descriptive) one and continuing, in order, to the last, simple one ("Harry nodded."). She then paraphrases the rest of each paragraph. She rushes the competing version to press before the original under the title: Ann Droid's Harry Potter 5.0. The knockoff flies off the shelves.

J.K. Rowling sues for copyright infringement. Ann's defenses: "But I wrote most of the words from scratch. Besides,

---

> this was fair use, because I copied only the portions necessary to tap into the Harry Potter fan base."
>
> Obviously, the defenses would fail.
>
> Defendant Google Inc. has copied a blockbuster literary work just as surely, and as improperly, as Ann Droid—and has offered the same defenses....

As many great advocates do, this duo analogizes something abstract and even cold—alleged infringement of software code—to something concrete and even personal—copying from a beloved book.

In another passage that's become famous in brief-writing circles, Chief Justice Roberts once explained why deciding which technology is "best" for controlling air pollution under the Clean Air Act is sort of like...asking people to pick the "best" car:

John Roberts, *Alaska v. EPA*

Determining the "best" control technology is like asking different people to pick the "best" car. **Mario Andretti may select a Ferrari; a college student may choose a Volkswagen Beetle; a family of six a mini-van. A Minnesotan's choice will doubtless have four-wheel drive; a Floridian's might well be a convertible.** The choices would turn on how the decisionmaker weighed competing priorities such as cost, mileage, safety, cargo space, speed, handling, and so on.

When I run into lawyers who have taken one of my brief-writing seminars, they often mention this example, even years after taking the workshop.

One reason the example sticks is that everyone grasps the concept right away. Soon you're thinking about your own favorite car and why you like it, forgetting that which car you like best is no doubt more subjective than whether a given technology is effective at fighting air pollution. As I mentioned, our personal lives are better fodder for analogies than our cerebral lives.

The Chief's example also soars through its language and rhythm. Roberts even toys with some rhetorical devices, like *conjunction deviation* when he drops the "and" before "a family of six" and *ellipsis* when he omits the verb before "a mini-van." His ear for language may be unsurpassed, at least in our humble legal profession.

For a very different way of using examples, let's turn to President Obama. As you know, he and Chief Justice Roberts have not always had the warmest relations. First there was that mishap with the Oath of Office during Obama's first term. (Things went better the second time.) Then they clashed over *Citizens United*, the campaign finance decision that the President criticized in his 2010 State of the Union address. Roberts's groundbreaking vote to uphold the Affordable Care Act might have helped mend fences, but then there was that Voting Rights Act decision....

In any event, when it comes to using examples in briefs, Roberts and Obama are simpatico.

Here is an example from a certiorari petition Obama signed in a case involving, yes, voting rights, his academic specialty at the University of Chicago Law School.

Voting rights law is a bit like environmental law in its complexity and abstraction. Obama understands that challenge, so he walks you through an example he and his team created—a bit like a hypothetical he might have given his law students—that makes his abstract point concrete:

Barack Obama, *Tyus v. Bosley*

Consider a city in which whites are **50%** of the total population, **54%** of the voting-age population, and all live on the south side of town; blacks are 50% of the total population,

> 46% of the voting-age population, and all live on the north side of town. **Also assume that** the city council is comprised of 50 single-member districts of equal population. Twenty five (**50%**) white-majority wards (proportionality based on total population) presumptively treat the two groups equally; 27 (**54%**) white-majority wards (proportionality based on voting-age population) do not. In the latter case, the map drawer can only "stretch" the white population to control two additional wards by "fracturing" black population that could have been used to create two additional black wards and putting them in white majority wards.

(In the last sentence, move "only" to right before "by 'fracturing,'" which is what "only" modifies. Also repeat "by" before "putting them" for parallelism.)

Addressing the reader in the second person, as Obama does here, is a particularly effective form of persuasion. Sure enough, another fan of this method is one of Obama's own Supreme Court Justice selections, Elena Kagan, who favors sentence openers like "Suppose" and "Take" in her opinions and dissents.

Yet another time for an example is when you're reporting a large number, something likely to fly by a judge's head unless you include a down-to-earth mental landmark. Here, Nancy Abell, along with some crack appellate lawyers from Gibson Dunn, wanted to give the Ninth Circuit a concrete reference point for what it means when 1.5 million women join a lawsuit:

Nancy Abell, *Dukes v. Wal-Mart*

[T]he district court concluded that their pay and promotion claims were representative of those that might be asserted under Title VII by each and every female Wal-Mart store employee in the United States over a six-year period—more

> than 1.5 million women, **a group that outnumbers the active duty military personnel in the Army, Navy, Marine Corps, and Air Force** *combined*. **The size of the putative class exceeds the entire population of at least 12 of the 50 States.**

Not that all your examples need to be teaching tools. Here, for instance, Joshua Rosenkranz's examples of famed creators of products—Albert Einstein and Charles Dickens—mock his opponent's position, rather than just explaining a legal principle:

> **Joshua Rosenkranz, *MGA Entertainment, Inc. v. Mattel, Inc.***
>
> **Albert Einstein would have been shocked to learn that his employer was claiming ownership over every idea he had while employed at the patent office. Dickens would have been infuriated if the *Morning Chronicle* had laid claim to *The Pickwick Papers* just because he wrote the novel while employed as a journalist.** So, too, a low-level employee in Bryant's position would be justified in assuming that Mattel was not laying claim to every idea that pops into his head—every doodle he makes and every word he writes—even if he came up with the idea in the shower, and even if it bears no relation to his job.

(In starting sentences with "So too," Rosenkranz oddly sounds like another J.R., John Roberts.)

Our next examples take us from Barbies and Bratz dolls to the heated "Obamacare" wars. Even so, the world of British literary giants remains a beacon:

> **Paul Clement, *Department of Health and Human Services v. Florida***
>
> To be clear, "applicable individual" is just the ACA's legalistic and **vaguely Orwellian way** of referring to virtually every human being lawfully residing in this country.

Clement's opponent here, the U.S. government, invokes an across-the-Atlantic author of its own:

> **Don Verrilli, *Department of Health and Human Services v. Florida***
>
> On petitioners' **through-the-looking-glass theory**, the better the bargain for the State, the more reason to conclude that the State has been impermissibly "coerced" into accepting it.

Patent guru Morgan Chu uses a similar tactic, though his examples have a more domestic flavor (what's more American than Chia pets?):

> **Morgan Chu, *Tessera v. United Test and Assembly Center***
>
> The truth is that United Test and Assembly Center would like to litigate this case in a vacuum, presenting it as a sort of bloodless logic puzzle in which accepting Tessera's contract interpretation means that UTAC is paying on products **(yo-yos? Chia pets?)** that have little or nothing to do with any licensed Tessera patents.

Chu's writing has great flair—something not often associated with patent litigation. A little bit of spunk can only help.

In that regard, Senator Ted Cruz, then representing the State of Texas in a dispute over a Ten Commandments monument on state property, incorporates below an aw-shucks reference to Texas football "fervor" to bring home a point about what the State is—or is not—endorsing:

Ted Cruz, *Van Orden v. Perry*

It is not at all clear how, standing in the midst of the Capitol Grounds's many stone monuments, an observer would reasonably understand the State to be officially endorsing the command, "Thou shalt not make to thyself any graven images." Nor is it clear how an observer would reasonably understand the State to be endorsing the command to "Remember the Sabbath day, to keep it holy." **For example, no one would reasonably think that the State has adopted a position, one way or the other, on whether the Dallas Cowboys should continue playing professional football on Sundays or whether the Texas Longhorns should continue playing college football on Saturdays (notwithstanding the seriousness, and even religious fervor, with which Texans approach their football, it would be a stretch to describe the game as "holy").**

All these examples are fun, or at least memorable.

Of course, you can also use examples and analogies for a more somber purpose: to make the judge feel queasy about ruling against you.

Here, for instance, Ted Olson and David Boies used a citizenship analogy in a trial brief to liken California's Proposition 8, which prohibited same-sex marriage, to another classification scheme that would make many a judge squirm:

Ted Olson and David Boies, *Perry v. Schwarzenegger*

Indeed, the discriminatory message conveyed by Prop. 8 is no different from the message that would be conveyed by a federal statute that **granted U.S.-born persons of Chinese ancestry all the benefits of U.S. citizenship but denominated them** "nationals of Chinese descent" rather than "United States citizens."

(This is the case that became *Hollingsworth v. Perry* at the Supreme Court.)

Another pair of name-brand lawyers invoke some closer-to-home examples, this time to discourage you from wanting to try Bolivian officials in a U.S. court:

Greg Craig and Alan Dershowitz, *Mamani v. Bustamante*

A U.S. court has no more (and in fact has less) authority to permit a trial of President Lozada or Minister Berzaín for their response to Bolivia's riots than it would have had to **try President Kennedy or Secretary of Defense McNamara** for their response to riots in the 1960s **or President George H.W. Bush** for his response to the Los Angeles riots of 1992.

A final way to use examples is through the classic parade of horribles.

In fighting civil claims that Duke lacrosse players wrongfully accused of sexual assault brought against Duke University, Jamie Gorelick needed to convince the court that no matter how much sympathy it had for the exonerated players, it should beware of burdening university officials with new duties of care when they give advice. But Gorelick doesn't just arouse sympathy for beleaguered administrators or sound the common theme of tort litigation run amok. Instead, she depicts a world where students and young employees are left to fend for themselves:

> ### Jamie Gorelick, *Carrington v. Duke University*
>
> **A professor who advises** a student on what courses to take to prepare for graduate school, **a coach who suggests** to a student how she might improve her chances of being drafted to play a professional sport, and **a guidance counselor who counsels** a student on the best approach to take in job interviews would be subject to liability under this "bad advice" theory—as would **an employee's mentor or supervisor who advises** her (mistakenly) about how best to "get ahead" at the company. Inevitably, people will be much less willing to become mentors and counselors, and those who do will limit their advice to a highly formal, bureaucratic realm.

Let's end with an example from the criminal world—or at least the criminal-law world. You may remember that Arthur Andersen, the corporation, was convicted of corporate crimes during the fallout over the Enron debacle. By the time Maureen Mahoney won its appeal 9–0 and got the conviction reversed, it was too late for the many employees who had already lost their jobs.

The case turned on the jury instructions for what it meant to "knowingly corruptly persuade" someone to withhold or alter documents in an official proceeding. In attacking those jury instructions, Mahoney parades horrible examples of all sorts of things that would be deemed felonies were the government's approach to prevail:

Maureen Mahoney, *Arthur Andersen v. United States*

In addition to the retention policies discussed above, the instructions given here would make any of the following into a felony:

- A **mother's advice to her son** that he should assert his Fifth Amendment privilege not to testify before a grand jury, because his testimony would incriminate him;
- A **manager's instruction to a custodian of** records not to comply with a voluntary request for documents from the SEC;
- A **CEO's instruction to her company's general counsel** to assert, not waive, the company's attorney-client privilege in response to an SEC subpoena;
- An **attorney's advice to her client** to answer only the question posed and not to volunteer information; or
- An **in-house attorney's suggested deletions** of potentially damaging statements in a draft memorandum prepared by a colleague.

In the end, then, shoot for one example, metaphor, analogy, or figure of speech in every motion or brief you write. If you choose carefully, your message may endure long after the brief is put back in the stack.

Jumpstart Your Sentences

In the words of Justice Ginsburg, "We simply don't have time to ferret out one bright idea buried in too long a sentence."[1]

---

1. Ruth Bader Ginsburg, *Remarks on Appellate Advocacy*, 50 S.C. L. REV. 567 (1999).

Read this typical sentence from a brief—not an especially bad sentence, mind you, but very much like the ones that judges see hundreds of times a day:

> Nothing in the law of this state suggests that to be actionable the actions of the party preventing performance must rise to the level of a separate standard of culpability beyond that inherent in preventing the performance.

What "bright idea" did you ferret out? Perhaps something like this:

> In this state, one party to a contract can sue if another party prevents performance of that contract.

Does this mini-experiment suggest that many briefs contain many "bright ideas" that the judges and clerks never see?

That's a frightening thought.

Perhaps it's better to think of sentences in a positive light—as tools for varying the prose and quickening the pace.

Here are six ways to spice up your sentences so that your "bright ideas" shine.

36

The Starting Gate: The one-syllable opener

One of the easiest ways to refine your style is to start more of your sentences with short, punchy transition words. In fact, the ability to do so is a hallmark of the best advocates' writing.

Consider how these three sentences begin:

However, the EPA cannot claim that ADEC's [the state agency's] decision was "unreasoned." **Moreover,** the EPA **also lacks the ability to** assert that ADEC's determination in any way results in emissions exceeding national standards or permitted increments. **The manner in which** emissions were controlled within those standards, without exceeding available increments, was for the State to decide.

Did you notice how slow and formulaic the openers were?

Now look at what Chief Justice Roberts actually wrote:

> **John Roberts, *Alaska v. EPA***
>
> **But** the EPA cannot claim that ADEC's decision was "unreasoned." **Nor** can the EPA assert that ADEC's determination in any way results in emissions exceeding national standards or permitted increments. **How** to control emissions within those standards, without exceeding available increments, was for the State to decide.

Adding speed in this way will push judges from one sentence to the next. And if you can weave together a series of three punchy openers like this, all the better. Especially if you run into naysayers, I've armed you below with three more examples, one appellate, one trial, one regulatory, all frontloaded with "and" and "but":

Stephen M. Shapiro, *Linde v. Arab Bank, PLC*

The Sanctions Order is severe and unjustifiable on its own. **But** it raises particular concerns because the court also eliminated traditional standards of causation and endorsed a sweeping theory of aiding and abetting liability. **And** it violated principles of international comity established in recent decisions of the Supreme Court.

Miguel Estrada, *Sanders v. Madison Square Garden*

In her original Complaint, ... [Plaintiff] sought an award to "compensate" her "for emotional distress" that she allegedly suffered as a result of sex discrimination. **But** in her First Amended Complaint she elected to withdraw her request for compensatory damages as well as any claim that she experienced "mental anguish" or "humiliation." **And** when she added a sex discrimination claim under Title VII in her Second Amended Complaint, she again affirmatively elected not to seek such damages.

Richard Wiley, *In re XM-Sirius Merger*

But it is well established that products in the same market need not be perfect substitutes for one another. **And** opponents conveniently ignore all of the innovative services that have been introduced recently or are likely to be available to consumers soon, such as HD Radio, streaming audio through

> mobile phones, podcasts, and mobile broadband Internet available in cars.

A superb writer can marshal this technique throughout an entire passage. In this passage from Justice Kagan's solicitor general days, for example, every sentence—and every clause—starts with a one-syllable word.

Elena Kagan, *United States v. Stevens*

And even if some of the depictions reached by Section 48 do express some sort of idea—for example, that gratuitous cruelty to animals is tolerable or appropriate—**they** may be prohibited because of the way the idea is expressed. **As** this Court has explained, certain narrow categories of speech are unprotected not because "they constitute 'no part of the expression of ideas,'" **but** because they constitute "'no essential part of any exposition of ideas'"; "their content embodies a particularly intolerable (and socially unnecessary) mode of expressing whatever idea the speaker wishes to convey." **So**, for example, child pornography may express an idea about the appropriateness of certain sexual behavior with children, **but** the Court nonetheless has declined to extend First Amendment protection to such material.

This single change can lighten your writing overnight, almost as if you were oxygenating your style.

Let's end with a quick before-and-after example:

Here's the original. Feel how heavy the openings to the second and third sentences are:

As this Court has recognized, "the relevant conduct or 'aggregation rule' grants the government a 'fearsome tool' in drug cases by allowing prosecutors to seek enhanced sentences by asking the sentencing court to consider types and quantities of drugs not specified in the counts of conviction." **Accordingly, the Court will** "carefully scrutinize uncharged relevant drug conduct" to ensure it bears "the necessary relation to the convicted offense" to be considered for sentencing. **Nevertheless, the Court also has** explained that a District Court's "finding that a defendant's relevant conduct includes uncharged drug quantities is a factual determination entitled to our deference 'unless we have a definite and firm conviction that a mistake has been made.'"

And now here's a revision:

As this Court has recognized, "the relevant conduct or 'aggregation rule' grants the government a 'fearsome tool' in drug cases by allowing prosecutors to seek enhanced sentences by asking the sentencing court to consider types and quantities of drugs not specified in the counts of conviction." **The Court will thus** "carefully scrutinize uncharged relevant drug conduct" to ensure it bears "the necessary relation to the convicted offense" to be considered for sentencing. **Yet the Court has also** explained that a District Court's "finding that a defendant's relevant conduct includes uncharged drug quantities is a factual determination entitled to our deference 'unless we have a definite and firm conviction that a mistake has been made.'"

(Note the lack of commas around "thus": putting commas around "thus" and "therefore" is grammatically incorrect and also drags sentences down.)

37

Size Matters: The pithy sentence

Everyone complains that lawyers' sentences are too long. But I wish the critics were as passionate about including short sentences. What makes prose sing, after all, is variety in sentence length and structure, not adhering to strict medium-sentence-only rules.

Let me propose a different goal, one that is also far more fun to strive for: on each page of your brief, include at least one sentence that starts and stops on the same line of text.

In that spirit, let's try another experiment. Cut the second sentence from sixteen words to five—or even fewer:

> Substituting one decisionmaker for another may yield a different result, but not in any sense a more "correct" one. **The aforementioned principle is applicable to the present issue in the instant case before this Court.**

Now here's the second sentence in the Chief Justice's original. It's just three words:

> **John Roberts, *Alaska v. EPA***
>
> Substituting one decisionmaker for another may yield a different result, but not in any sense a more "correct" one. **So too here.**

Roberts uses this short quip to analogize. But what are some other times to include a short sentence?

How about to disagree with your opponent?

Do you think any judge wants to read even one more sentence like this: "The premise upon which Defendants rest their argument is fundamentally flawed as a matter of law and fact"?

Far more refreshing—and far less common—is "Defendants' argument is wrong."

Here are some more short sentences used to good purpose—all in the negative:

John Quinn, *Mattel v. MGA Entertainment*

MGA argues that reading Paragraph 4 to require more than a "request" to retailers would render Paragraph 6 "surplusage." **That has it backwards.**

John Payton and the NAACP, *Greater New Orleans Fair Action Housing Center v. HUD*

Rainwater argues that § 3604(a) applies only to prospective homeowners, and does not apply to Plaintiffs here because they were already homeowners before Hurricane Katrina. **This argument is incorrect.**

Morgan Chu, *TiVo v. EchoStar*

EchoStar's argument rests on the flawed legal premise that as long as an infringer modifies the precise elements of a device identified at trial as meeting a particular limitation, it cannot be held in contempt no matter how clearly the device still infringes. **That is not the law.**

Bernie Nussbaum, *IBP v. Tyson Foods*

Rather than address *any* of these points, Tyson merely argues that IBP has not shown irreparable harm because, as Tyson would have it, the only irreparable harm IBP has alleged is "the issuance of a single commission for a discovery subpoena in the Arkansas Action." **But IBP has never said that.**

Don Verrilli, *United States v. Jones*

Although the court of appeals did not address the question, respondent also contends that the attachment of the GPS device to his vehicle, as distinct from the use of the device to monitor the vehicle's public movements, violated the Fourth Amendment. **It did not.**

Nancy Abell, *Doiwchi v. Princess Cruise Lines*

So, too, is [the record] devoid of the requisite proof that those accused of failing to accommodate knew that Doiwchi had a covered disability and a disability-caused work-related limitation that required accommodation. **Doiwchi never told them.**

Fred Bartlit, *Stumpf v. Garvey*

No alleged disclosure provides any indication that The Yankee Group's predictions, or any other predictions about demand, were *wrong as of July 26, 2000.* **Nor does Hallman so claim.**

Richard Taranto, *Morgan Stanley v. Public Utility District No. 1 of Snohomish County*

The *Mobile* and *Sierra* opinions plainly do not remove contract rates from the statutory "just and reasonable" standard. **Nor do their holdings.**

Carter Phillips, *Fifth Avenue Presbyterian Church v. City of New York*

[F]or Section 435 to apply even when the Church closes its property to the public at night in order to conduct its ministry, that property must still be either a "public sidewalk" or a "public place." **It is neither.**

Roy Englert, *Choose Life Illinois v. White*

In a final effort to muddy the waters, respondent claims that this case boils down to a disagreement about the factual record. **That is false.**

Ken Starr and Eric Holder, *McDonald v. United States*

The Ninth Circuit's decision permits prosecutors to gerrymander an African-American defendant's case into a forum where the government is assured of obtaining a predominately white jury pool. **In the Twenty-first Century, this should not be.**

A short sentence is also a fine way to start a section:

> **Paul Clement, *Department of Health and Human Services v. Florida***
>
> *Printz* is no different.

> **Greg Garre, *Weber v. Infinity Broadcasting***
>
> The jury got this case right.

A pair of contrasting short sentences can work well, too:

> **Ted Wells, *NAACP v. Ameriquest Mortgage Company***
>
> CitiMortgage served its requests by the deadline. Plaintiff did not.

Let me close with two more variations that are not for the faint of heart: the sentence fragment and the contraction.

One thing you should know is that many linguists disagree with the whole a-sentence-must-have-a-subject-and-verb test. These linguists would define a sentence as a complete unit of thought, not necessarily as a clause containing a subject and verb. That's one reason you'll often find so-called "fragments" in many first-rate newspapers and magazines—and even in the work of some of the best judges and brief writers:

> **Paul Clement, *Department of Health and Human Services v. Florida***
>
> Individual's surprising unreceptiveness to substantial incentives to invest in 401(k) accounts could be overcome by mandating such investments. **And so on.**

Pattie Millett, *United States v. Stevens*

The government cannot possibly believe its own argument. **Or so its amici should hope**.

Maureen Mahoney and Greg Garre, *Christian Legal Society v. Martinez EchoStar*

Petitioner claims that Hastings' policy is viewpoint-discriminatory in that only religious groups are forbidden to restrict their membership to persons sharing the group's ideology or beliefs. **Not so.**

Bernie Nussbaum, *IBP v. Tyson Foods*

Tyson argues that "[t]he Court was not asked to, and did not, preclude Tyson from prosecuting any claims in the Arkansas Action." **Another technically correct, but disingenuous, assertion**.

And finally, are you brave enough to include an occasional contraction—one of the most enduring taboos in legal writing. Top trial lawyer Phil Corboy uses one here:

Phil Corboy, *Boyle v. RJW Transport*

The facts presented in Wilson-McCray are very easily distinguishable from those presented herein. First, the record in Wilson-McCray indicates that the carrier was simply required

> to make drivers available to transport loads for the shipper, Birmingham Steel. **That's it; nothing more.**

But if you think that contractions are only for hip plaintiffs' lawyers, I'll show you one from Miguel Estrada, as august a member of the defense bar as you'll ever find. Maybe the subject matter just got to him; this Supreme Court case was about the FCC's efforts to ban the F-word from television broadcasts:

Miguel Estrada, *FCC v. Fox*

The only argument remotely resembling an explanation for the Commission's change in course came to the Commission as an afterthought: "Moreover, in certain cases, it is difficult (if not impossible) to distinguish whether a word is being used as an expletive or as a literal description of sexual or excretory functions." **That's it.**

Estrada's contraction could make some judges launch into expletives themselves, but at least he's pushing the right limits. On the other hand, if you're ever before Justice Scalia, using contractions might make him accuse you of trying to be too "buddy-buddy."[1]

---

1. http://www.npr.org/templates/story/story.php?storyId=90001031.

38

Freight Train: The balanced, elegant long sentence

Having lauded the short, pithy sentence, I will now embrace the long, rich one. After all, are we so averse to long sentences today that we've lost much of the elegant writing of times past?

If so, some nostalgia may be in order. As style expert Joseph Williams puts it, "[W]hile most readers prefer bald clarity to the density of institutional prose, they sometimes feel that the relentless simplicity of the plain style can eventually become dry, even arid....A touch of class, a flash of elegance can mark the difference between bland clarity and a thought so elegantly shaped that it not only fixes itself in the minds of your readers, but gives them a flicker of pleasure every time they recall it."[1]

I can't remember the last time I felt a "flicker of pleasure" in recalling a sentence from a motion *in limine*. But that doesn't mean that elegance and brief writing can never go hand in hand.

Take the following passage from Justice Ginsburg's advocacy days. The facts are prosaic—beer-drinking ages in Oklahoma in the 1970s—but the legal issue is gender equality, Ginsburg's lifelong passion. Perhaps that passion is what inspired her to create a passage like this, a passage long on balanced and symmetrical phrases as well as parallel contrasts and comparisons.

---

1. JOSEPH WILLIAMS, STYLE: LESSONS IN CLARITY AND GRACE 211 (5th ed. Longman 2006).

Ruth Bader Ginsburg, *Craig v. Boren*

Just as age of majority gender-based differentials have been declared inconsonant with the equal protection principle, **so** have sharp lines between the sexes relating to the purchase, sale or consumption of alcoholic beverages. The decision below apart, the sole authority for differential treatment of the sexes in relation to alcoholic beverage association is *Goesaert v. Cleary*, 335 U.S. 464 (1948). Widely criticized in commentary, **in square conflict** with decisions of this Court in the current decade and with national equal employment opportunity policy, **and politely discarded** by the nation's lower courts, *Goesaert* is a decision overdue for formal burial. **On the surface**, Oklahoma's 3.2 beer sex/age differential may appear to accord young women a liberty withheld from young men. Upon **deeper** inspection, the gender line drawn by Oklahoma is revealed as a **manifestation** of traditional attitudes about the expected behavior of males and females, part of the **myriad signals** and messages that daily underscore the notion of **men** as society's active members, **women** as men's quiescent companions.

You've just read an example of one of the rare times a sentence in a brief approaches the rhythms and patterns of literature.

And yet if Ginsburg's style is still too much for you, I can accept that.

As a fallback, let me suggest a less lofty technique that *Wall Street Journal* writing guru William Blundell calls the "freight-train sentence."

Blundell offers this "before" version as an example of why thin sentences are not *always* beautiful:

> The engineer proved this with precise, relentless logic. First, he showed that the ground-water supply was connected to the mainstream of the river. Then he was able to prove that pell-mell pumping would diminish the river's flow because the two water sources were linked. This meant, he argued, that New Mexico would be unable to meet its legal obligation to Texas. The result: before long, users in the basin would have to be cut off to make up the Texas share, thus turning boom into bust.[2]

Then Blundell proposes this single-sentence "freight train" version that's speedier—and shorter—than the plodding passage above. The revision builds on a series of "that" clauses:

> In his precise, relentlessly logical way, the engineer showed **that** the ground-water supply was connected to the river's mainstream; **that** pell-mell pumping would thus diminish the river's flow; **that** New Mexico would be unable to meet its legal obligation to Texas; **and that** before long, users in the basin would have to be cut off to make up the Texas share, turning boom into bust.

Lisa Blatt may not be a *Wall Street Journal* alum, but her writing style has served her well as the head of Arnold & Porter's Appellate and Supreme Court Practice. Here she uses a similar *Freight Train* technique in a 64-word sentence that chugs along in crisp parallel form:

---

2. WILLIAM BLUNDELL, THE ART AND CRAFT OF FEATURE WRITING 181 (Plume 1988).

Lisa Blatt, *Sorrell v. IMS Health*

The law thus seeks to alter "[t]he marketplace for ideas on medicine safety and effectiveness," **even though** the manufacturer's speech is truthful, non-misleading and extensively regulated by the Food and Drug Administration; **even though** physicians are trained to use their medical judgment in the best interest of patients; **and even though** physicians have total control over whether, when, and how they communicate with manufacturers.

Former U.S. Attorney Patrick Fitzgerald did something similar when a federal court was poised to sentence former Illinois governor Rod Blagojevich. When you're cataloguing a defendant's supposed sins, the whole can be greater than the sum of the parts:

Patrick Fitzgerald, *United States v. Blagojevich*

Over the course of a relatively brief period of time, during his machinations surrounding the appointment of a United States Senator, and the shakedowns of hospital and racetrack executives, the defendant revealed his corrupt, criminal character. But, as the evidence and Blagojevich's conduct at his trials established, these were not isolated incidents. They were part and parcel of an approach to public office that defendant adopted from the moment he became governor in 2002. **In light of** Blagojevich's **extensive corruption** of high office, **the damage he caused** to the integrity of Illinois government, **and the need to deter** others from similar acts, the government suggests a sentence of 15 to 20 years imprisonment is sufficient but not greater than necessary to comply with § 3553.

Our last *Freight Train* example comes from John Roberts's brief for Alaska in *Alaska v. EPA*. Clocking in at an impressive seventy-six words, Roberts's freight-train sentence anchors the reader with "that," guaranteeing a smooth ride:

John Roberts, *Alaska v. EPA*

Because there is no "correct" [Best Available Control Technology] determination for any particular source, the EPA cannot conclude **that** a State failed to include the "correct" BACT limitation in a PSD permit, the way the EPA can conclude, say, **that** the State failed to require a PSD permit, **that** the State failed to include a BACT limitation at all in a PSD permit, or **that** the State issued a permit allowing emissions to exceed available increments.

39

Leading Parts: Two sentences joined as one

Now let me sell you on a different type of complex sentence that can add variety and sophistication.

How well do you think this passage flows?

> Plaintiff was frustrated with the glass ceiling at [her employer] and was unable to do anything about it from within. Therefore, plaintiff filed a charge of discrimination with the EEOC for violation of Title VII.

Now here's what Greg Garre actually wrote:

> **Greg Garre, *Weber v. Infinity Broadcasting***
>
> Frustrated with the glass ceiling at [her employer] and unable to do anything about it from within, plaintiff filed a charge of discrimination with the EEOC for violation of Title VII.

The technique Garre uses is what writing expert Bruce Ross-Larson, author of the fantastic little book *Stunning Sentences*, calls "leading parts." Consider this technique when you have two sentences about the same subject, such as a court or a party. Convert the first sentence to an introductory clause, and you'll have much more elegant and efficient prose.

Ross-Larson offers this before-and-after example:

Before

Mr. Gorbachev is esteemed in the West as the statesman who ended the cold war. But he is extremely unpopular in Russia, where he is blamed for allowing the Soviet Union to fall apart and for not having pushed reform of the command economy far enough.

After (from *The Economist*)

Esteemed in the West as the statesman who ended the cold war, Mr. Gorbachev is extremely unpopular in Russia, where he is blamed for allowing the Soviet Union to fall apart and for not having pushed reform of the command economy far enough.

This technique is well known to the nation's top legal writers. In its *Federal Appellate Practice* treatise, for instance, the stellar appellate group at Mayer Brown endorses the same edit to "make the writing more interesting than using the standard 'noun-verb' form in sentence after sentence." Here's Mayer Brown's before-and-after example:

Before

Smith asserts that the district court's instruction correctly stated the elements of a claim for tortious interference with contract. **This argument ignores** the welter of authority cited in our opening brief.

After

Ignoring the welter of contrary authority cited in our opening brief, Smith asserts that the district court's instruction correctly stated the elements of a claim for tortious interference with contract.[1]

Now let's turn to some real-life *Leading Parts* examples about a court, a city, a state, and the federal government:

Miguel Estrada, *FCC v. Fox*

Recognizing that the words used in Carlin's monologue were "not entirely outside the protection of the First Amendment," and that even Carlin's "monologue would be protected in other contexts," **this Court** narrowly upheld the Commission's sanction.

Carter Phillips, *Fifth Avenue Presbyterian Church v. City of New York*

Having substantially burdened three First Amendment rights, **and having failed** to demonstrate that there is any neutral, generally applicable law at issue here, **the City** must demonstrate that it has narrowly tailored its actions to further a compelling government interest.

---

1. *Federal Appellate Practice*, at 302.

Lisa Blatt, *Sorrell v. IMS Health*

Having crippled the "deeper" privacy interest in protecting doctors from economically motivated communications, **Vermont** can hardly seek refuge in a concededly lesser-included privacy interest in the information generally.

Seth Waxman, *Boumediene v. Bush*

Recognizing the weakness of its evidence on that score, **the Government** attempts to engage in "profiling," arguing that, because Petitioners have engaged in certain types of conduct in the past, the Court should find that they were planning to engage in combat in the future (even absent direct or circumstantial evidence of such a plan).

Note that *Leading Parts* can work well at the end of a sentence, too:

Frank Easterbrook, *Kissinger v. Reporters Committee for Freedom of the Press*

The disputed telephone notes are in the possession of the Library of Congress. They are the property of the United States, **Kissinger having surrendered whatever interest he had.**

40

Talk to Yourself: The rhetorical question

Before writing this book, I had always thought that rhetorical questions in briefs were pompous, if not offensive. I shuddered at the thought of a lawyer penning this rhetorical question from Justice Scalia's dissent in *PGA v. Martin*, the case about whether disabled golfer Casey Martin should be allowed to use a golf cart during tournaments:

> I am sure that the Framers of the Constitution, aware of the 1457 edict of King James II of Scotland prohibiting golf because it interfered with the practice of archery, fully expected that sooner or later the paths of golf and government, the law and the links, would once again cross, and that the judges of this august Court would someday have to wrestle with that age-old jurisprudential question, for which their years of study in the law have so well prepared them: **Is someone riding around a golf course from shot to shot really a golfer?**

I've since done an about-face. I still don't think you should try to be as sarcastic and scathing as Justice Scalia can be, but many advocates do use rhetorical questions to great effect.

The sharpest questions often put the court on the defensive, suggesting that unless the judge can answer the rhetorical question posed, the judge has no choice but to find for the writer's client:

Kathleen Sullivan, *SEC v. Siebel Systems*

[T]he Complaint asserts that Mr. Goldman's "body language was positive" during the meeting on April 30. **Would [the SEC] have interpreted negative body language—crossed arms and a furrowed brow perhaps—to constitute a violation as well?**

Bob Bennett, *United States v. Scooter Libby*

How can it possibly be maintained that Ms. [Judy] Miller's notes of discussions with persons other than Mr. Libby, regarding topics unrelated to the instant case, have any bearing on his, hers, or anyone's recollection of the salient facts regarding her conversations with him?

Maureen Mahoney, *Arthur Andersen v. United States*

Under the Government's interpretation, therefore, § 1515(a)(6) would have to provide a defense for someone who accidentally lies to a witness even if their purpose is to impede agency fact-finding. But telling the truth to impede agency fact-finding would remain criminal. **So a defendant who thinks he is telling the truth to impede an official proceeding has committed a crime if he is right, but not if—entirely unbeknownst to him—he happens to be wrong?**

If you have a literary bent, you can also even pose a rhetorical question from someone else's perspective:

Deanne Maynard and Joshua Rosenkranz,
TiVo v. EchoStar Corporation

It would be imprudent for any company that devised a brilliant design-around after being enjoined for infringement to implement its innovation. Any such company would have to ask itself: **"If all the effort EchoStar expended, every precaution EchoStar took, and everything EchoStar achieved were not enough to protect EchoStar from contempt, how exactly can we protect ourselves from contempt?"**

Larry Tribe, *Larkin v. Grendel's Den*

And if the state *were* to capitulate to such supposed desires for total disentanglement from others or total power over others, it is hard to see why such appeasement should start—or stop—with schools and churches. **Are we to suppose that church leaders are more likely than homeowners to find unbearable the prospect of nearby drinking or the burdens of submitting their objections peacefully to public scrutiny?**

Or you can try your hand at a whole series of questions:

Judy Clarke, *United States v. Loughner*

The actual [psychiatric] commitment orders [for accused Arizona mass shooter Jared Loughner] themselves placed no limitations on any medication changes the prison may decide to make, and the [district court's] *post hoc* reference to "minor modifications" is too vague to subject the prison to any meaningful judicial oversight. **Would it prevent a change to a different second-generation antipsychotic drug or different antidepressant? An increase from 6 mg to 10 mg of risperidone? To 12 mg? What about in light of the fact that "the scientific literature is clear" that there is no difference in efficacy between 2–4 mg and 16 mg daily, but only an increase in "side effects" with the higher dose?**

Brendan Sullivan, *United States v. Ted Stevens*

Which of these two questions did Senator Stevens allegedly answer falsely? **Who** exactly gave Senator Stevens the thing of value that allegedly had to be disclosed? **Was** it a gift or liability? **Why** did this alleged gift or liability qualify as such under the applicable rules for completing the form in question?

Richard Taranto, *Holder v. Humanitarian Law Project*

The government now proposes that "expert advice" encompasses speech derived from knowledge that is "specific, practical, and related to a particular branch of science or a profession," or from "knowledge relating to subject matter and based on experiences not usually possessed or shared by the general public." These definitions do not clarify matters. **Is advice based on human rights, political advocacy, or peacemaking derived from "specific" and "practical" knowledge? Where does one find a gauge of what knowledge or experiences are "usually" possessed by the "general public"? And even if these questions could be answered, how is a citizen**

> supposed to know that they are the right questions to ask,
> given that these are not the statute's terms?

Roy Englert and the State of Alaska offer an interesting twist below—what you might call a "preemptive rhetorical strike"—in a case about convicted defendants' rights to DNA testing. If rhetorical questions are so appealing—and thus dangerous—why not pose one from your opponent's point of view just so you can shoot it down before it sticks?

Roy Englert, *District Attorney for the Office for the Third Judicial District v. Osborne*

Osborne's due-process arguments can be distilled to a single question: **If it costs the State nothing, why not test? But it does not cost the State nothing.** The State's interest in limiting meritless attacks on its criminal judgments—sometimes referred to as "finality"—is no mere abstraction. Beyond the victims' interests, there is the State's need to husband the resources that must be expended in reviewing, processing, and (when necessary) litigating these requests. And those burdens—which are borne by prosecutors' offices, crime laboratories, and courts—increase when the standards for requesting testing are set so low as to encourage gamesmanship by prisoners with no valid claim of innocence but nothing to lose by requesting testing.

(Note the use of dashes as well as the effective *Starting Gate* openers "But" and "And." But toward the end, repeat the "with" before "nothing to lose" for parallelism purposes.)

Finally, you can also use rhetorical questions to impugn the other side directly:

Bernie Nussbaum, *IBP v. Tyson Foods*

Tyson asks the Court to "dissolve" the existing temporary restraining order. The obvious questions presented to IBP and the Court by this request are: **"Why? What does Tyson intend to do if the restraining order is lifted? Why should the Arkansas proceeding be revived prior to the resolution of the claims before this Court?"**

(Consider rewriting the lead-in as follows: "This request presents IBP and this Court with some obvious questions." That rewrite has four advantages: (1) moving "this request" closer to the request, (2) moving the "obvious questions" closer to the questions, (3) avoiding the passive voice while saving a few words, and (4) avoiding the improper colon after "are" (lead-ins to quotations take colons only when they are complete sentences).)

Phil Corboy, *Rodriguez v. Voss*

Incredibly, Thomas Voss, the supposed intended beneficiary of the tape measure, cannot even remember asking/telling/ordering/suggesting Voss Jr. to bring him anything, much less a tape measure. **Is Voss Jr. telling the truth? Is he hiding something?**

41

Parallel Lives: The parallel construction

Like all great writers, great legal writers have an eye and an ear for parallel construction: the use of words, phrases, or clauses of similar form and length. Strunk & White's Elements of Style offers this example:

> **Not parallel**: Formerly, science was taught by the textbook method, while now the laboratory method is employed.
>
> **Parallel**: Formerly, science was taught by the textbook method; now it is taught by the laboratory method.

The second version is preferred because "science" is the subject of both clauses and because the "by" construction is repeated. Yet parallelism is not just a stylistic device or a grammatical challenge. It's a way to streamline information, to make your points stick and, as Strunk & White point out, to project confidence.

Let's consider two ways to include such constructions: first in lists, and then in comparisons and contrasts.

Take lists. Many intellectual property lawyers describe technology—say, Microsoft Outlook's calendar function—like this:

> Technically, the software **creates** the month display, dates are **filled in** (shown as falling on the correct day of the week), and then **tracking** of the correct order of dates and times occurs.

Do you feel as though you don't know what day of the week it is yourself?

Now look how Carter Phillips describes the same technology through a parallel series of simple active verbs:

> **Carter Phillips, *Lucent Technologies v. Gateway***
>
> Technically, the software **creates** the month display, **fills** it in with dates (shown as falling on the correct day of the week), and **tracks** the correct order of dates and times....

Even if you use the passive voice, as Richard Taranto does here to focus his sentences on actions and not actors, parallel verb form helps bind a list together:

> **Richard Taranto, *Holder v. Humanitarian Law Project***
>
> The challenged provisions force plaintiffs to guess whether their proposed political advocacy, human rights training, and peacemaking assistance **is derived** from or imparts "general" or "specialized" knowledge, **is done** "for the benefit of" the recipient group or for other purposes, **or is conducted** independently or in some unspecified coordinated fashion.

(On the other hand, you don't "do" advocacy, training, or assistance. Maybe "engaged in"?)

Parallel structure can help you persuade, not just explain. The series of participles in the next example—"feeding," "clothing," "sheltering"—packs a punch for the States opposed to the "Obamacare" individual mandate:

> **Paul Clement, *Department of Health and Human Services v. Florida***
>
> The federal government spends billions of dollars **feeding** the hungry, **clothing** the poor, and **sheltering** the homeless.

Alan Dershowitz used a similar parallel sequence in the next example. His goal was to convince the court that failing to revoke the People's Mojahedin Organization of Iran's designation as a terrorist organization would harm defenseless Iraqi civilians. It apparently worked, because in late 2012, the organization was removed from the list:

Alan Dershowitz, *In re People's Mojahedin Organization of Iran*

Grave circumstances require timely and decisive action. Any less would **devalue** the rule of law, **encourage** the mistreatment or murder of thousands of human beings, and **operate to preserve** an obstacle to the protection and rescue of persons in clear and present danger.

(The sequence would have been even stronger had he written just "preserve" and not "operate to preserve." Also prefer verbs or gerunds to "the _____ of": "an obstacle to protecting and rescuing.")

For a more sophisticated approach, you can repeat a word or phrase throughout a list to create a parallel effect, as Solicitor General Don Verrilli does here in objecting to Arizona's immigration statute on preemption grounds:

Don Verrilli, *Arizona v. United States*

A scheme that depends on national uniformity cannot coexist with a patchwork of different state regimes, whether that patchwork involves **50 different** decision-makers, **50 different** remedies, or **50 different** substantive rules.

The alliteration of "D" below—not in "different" this time but in "dismantling," "discrediting," and "dismissing"—doubles down on behalf of Steven Donziger, a lawyer who represented thousands of Amazon villagers in an environmental case against Texaco:

Larry Robbins, *Chevron Corp. v. Donziger*

Two weeks later, the district court displayed its handiwork to the world: a 126-page preliminary-injunction order [preventing enforcement of a $19 billion Ecuadorian judgment for the villagers] that refers to Donziger by name 190 times, **dismantling** his reputation, **discrediting** his life's work, and **dismissing** the entire government of Ecuador as corrupt and inept.

(Both Donziger and Ecuador regained whatever they might have lost: Robbins got the Second Circuit to lift the district court's order.)

From the NAACP on the plaintiffs' side, the repetition of "S"—"small," "small," "simple"—similarly belies the defendant's claims of high costs:

John Payton and the NAACP, *In re Alper Holdings USA*

Certainly Alper's case—which involves a **small** number of creditors, a **small** number of appealed claims and a **simple** asset base—is not so complex that such information would prove to be too costly to provide, and its benefits to Alper's creditors are apparent.

Sometimes this technique can create a quasi-literary effect. Here, Ken Starr and John Roberts sound the word "what" three times while defending the first George Bush administration's position on abortion access:

Ken Starr and John Roberts, *Rust v. Sullivan*

Even assuming **what** we do not concede, **what** has not been shown, and **what** is hardly intuitive—that a woman may encounter difficulty in obtaining abortion information if Title X projects do not provide abortion counseling, referral, or advocacy—that difficulty is not a government-created obstacle.

I almost wonder if Starr and Roberts were channeling Lincoln's Gettysburg Address here: "The world will little note, nor long remember what we say here, but it can never forget what they did here."

The Starr-Roberts example repeated "what" three times in a sentence. How about repeating a word several times over a series of sentences, making an entire passage gel and cohere?

One-upping the Don Verrilli quotation above, Nancy Abell and an appellate team from Gibson Dunn morphed "different" into a drumbeat, helping to drive home Wal-Mart's point as it sought to defeat the largest civil-rights class action in history:

Nancy Abell, *Dukes v. Wal-Mart*

The named Plaintiffs are four former and two current Wal-Mart employees. They worked at **different** stores, at **different** times, in **different** positions. They were promoted to (and demoted from) **different** job classifications, disciplined for **different** offenses, and paid **different** amounts for performing **different** jobs. They transferred to **different** stores and **different** positions within stores, applied for **different** management training opportunities, and quit (or were fired) for **different** reasons. They claim to have been discriminated against on the basis of sex in **different** ways, by **different** managers, in **different** circumstances. These are their **different** stories.

Now let's turn to a third and final way to use parallelism: to draw contrasts through the rhetorical device known as "antithesis."

President Obama used this strategy in a case involving voting. Here's an excerpt from a certiorari petition, contrasting the districting of black voters with that of white voters:

Barack Obama, *Tyus v. Bosley*

Plaintiffs' expert's affidavit presented evidence of the type of unevenhanded boundary manipulations that, according to *Voinovich v. Quilter*, 507 U.S. 146 (1993) should be of singular concern in a voting rights challenge to a single-member districting plan—namely that in drawing the 1991 boundaries, **defendants intentionally reduced black population in specific wards to enhance white voting strength, systematically "fractured" black voters to cancel out their voting strength** and "packed" black voters in neighboring wards to waste their voting strength. **Not one example exists of defendants' similarly reducing white population to enhance black voting strength,** or of systematically wasting white votes by fracturing and packing white population.

(To avoid the flat verb "exists" and to perfect the parallel in the second bolded phrase, perhaps Obama could have written "Yet not once have defendants ever reduced white population to enhance black voting strength." Also lose the almost-always-useless word "namely" after the dash.)

It seems fitting to end with another example from Paul Clement, one of President Obama's nemeses, at least when it comes to the Supreme Court. Here is a great example of antithesis from his brief against the Affordable Care Act:

> **Paul Clement, *Department of Health and Human Services v. Florida***
>
> The focus on the purported "uniqueness" of the health care market and the centrality of the individual mandate might explain why **this is the first time** Congress has asserted this unprecedented power, but it does not explain why **it will be the last.**

Creative Punctuation

Literary agent Noah Lukeman wrote a book called *A Dash of Style: The Art and Mastery of Punctuation*. It's about how great writers—from Ernest Hemingway to Emily Dickinson—use punctuation to add elegance and flair.

An agent for many bestselling authors, Lukeman says that after having read tens of thousands of manuscripts, he's learned that "punctuation, more than anything, belies clarity—or chaos—of thought."[1] His point is as true for great legal writers as it is for any other great writer. "The benefits of punctuation for the creative writer are limitless," he says, "if you know how to tap them."[2]

Let's look now at how the best legal writers tap those benefits by using dashes, semicolons, and colons in creative and effective ways.

---

1. Noah Lukeman, A Dash of Style: The Art and Mastery of Punctuation 15 (W. W. Norton 2006).

2. *Id.*

42

A Dash of Style: The dash

As Lukeman puts it, "The dash is built to interrupt. It can strike with no warning, cut you off, stop conversation in its track, and redirect content any way it pleases."[1]

Doesn't that sound like the sort of thing that would help a lawyer add emphasis and vary the prose?

It is, for two reasons: first to explain or emphasize something in the middle of your sentence, and second to elaborate on something at the end of your sentence.

Let's start with how to use a pair of dashes to explain or emphasize.

Because then-Solicitor General Elena Kagan was mocking the idea that gratuitous cruelty to animals could constitute an "idea," she put that phrase between dashes rather than between such yawn-inducing marks as commas or parentheses:

Elena Kagan, *United States v. Stevens*

And even if some of the depictions reached by Section 48 do express some sort of idea—**for example, that gratuitous cruelty to animals is tolerable or appropriate**—they may be prohibited because of the way the idea is expressed.

And here, Deanne Maynard uses dashes to contrast knowledge standards in a case she's citing with the ones that would apply to her own client:

---

1. *Id.* at 112.

Deanne Maynard, *In re Tremont Securities*

[T]he auditor [in the case] had signed off on financial statements even though it knew—**not "should have" or "would have" known**—that the audited company's revenues being certified were at best uncertain and almost certainly overstated.

Not that dashes are just for doctrine. Bankruptcy guru Harvey Miller uses dashes below to mock his Chapter 11 opponent, whom he elsewhere calls a "proven serial filer," for being litigation-happy, especially when it comes to suing Miller's client General Motors:

Harvey Miller, *In re Motors Liquidation Co.*

Mr. Washington's fondness for litigation—**including litigation against General Motors Corporation**—is not limited to this bankruptcy.

You can also use a dash to elaborate or expand on a point:

John Roberts, *Alaska v. EPA*

Described as an "experiment in federalism," the Clean Air Act assigns to the States an important—**indeed primary**—role in air pollution prevention and control.

Sri Srinivasan and Deanne Maynard,
CompuCredit Corp. v. Greenwood

It is one thing to declare an arbitration agreement unenforceable, as Congress has done in certain provisions through explicit and direct language. It is quite another to conclude that Congress intended to deem the mere existence of an arbitration agreement—**indeed, the mere *offer* to enter into an arbitration agreement**—a *violation of federal law* subject to damages liability and administrative enforcement.

(Italicizing key language like "offer" and "a violation of federal law" can work in small doses for a particularly passionate point. Don't do it more than once or twice per brief, though.)

For an effect that's both literary and persuasive, you can even put dashes around a repeated word, as Tom Goldstein does here to emphasize how remote he thinks a chain of events truly is:

Tom Goldstein, *Christopher v. SmithKline Beecham*

A conversation between a [pharmaceutical] detailer and a physician might–***might***–set in motion a chain of events in which a prescription is written, which a patient then takes to a pharmacy, which as a consequence orders more of a drug from a wholesaler, which then consummates a "sale" with the drug company.

As I mentioned, yet another way to use a dash is to emphasize a trailing thought at the end of a sentence. The dueling sides in *United States v. Stevens* both use that technique to good effect:

Elena Kagan, *United States v. Stevens*

[The prohibited material] also includes videos of dogfights, hog-dog fights, and cockfights—**bloody spectacles of vicious animals forced to fight to the point of exhaustion or death.**

> **Pattie Millett, *United States v. Stevens***
>
> The government cannot suspend the First Amendment just because the conduct depicted is illegal—**somewhere.**

As does Senator Ted Cruz, defending the Great State of Texas as its solicitor general:

> **Ted Cruz, *Van Orden v. Perry***
>
> Nothing in the monument's history could lead [Plaintiff] to conclude that it was intended to or did in fact send a message of religious endorsement. On the contrary, the monument's history reinforces the perception of the same message suggested by its context and content—**a message highlighting the Ten Commandments' historically significant civic impact.**

Finally, let me answer some common formatting questions: Yes, the dash should touch the word before and after it, and no, you cannot just type two hyphens. And speaking of hyphens, read on.

Interlude: The hyphen

What's the difference between a "little used car" and a "little-used car"? Between "more critical attacks" and "more-critical attacks"? Or, for that matter, between "toxic tort litigation" and "toxic-tort litigation"?

Friends don't let friends worry about what modifies what. That's why grammarians invented rules for multiword phrases known as "compound modifiers" or "phrasal adjectives." In general, if two or more words modify another word and precede that word, hyphenate them. If you think this country has too many lawsuits, you may very well complain about the "toxic tort litigation" that's ruining the economy. But if you're on the plaintiff's side, you likely believe that "toxic-tort litigation" helps make us safer. No need to obsess here: if your meaning is obvious, don't feel obliged to hyphenate. So "criminal law attorney" and "affirmative action plan" are fine as is.

Here are some models from the Chief Justice, who is also known to be one of the profession's Chief Grammarians:

John Roberts, _Alaska v. EPA_

state-issued permit
orange- and red-stained creekbeds
emissions-netting approach
site-specific conditions
four-wheel drive
then-current regulations
bright-line rule
eighteen-month process
diesel-fired electric generators
case-specific policy judgments
per-ton-removal basis
cost-effectiveness data
policy-laden discretionary judgment
year-round employment

One more thing: If your multiword phrase modifies another word but the first word in that phrase ends in *-ly*, there's no need to hyphenate the phrase:

John Roberts, _Alaska v. EPA_

critically important employer
potentially competing demands

43

Good Bedfellows: The semicolon

One of the famous lines in the history of Supreme Court advocacy is from Alexander Bickel, who represented the *New York Times* in the Pentagon Papers case: "A criminal statute chills; prior restraint freezes."

If some of today's lawyers had been around then, the Justices might have heard something like this: "It is of the nature of a criminal statute to create a chilling effect. However, by contrast, prior restraint is defined with reference to its inherent freezing qualities."

I'll take Bickel's version any day. In fact, I wish many lawyers hated strings of choppy, disjointed sentences as much as they hate the semicolon.

Here's a good example from Justice Stevens of how to use semicolons: "Some of those decisions will be controversial; many will have differential effects across populations; virtually all will entail value judgments of some kind." And here's a good example from a litigator: "Congress did not refer to 'pot,' 'grass,' or 'weed'; it identified the substance as 'marijuana,' and then further defined that term using its formal botanical classification."

What's the pattern? These writers are using semicolons not to join just any old vaguely related points, but to compare or contrast like things: decisions in one case, and references to drugs in another.

Here's how to make this technique work for you. What is the lawyer trying to contrast in this example?

In clean air areas, the federal government determines the maximum allowable increases of emissions for certain pollutants. However, the decision as to the mechanism for allocation

> of the available increments among competing sources for economic development and growth rests with the State.

Now look at the same contrast in the hands of the Chief Justice. Note the contrast between the federal government and the states, as well as the parallel structure between "determines" and "decides":

> **John Roberts, *Alaska v. EPA***
>
> In clean air areas, **the federal government determines** the maximum allowable increases of emissions for certain pollutants; **the States decide** how to allocate the available increments among competing sources for economic development and growth.

Roberts, unlike many attorneys, does not put "however" after the semicolon. That would ruin the parallel—a bit like saying, "To err is human; however, to forgive is divine."

Here's another great use of a semicolon in the same brief, again to draw a contrast through parallel structure:

> **John Roberts, *Alaska v. EPA***
>
> **Deciding that a more stringent and more costly control is "best"** for a particular source may reflect a judgment that the economic benefits of that particular expansion are worth consuming only so much of the available increment; **deciding that a less stringent and less costly control is "best"** for a different source may reflect a different judgment about the value of that specific project.

And here's a very different example from J. K. Rowling's lawsuit over the Harry Potter lexicon. Larry Lessig is contrasting the purpose of his client's work with the purpose of the works cited by J. K. Rowling and her publisher:

> **Larry Lessig, *Warner Bros. Entertainment v. RDR Books***
>
> **None of the works** at issue in those cases served a purpose comparable to the Lexicon's; **each** was essentially an abridgment that retold the original story in its original sequence, albeit in shortened form.

And from another litigation superstar, an even more straightforward example:

> **Stephen Susman, *Sklar v. Bank of America***
>
> In other words, **this case** involves an actual conflict; *Aronson* did not.

You'll find something similar from Seventh Circuit Chief Judge Frank Easterbrook during his deputy-solicitor-general days:

> **Frank Easterbrook, *Kissinger v. Reporters Committee for Freedom of the Press***
>
> The Library of Congress **desires to keep the notes**; the State Department, so far as this record discloses, **does not want them back**.

And, complete with alliteration, from Solicitor General Don Verrilli:

Don Verrilli, *Arizona v. United States*

Arizona's attempt to set its own policy for enforcement of federal immigration law **is not cooperation; it is confrontation.**

Our final example, which uses semicolons not to contrast but to overwhelm the reader with parallel reasons, is even more ambitious. Watch how Tom Goldstein strings together four ways that a "detailing" conversation with doctors about a drug is hardly a "sale" of that drug:

Tom Goldstein, *Christopher v. SmithKline Beecham*

At the end of the detailing conversation [between a pharmaceutical sales rep and a physician], the very most that [SmithKline Beecham] can hope is that the physician will offer a gratuitous, unenforceable, and qualified promise: that in a medically appropriate situation, the physician will prescribe a drug. That simply is not a sale. **The detailer never delivers, nor promises to deliver, the drug; the physician never pays, nor promises to pay, any money; no particular patient is identified; and no enforceable commitment is made.**

44

Magician's Mark: The colon

Literary agent Noah Lukeman calls the colon the "magician" of punctuation, "one of the most powerful tools in the arsenal of a creative writer."[1]

And no, he doesn't mean using a colon for such pedestrian purposes as introducing a list or a block quote.

Consider Lukeman's contrasting examples:

Before

I grabbed my bag, put on my coat, and stepped out the door, as I wasn't coming back.

After

I grabbed my bag, put on my coat, and stepped out the door: I wasn't coming back.

Do you see how the colon makes the second version so much more dramatic?

Many great brief writers use colons the same way: to announce that they're going to explain something they've just discussed. In other words, they use a colon when many other writers would just insert "because" or "due to the fact that":

---

1. LUKEMAN, *supra* note 7, at 91.

Larry Tribe, *Larkin v. Grendel's Den*

Whether Grendel's is "entitled" to a liquor license is irrelevant to the due process analysis: even if Grendel's is not "entitled" to serve liquor and its patrons are not "entitled" to consume it, the state is hardly free to dispense with the dictates of the Fourteenth Amendment in ruling on Grendel's application.

Barack Obama, *Tyus v. Bosley*

In effect, the lower court has turned the Voting Rights Act into **a ceiling or cap on black representation**: as long as proportionality is provided, political actors are free to engage in the most blatant schemes to fragment and pack black population to maximize white political power. This cannot be the law.

Walter Dellinger, *Bank of America v. City of Cleveland*

The City's objective in *City of Cleveland v. Deutsche Bank Trust Company*, **could not be clearer**: to regulate the real estate lending activities of virtually every major non-local financial institution in the country.

Brendan Sullivan, *United States v. Ted Stevens*

Witness C's criminal history is also relevant and admissible **for a separate reason**: It affects his exposure for any crimes for which he is currently under investigation, including in connection with the allegations of this case.

(Sullivan capitalizes the first word of an independent clause introduced by a colon. Usage authorities suggest that you can go either
way on this one.)

Herbert Wachtell, *NFL Enterprises v. EchoStar Satellite*

This is a matter of common sense: an injunction that would
require the party that is likely wrong in its interpretation of
a contract to have the benefit of a valuable service while not
paying for it is hardly "equitable"—not even "by halves."

Seamless Flow

Read this passage and note how you feel each time you start a new
sentence:

The correctness of Plaintiffs' contention with regard to their
need to allege only that the employer knew that the illegal
workers it hired had been "brought into" this country illegally
would not render Plaintiffs' allegations sufficient. Plaintiffs
only allege that Mohawk hired, harbored, and encouraged illegal workers. Plaintiffs do not allege that any of these workers
were "brought into" the United States illegally. None of the
allegations cited by Plaintiffs allege that anyone brought the
workers into the country illegally. Plaintiffs' own erroneous
interpretation of § 1324(a)(3) does not allow their allegations
to state a claim.

Do you feel as though you're inside a bumper car?

Now here's the same passage again, this time with the transitions
that Virginia Seitz used in the actual passage:

> **Virginia Seitz, *Williams v. Mohawk Industries***
>
> **Even if** Plaintiffs were correct that they need only allege that the employer knew that the illegal workers it hired had been "brought into" this country illegally, Plaintiffs' allegations are still insufficient. **In short**, Plaintiffs only allege that Mohawk hired, harbored, and encouraged illegal workers; Plaintiffs do not allege that any of these workers were "brought into" the United States illegally. **In fact**, none of the allegations cited by Plaintiffs allege that anyone brought the workers into the country illegally. **Thus**, even under Plaintiffs' own erroneous interpretation of § 1324(a)(3), their allegations still do not state a claim.

In advocacy writing, sprinkling in such "signpost" words and phrases helps clarify your logic and push your prose ahead. Of course, before you can insert these signposts, you'll need to figure out how your sentences and thoughts relate to one another. By filling in those missing links, you'll make your writing flow.

Here are some ways to do so.

45

Take Me by the Hand: Logical connectors

All brief writers use at least some logical connectors. The most popular ones include *moreover, additionally, however, furthermore*, and *nevertheless*. Heralded in law school writing classes, these words also pepper the canned "model" memos and briefs in many legal-writing textbooks.

So what's the problem? First, these words get old fast. You need to have dozens of transitions words at your disposal, not just a handful. Second, they're formulaic and heavy—the last things you want if you're trying to lighten your prose. Third, they're generic. When lawyers use *moreover, furthermore*, or *additionally*, they usually just want to make a new point, regardless of whether it's related to the old one: "The statute is on point. Additionally, Petitioner misrepresented what we said at the hearing." In a similar way, *nevertheless* and *however* become catch-alls for all sorts of vague contrasts, counterarguments, and exceptions.

You can still use such transitions to good effect—in small doses. But you should also broaden and deepen your repertoire.

In his much-heralded brief for the state of Alaska in *Alaska v. EPA*, for example, Chief Justice John Roberts used a few *moreovers* and *furthermores*. But he also included such varied signals as *at bottom, also, under that approach, in short, to this end, because, then, for example, in each case, in any event, of course, instead, to begin with, indeed*, and *thus*.

In that spirit, let me share what I believe is the most comprehensive list available of transitions for lawyers and other advocates. I've arranged these 135 signposts according to your goal for the sentence. In general, favor the shorter options in each category:

135 Transition Words and Phrases

To Provide Another Point

Additionally	Further
Along with	Furthermore
Also	In addition
And	Moreover
Another reason	Nor
As well (as)	To X, Y adds Z
Besides	What is more

To Conclude

Accordingly	In summary
All in all	In the end
Consequently	Then
Hence	Therefore
In brief	Thus
In conclusion	To summarize
In short	
In sum	

To Extract the Essence

At bottom
At its core
At its root
In effect

In essence
In the end
The bottom line is that

To Show Cause and Effect

And so

And therefore

And thus

As a result

Because

For

For that reason

In consequence

On that basis

So

That is why

To that end

To this end

With that in mind

To Draw an Analogy or Comparison

As in X, Y

As with X, Y

By analogy

By extension

Here

In each case

In like manner

In the same way

Just as X, so Y

Like X, Y

Likewise

Similarly

So too here

So too with

To Draw a Contrast

At the same time

But

By contrast

Despite

For all that

However

In contrast

In the meantime

Instead

Nevertheless

Not

Rather

Unlike (in)

Yet

To Give an Example

As an example	Including
As in	In that regard
By way of example	Like
First, second, third, etc.	Say
For example	Such as
For instance	Suppose (as first word of sentence)
For one thing	Take (as first word of sentence)
Imagine (as first word of sentence)	To illustrate

To Concede a Point or to Preempt a Counterargument

All of that may be true, but	For all that
All the same	Of course
Although	On the other hand
At least	Otherwise
At the same time	Still
Even assuming	That said
Even if	Though some might argue
Even so	To be sure
Even still	True enough
Even though	
Even under	

To Redirect

At any rate
(Even) more to the point
In all events
In any event

To Emphasize or Expand

Above all	In fact
All the more because	In other words

All the more reason	In particular
All the more X because Y	Indeed
By extension	Not only X, but (also) Y
Especially	Particularly
Even more (so)	Put another way
If anything	Put differently
In effect	Simply put

Let me share some examples of these transition words in context. We already saw one example at the beginning of this section, when I showed you a Virginia Seitz paragraph, first without her transition words and then with them. Here's another example—produced by six former federal judges in an amicus brief on the detainee side in *Hamdi v. Rumsfeld*, one of the first cases about detainee rights during the war on terror. To paraphrase a famous E. F. Hutton saying from the 1980s, "When federal judges write briefs, people should listen":

Six former federal judges, *Hamdi v. Rumsfeld*

None of the cases relied on by the Government, or by the Fourth Circuit, supports the contention that because this nation is at war a federal habeas court may be bound by the executive's assertion of the jurisdictional facts underlying its authority to detain the petitioner. **In particular**, in both *Ex parte Quirin* and *In re Territo*, petitioners did not dispute the factual findings underpinning the determination of their status. **Nonetheless**, they had full access to a tribunal in which any disputed facts could be tried. **Indeed**, in *Quirin*, this Court reached the merits of the habeas petitions despite a presidential order that purported to deny the petitioners access to U.S. courts.... The executive's supposed primacy in "war making" therefore does not support the surrender of the judicial power wrought by the decision below. **Nor** does the Fourth Circuit's reliance on the alleged (but unproved) fact that Mr. Hamdi was seized in a "war zone" justify his continued detention without effective judicial review. **If** the place of the petitioner's capture were determinative, all the more reason that this vital jurisdictional fact be subject to court review. The notion that the scope of court review of a habeas corpus petition should depend on whether the petitioner was captured on a battlefield is, in any event, wrong.

Let's return to the world of practicing attorneys. On the trial side, here is Seth Waxman seeking a permanent injunction against eBay for MercExchange:

Seth Waxman, *MercExchange v. eBay*

Nor is the eBay holding limited to permanent injunctions. The Court's reasoning applies with even greater force at the preliminary injunction stage, where a plaintiff has at best shown a likelihood of success, not actual success on the merits. **Indeed**, eBay rested its holding on *Amoco Production Co. v. Gambell*, which itself involved a preliminary injunction and rejected a presumption of irreparable harm in favor of traditional equitable factors. The Supreme Court's *eBay* decision **therefore** solidified the rule set out in Amoco that presumptions "contrary to traditional equitable principles" are not permissible for any type of injunction.

And here, with an even lighter touch, we see liberal use of short transition words and links in a high-profile dispute about the Copyright Term Extension Act:

Larry Lessig and Kathleen Sullivan, *Eldred v. Ashcroft*

Petitioners have adopted the meaning of "progress" employed by this Court. That "progress" is the "creation of useful works." **But** even if this different conception of "progress" were adopted, [Copyright Term Extension Act] would still be at odds with the structure of the Clause and its framing history. For as petitioners have also demonstrated, whatever the meaning of "progress," the Framers granted copyright only as part of a quid pro quo. **Thus**, even if "progress" means "spread," or "dissemination," or (anachronistically) "restoration," the monopolies that the Framers spread were not granted on the mere hope that something would be given in return. Their monopolies were offered upon the condition that something was given in return. **It is for this reason**, among others, that the author of the primary source Senator Hatch relies upon herself concludes that [the Act] is "unconstitutional per se."

In great persuasive writing, you will often find several transition words or phrases in a short passage. Consider this example from appellate guru Roy Englert on behalf of Saudi Arabia:

Roy Englert, *Federal Insurance Company v. Kingdom of Saudi Arabia*

Here, Saudi Arabia is alleged to have provided material support for terrorism, so, as the Second Circuit recognized, the relevant exception is the [Foreign Sovereign Immunities Act's] terrorism exception. That exception, **however,** applies only when the U.S. Department of State has designated the defendant state as a state sponsor of terrorism. The State Department has never so designated Saudi Arabia. **To the contrary,** the State Department has identified Saudi Arabia as a crucial ally, emphasizing that the United States and Saudi Arabia are "united in the war against terror."

(Note that Englert moves "however" inside the sentence close to the verb rather than sticking it out front—a great writing trick that will improve your cadence.)

46

Bridge the Gap: Linked paragraphs

I don't mean to suggest that including a "signpost" word from the list of 135 words and phrases in the previous section is the only way to link your points logically.

You can also "bridge" between two sentences or paragraphs.

Consider these sentence pairs. In each case, the first sentence will be the end of one paragraph. That sentence will stay the same. The second sentence will be the beginning of a new paragraph. That sentence will change as we work through the series.

Here's Version 1:

> Except in one specified instance—not applicable here—the [Clean Air] Act nowhere requires the EPA to approve a State's BACT determination.
>
> **A broader principle stems** from the Act's scheme of rules and exceptions, i.e., that Congress otherwise did not intend the EPA to have the "ultimate authority" to determine BACT for particular sources.

Do you have any idea how the new paragraph relates to the end of the one before? I didn't think so.

Now here's Version 2:

> Except in one specified instance—not applicable here—the [Clean Air] Act nowhere requires the EPA to approve a State's BACT determination.

> **That single departure** is evidence of a broader principle—that Congress otherwise did not intend the EPA to have the "ultimate authority" to determine BACT for particular sources.

Better, right? At least we know that the phrase "that single departure" points back to the paragraph before, so we know there's some connection, somewhere.

And now for the grand finale. Read what the Chief Justice actually wrote:

John Roberts, *Alaska v. EPA*

Except **in one specified instance**—not applicable here—the Act nowhere requires the EPA to approve a State's BACT determination.

Indeed, that **one instance** is the exception that proves the rule—that Congress otherwise did not intend the EPA to have the "ultimate authority" to determine BACT for particular sources.

Because Roberts repeated the words "one" and "instance," the connection between the paragraphs becomes crystal clear.

Using this technique is one of the easiest ways to help make your writing flow.

I've reproduced in that regard the opening of a key section in Thurgood Marshall's brief in *Brown v. Board of Education*. Look how the sentences in the first paragraph flow one into the next—and how the end of the first paragraph flows right into the second:

Thurgood Marshall, *Brown v. Board of Education*

While the State of Kansas has undoubted power to confer benefits or impose disabilities upon selected groups of citizens in the normal execution of governmental functions, **it must conform to constitutional standard**s in the exercise of this authority. **These standards** may be generally characterized as a requirement that **the state's action be reasonable**. **Reasonableness** in a constitutional sense is determined by examining the action of the state to discover whether **the distinctions or restrictions** in issue are in fact based upon real **differences** pertinent to a lawful legislative objective.

When the **distinctions** imposed are based upon race and color alone....

Let's turn to some more modern examples. Representing amici opposed to a tough Arizona immigration statute, Seth Waxman builds a bridge through "Executive" and "discretion":

Seth Waxman, *Arizona v. United States*

But because Congress has also recognized that immigration is "a field where flexibility and the adaptation of the congressional policy to infinitely variable conditions constitute the essence of the program," Congress has thus granted the **Executive** considerable **discretion** in enforcing those laws.

In exercising that **discretion**, the **Executive** has traditionally taken into account many factors that implicate foreign affairs.

To create this effect, you need not repeat the exact words. Sometimes, you can simply refer to the paragraph before through a pithy "pointing" sentence, as Larry Tribe and Kathleen Sullivan do in this gay-rights case:

Larry Tribe and Kathleen Sullivan, *Romer v. Evans*

But it is quite another matter for a state's constitution absolutely to preclude, for a selected set of persons, even the possibility of protection under any state or local law from a whole category of harmful conduct, including some that is undeniably wrongful.

Amendment 2 does just that. It does not simply write into the state's constitution a substantive rule that a particular sphere of conduct—for example, expelling a guest from one's home on whatever basis one wishes, however "prejudiced" one's reasons for finding the guest unwelcome—is a matter for private choice that inflicts no wrong at all and accordingly may not be made the basis of any claim for legal redress by anyone.

Or even through a short "this," "that," "these," "or those" phrase, as Carolyn Lamm does here:

Carolyn Lamm, *Globe Nuclear Services and Supply v. AO Techsnabexport*

The statute also provides that, in an action brought against an agency or instrumentality, an answer to the complaint or other responsive pleading is due "within sixty days after service has been made under this section."

When these provisions are construed as a whole (as they must), it is apparent that Congress has gone to great lengths to carefully circumscribe the Court's subject matter jurisdiction and the requirements of personal jurisdiction in those cases that involve a foreign state.

(Note that Lamm mercifully uses "these" and not the stiff and legalistic "such" that's so common elsewhere.)

Here's another example from Patrick Fitzgerald in the fallout over who revealed the covert identity of CIA agent Valerie Plame. Fitzgerald is addressing the thorny question of when prosecutors can subpoena a reporter's confidential notes, in this case notes belonging to *New York Times* reporter Judy Miller:

Patrick Fitzgerald, *Miller v. United States*

The Court rejected the suggestion that courts should conduct a case-by-case balancing of interests each time a reporter is subpoenaed by a grand jury. Instead the Court struck **a one-time balance**: the state's interest in "law enforcement and in ensuring effective grand juries" justifies the "burden on First Amendment rights" when "reporters [are required] to give testimony in the manner and for the reasons that other citizens are called." The Court refused to grant news sources a privilege not granted to law enforcement informants in criminal cases.

In striking this balance, the Court carefully analyzed the competing interests. The reporters claimed that newsgathering would be significantly impeded, but the Court concluded that requiring testimony from reporters in cases where news sources are "implicated in crime or possess information relevant to the grand jury's task" would not seriously impede newsgathering.

Supreme Court stalwarts Stephen Shapiro and Ted Olson construct bridges of their own below:

Stephen Shapiro, *Stoneridge Investment Partners v. Scientific Atlanta*

Virtually all commentators now recognize that, over time, a diversified investor buys and sells in roughly equal amounts, meaning that securities fraud settlements simply "transfe[r] money from one pocket to the other, with about half of it dropping on the floor for lawyers to pick up."

In such a regime, securities fraud litigation serves only as "a grotesquely inefficient form of insurance against large stock market losses."

(Note that Shapiro's use of "such a regime" here, as in "a regime like this one," is perfectly sound. It's using "such" for "this" or "these," as in "I know you're looking for our agreement but I haven't seen such document," that's so jarring to the ear.)

Ted Olson, *Viacom v. YouTube*

Indeed, service providers that induce infringement [] have at the very least "[a]wareness of facts or circumstances from which infringement is apparent." Otherwise, Congress's narrow safe harbor would be converted into a haven for intentional piracy.

And that is a world in which copyright owners cannot long survive.

Interlude: Streamlining paragraphs

Bridge transitions work within paragraphs as well. Take this paragraph from the "red sole shoes" suit between Christian Louboutin and Yves Saint Laurent. In April 2011, French shoemaker Louboutin alleged that Yves Saint Laurent violated its trademark by selling red-soled shoes. Note how the subjects of the sentences shift from "evidence" to "Mr. Louboutin" and to "much of the material."

> The evidence in this case demonstrates that use of the color red on the outsoles of shoes is aesthetically functional. **Mr. Louboutin** himself admits that he started using red on outsoles, not as a source-identifier, but rather to give life to a creative concept. He chose **red** because it gives his shoes "energy," "is engaging, flirtatious, memorable and the color of passion," and because it "appeals to everyone and is sexy." Similarly, **much of the material** Louboutin submits to the Court purportedly to establish secondary meaning highlights instead the beauty—the aesthetic function—of the design feature. *See, e.g.,* Mourot Decl. Ex. B, p.87 ("Part of the genius of the red sole is that it is beautiful.").

Now consider this rewrite, which uses "red" as an anchor to link the sentences:

> The evidence shows that using red on the outsoles is aesthetically functional, as Mr. Louboutin himself admits: He used **the red** to give life to a creative concept, not as a source identifier. **Red** gives his shoes "energy," "is engaging, flirtatious, memorable and the color of passion," and "appeals to everyone and is sexy." In fact, the beauty of **red**—the aesthetic

> function—inspires much of the material that he has submit-
> ted to establish secondary meaning. *See, e.g.,* Mourot Decl. Ex.
> B, p.87 ("Part of the genius of the red sole is that it is beauti-
> ful.").
>
> (The rewrite also shaves off twenty-two words.)

Visual Appeal

We've talked a lot in this section about how to make your words
sound good. Now let's talk about how to make them look good.

A great source of general advice comes from the Seventh Circuit's
Practitioner's Handbook: "[R]ead some good books and try to make
your briefs look more like them.... [M]aking your briefs typograph-
ically superior won't make your arguments better, but it will ensure
that judges grasp and retain your points with less struggle."[1]

So what are some ways to be "superior" on the visual front?

First, here are four things to avoid:

- **Avoid excess emphasis**. Judge Dan Friedman: "Effectiveness
  is lost by extensive capitalization, underlining, boldface type,
  or italics."[2]
- **Avoid excess definition.** According to former Wisconsin Court
  of Appeals Chief Judge William Eich, defining obvious terms
  is "excusable, perhaps, if the lawyer is 127 years old and was
  apprenticed in his youth to Silas Pinney, but never welcome
  in any piece of writing by anyone younger." He offers this
  example of what *not* to do: "This appeal arises out of a note

---

1. United States Court of Appeals for the Seventh Circuit, *Practitioner's Handbook for Appeals* 78–79 (2003).

2. Daniel M. Friedman, *Winning on Appeal*, 9 LITIG. 15, 17 (Spring 1983).

(the 'note') that Peter and Patricia Smith (collectively 'Smiths') executed to Patrick Brown ('Brown'). To secure the note, Smiths executed a mortgage ('the mortgage') for certain real property ('the real property') and a lien on certain personal property ('the personal property') as further security for the note."[3]

- **Avoid excessive acronyms.** Ninth Circuit Chief Judge Alex Kozinski has mocked this example from a brief: "LBE's complaint more specifically alleges that NRB failed to make an appropriate determination of RPT and TIP conformity to SIP." As Kozinski put it, "Even if there was a winning argument buried in the midst of that gobbledygook, it was DOA."[4] The D.C. Circuit has launched a similar diatribe: "The parties abandoned any attempt to write in plain English, instead abbreviating every conceivable agency and statute involved, familiar or not, and littering their briefs with references to 'SNF,' 'HLW,' 'NWF,' 'NWPA,' and 'BRC'—shorthand for 'spent nuclear fuel,' 'high-level radioactive waste,' the 'Nuclear Waste Fund,' the 'Nuclear Waste Policy Act,' and the 'Blue Ribbon Commission.'"[5]

- **Avoid writing out numbers in both figures and letters.** Former Ohio Judge Mark Painter: "Never clutter your document with both words and numbers: 'There were four (4) plaintiffs and six (6) defendants.' Never."[6]

---

3. William Eich, *Writing the Persuasive Brief*, 76 WIS. LAW. 20, 55 (Feb. 2003).

4. Alex Kozinski, *The Wrong Stuff*, 1992 B.Y.U. L. REV. 325, 329.

5. *National Assoc. of Regulatory Utility Commissioners v. United States Dept. of Energy*, No. 11-1066 (D.C. Cir. June 1, 2012) (Silberman, J.)

6. Mark P. Painter, *The Legal Writer: 40 Rules for the Art of Legal Writing* 61–72 (2d ed. Jardyce & Jardyce 2003).

Now that I've let these judges blow off steam, let's turn to some happier ways to enhance your brief's visual appeal.

Interlude: Looking good

The judges of the Seventh Circuit have thought a lot about how to make a brief look good—"and thus more likely to be grasped and retained."

Here are some of their suggestions:

- Use proportionally spaced fonts designed for books. Both the Supreme Court and the Solicitor General use Century, the Seventh Circuit points out. The court also endorses such book-friendly fonts as New Baskerville, Book Antiqua, Calisto, Century, Century Schoolbook, and Bookman Old Style.
- Consider avoiding Garamond and Times New Roman. (Note that although the Seventh Circuit doesn't like these fonts, they are both wildly popular among great brief writers.)
- Use italics, not underlining, for case names and emphasis.
- Use "smart quotes" and "smart apostrophes" (the curly kind, not the straight kind).
- Use one space after periods, not two. (Matthew Butterick, the author of the typography book mentioned below, offers the same advice, though two-spacers still appear to dominate the upper ranks of firms and agencies.)
- Avoid all-caps for headings. Use title case instead, as I do for the techniques in this book. (Capitalize all words except for articles, prepositions, and conjunctions that have four letters or fewer.) Here is a model that the judges provide:

ARGUMENT

I. The Suit is Barred by the Statute of Limitations
   A. Perkins had actual knowledge of the contamination more than six years before filing suit[7]

For more on looking good in your work product, visit http://www.typographyforlawyers.com or better yet, buy Matthew Butterick's terrific book *Typography for Lawyers*.

---

7. Seventh Circuit Court of Appeals, *Requirements and Suggestions for Typography in Briefs and Other Papers*, *available at* http://www.ca7.uscourts.gov/Rules/type.pdf.

47

Join My Table: Tables and charts

One of the best ways to add interest and streamline information is to include an image, timeline, table, or chart.

"Wherever possible, use pictures, maps, diagrams, and other visual aids in your briefs," said Judge Posner in a recent article on effective brief writing. He shared the story of a trademark dispute between the Indianapolis Colts and the Baltimore CFL Colts in which the briefs never showed a picture of the hats and other trademarked products at issue. Luckily for the Indianapolis Colts lawyer, when Posner asked him for a visual aid he was able to pull out a couple of caps from his briefcase. "The caps looked identical. He won the case at that moment. He was lucky that he was asked that question," Posner said. "*Seeing* a case makes it come alive to judges."[1]

It's no surprise, then, that the following examples come from renowned trial lawyers adept at swaying jurors. Who better understands the appeal of visual aids in cases with dry, complicated material?

Some lawyers push these strategies to their limits. In fact, perhaps you heard about the reply brief filed in an antitrust case against publishers of e-books: it was a self-proclaimed "graphic novelette" consisting solely of cartoons. "I thought of the idea of using pictures which, as we know, paint a thousand words," the lawyer told Bloomberg News, adding that he was faced with a five-page limit.

If you're a bit more risk-averse, though, I'll share two tables that lawyers used to their advantage. Each time, I'll show you just the first row of the table.

---

1. Richard Posner, *Effective Appellate Brief Writing*, *available at* http://apps.american-bar.org/litigation/litigationnews/trial_skills/appellate-brief-writing-posner.html.

In this first example, David Boies uses a table to present the plaintiff's response to defense claims that the plaintiff cannot establish the standard class-certification factors. Here is the opening point and counterpoint on the "numerosity" factor:

David Boies, *Renton v. Kaiser*

Kaiser's Argument	Plaintiff's Response
"Plaintiff has offered no proof that numerosity can be met once the putative class is cut down and it is not clear that there is anyone beside plaintiff herself whose claims are reasonably coextensive with hers."	Plaintiff's proposed class consisting of millions of Kaiser subscribers and former subscribers who are located throughout the United States is so numerous as to make joinder impracticable.

And in this example, Morgan Chu uses a table to organize his objections to various kinds of evidence that his opponent seeks to have admitted:

Morgan Chu, *Tessera v. United Test and Assembly Center*

Material Objected To	Grounds for Objections
Jager Declaration, page 4, lines 19–23 and associated footnote at line 28: "The bedrock foundation of a patent license, and the basis on which a licensor can collect royalties from a licensee, is the manufacture and sale of a product that practices a valid patent owned by the licensor . . . ."	Improper legal argument and conclusion. (Evid. Code §§ 310, 801, 803; *California Shoppers*, 175 Cal. App. 3d at 67; *Summers*, 69 Cal. App. 4th at 1178.)

48

Bullet Proof: Bullet points and lists

Here are more visual aids for your brief-writing arsenal: bullet points and lists. These formatting tricks make it easier for readers to absorb all manner of information:

- The main issues in the case
- The main reasons you should win
- Procedural history
- The content of trial exhibits
- Trial testimony
- A witness's qualifications
- Your own argument
- Flaws in the other side's argument
- Contrasts between your opponent's argument and your own

Let's start with an example from SEC Chair Mary Jo White. The former Manhattan U.S. Attorney knows that looks matter when you share information with a jury or judge. Here, she uses bullets to spin a discovery tale designed to make Donald Trump's team squirm:

Mary Jo White, *Trump v. O'Brien*

Trump's frivolous claims for mitigation damages arising from his meeting with Forbes, his communications with The Times, and his attorneys' fees in this litigation also fail. As with his other expenses, Trump has completely failed to provide discovery in support of these claimed damages, despite numerous opportunities to do so. By way of procedural background:

- On July 7, 2007, the Court **ordered plaintiff** to "respond fully" to various interrogatories interposed by defendants on August 21, 2006, including interrogatories about his damage claims.
- Because Trump did not comply with this Order, defendants moved to enforce litigants' rights, and the Court **again ordered plaintiff** to "respond fully to each subpart" of defendants' damages interrogatory, which requested, among other things: (1) information about the amount of such alleged damages; (2) any data allegedly supporting such damages; and (3) any documents relevant to calculating such alleged damages.
- On January 7, 2008, **in response to this Order**, plaintiff for the first time claimed mitigation damages, including advertising expenses, meeting with Forbes, and communicating with The Times....

On the case-law side, you could use bullets to explain why your opponent's argument lacks support, as Nancy Abell does:

Nancy Abell, *Jackson v. Microsoft*

[Plaintiff] Jackson can cite no case in which the court reversed dismissal of a case where, as here, the wrongdoer
- Either procured, or at a minimum paid an "appreciation" fee, to get "valuable" stolen attorney-client privileged documents setting forth some of his opponent's strategy for defending the thief's lawsuit;
- Admitted that he intended to use the stolen evidence to advance his case;

- Reviewed and sent to his counsel "important" attorney-client privileged communications pertaining to his claims, thereby giving them all knowledge that could never be unlearned....

As this example from Harvey Miller shows, bullet points can also spill into a parade of horribles, highlighting the consequences of not doing what your client wants:

Harvey Miller, *In re General Motors*

For example, a protracted bankruptcy process, among other things, would:

- dramatically and irreversibly **erode** sales and GM's market share....
- **endanger** the viability of GM's dealers and suppliers that depend on volume sales to GM, causing systemic failures;
- **distract** managerial and union employees from the performance of their duties or, worse yet, cause them to seek other job opportunities, while, at the same time, rendering it extremely difficult, if not impossible, to attract new employees;
- lead many of GM's suppliers, dealers and partners (including certain joint-venture partners) to **terminate** their relationships with GM...and
- **foreclose** GM's ability to obtain debtor in possession financing sufficient to sustain operations during case administration, which likely would force the Debtors' liquidation.

(In the final bullet, putting "likely" before "would" is the stuff of myth. Those who insist it should go before claim that they're avoiding splitting an infinitive. But there's no infinitive here (an infinitive requires "to," as in "to boldly go where no one has gone before"). "Which would likely force" is standard and more lyrical.)

Also consider bullets for facts that sound your legal theme. Here, Miguel Estrada's four bulleted examples of alleged "fleeting expletives" paint the FCC as too quick to take offense when it sought to fine Fox for indecency:

Miguel Estrada, *FCC v. Fox*

[T]he Commission adjudicated as "indecent" and "profane" the broadcast of fleeting expletives in four programs:

- The **isolated** use of the word "bullshit" by New York City police detective Andy Sipowicz in episodes of ABC's NYPD Blue.
- The **single use** of the word "bullshitter" during a live news interview on CBS's The Early Show. The word was unexpectedly used by a castaway contestant from Survivor: Vanuatu when referring to an unscrupulous competing contestant.
- A **single, unscripted use** of the phrase "fuck 'em" by the performer Cher during a live broadcast by FOX of the 2002 Billboard Music Awards.
- An **unscripted** moment during FOX's 2003 Billboard Music Awards live telecast, during which presenter Nicole Richie stated, "Have you ever tried to get cow shit out of a Prada purse? It's not so fucking simple."

By bulleting these stray, isolated, unscripted utterances, Estrada helps make the FCC sound prim and out of touch.

Finally, consider using bullets to contrast your opponent's claims with your own. Particularly in opposition or reply briefs, this technique is one of the best antidotes to long, repetitive paragraphs stuffed with "My opponent's contention is erroneous" or "Contrary to my opponent's contention" and other filler:

Walter Dellinger, *Bank of America v. Cleveland*

A comparison of the allegations in Deutsche Bank to Bank of America's allegations here conclusively establishes that Bank of America's real estate lending-related activities are the real target of the City's claims against BAC:

- The City alleges that the use of improper underwriting standards permitted BAC to "originate[] loans that made no economic sense." **As the Complaint here makes plain**, BAC does not originate loans; instead, Bank of America (inclusive of its operating subsidiaries) is the BAC-affiliated entity that does so.
- The City alleges BAC violated state nuisance law by offering "Hybrid Adjustable Rate Mortgages"; offering "Low- and No-Documentation Loans"; and offering "Interest-Only Loans." Yet BAC does not establish terms of credit for real estate loans; Bank of America is the BAC subsidiary that carries out such activity....

As you can see, these varied uses of bullets add visual appeal while highlighting your key points.

A final thought on style: great advocacy writing is simply great writing that happens to be about the law. From word choice and sentence structure to transitions, punctuation, and even formatting, seize every opportunity to mold dense, dry law into fresh, varied language. In other words, you should write the sort of prose that you would enjoy reading.

The end of a motion or brief—the conclusion—brings us to our next and final family of techniques.

PART FIVE

THE CLOSE

Part Five will share two techniques for generating conclusions:

Part Five: The Close

The Last Word

In Part Two, I shared some nonfiction writing tips from Pulitzer Prize winner James Stewart, whose bestselling books on Whitewater and the 1980s insider trading scandals have deep legal dimensions that make them priceless to any writer of legal prose.

For Stewart, "the ending is the most important part of a story. If the lead provides the first impression necessary to propel readers through a story, the ending provides the last. What is freshest in readers' minds is what they read most recently, which is the ending."[1]

Stewart cites his own conclusion to *Blood Sport*, his magisterial book on the Whitewater investigation during the Clinton years. After

---

1. James B. Stewart, Follow the Story 272 (Simon & Schuster 1998).

having told such a torrid tale, Stewart offers the reader this final reflection:

> Whitewater is not solely about events and crimes and Little Rock. It is also about questions—and I stress that they are only questions, which we are not very far along in examining—about the official processes of government in Washington. It is about whether participants in Washington deceived federal investigators trying to reconstruct those processes of government. It is about the White House travel office....It is about contact between the Treasury Department and the White House concerning law enforcement matters....It is, in short, about public trust.[2]

Few litigated disputes have such grand dimensions, but you can still adopt the spirit of Stewart's model closing. After all the lists and standards, the record cites and analogies, the various points and counterpoints, what exactly is your own dispute "about"?

Once you settle on an answer to that question, you have some flexibility in where you put it:

Option One: You follow the classic approach, which is to make your "conclusion" section a formulaic sentence or two: "For the foregoing reasons, the Court should grant Plaintiffs' motion for partial summary judgment." You would then put your "real" conclusion at the end of your argument section.

Option Two: You make your "conclusion" section more than just a formula. It also includes expansive final thoughts that strike your themes, sum up your argument, or both.

Let's consider those options in turn.

2. *Id.* at 291.

49

Parting Thought: End the argument with a provocative quotation or pithy thought

As with the end of any good story or essay, the last sentence in your argument section gives you a chance to crystallize your message and leave the court with a parting thought.

One way to do so is through an apt quotation. How's this for a dream scenario: you manage to work in something from the dissent in *Plessy v. Ferguson*:

Paul Smith, *Lawrence v. Texas*

Because it discriminates at the core of the private sphere that is constitutionally protected against state intrusion, the Homosexual Conduct Law is **"inconsistent not only with that equality of rights which pertain to citizenship..., but with the personal liberty enjoyed by everyone within the United States."** *Plessy v. Ferguson*, 163 U.S. 537, 555 (1896) (Harlan, J., dissenting).

You can also include a more mundane quotation that fits the bill, as then-U.S. Attorney Patrick Fitzgerald does at the end of the government's argument in a kickback case against a former hospital CEO:

Patrick Fitzgerald, *United States v. Rogan*

Under the common law, the United States has a right to recover funds lost through the erroneous acts of its agents—i.e., payments made under a mistake of fact. Thus, if agents of the federal government, acting on behalf of the United States, paid claims submitted by Edgewater as a result of Rogan's actions **"under an erroneous belief which was material to the decision to pay, [the Government] is entitled to recover the payments."** *United States v. Mead*, 426 F.2d 118, 124 (9th Cir. 1970). Here, the express and implied certifications of compliance with the Anti-kickback and Stark Statutes contained in Edgewater's cost reports and UB-92 forms were material to the United States' decision to pay Edgewater, and as these certifications were false, **the United States erroneously paid Edgewater and is entitled to recover the amounts improperly provided to the hospital.**

Sometimes, even shorter quotes are ideal. In his brief for the state of Alaska against the federal EPA, John Roberts ended with six quoted words that sound his theme that the states need flexibility to decide which technology is truly "best":

John Roberts, *Alaska v. EPA*

When it came to [Best Available Control Technology], however, Congress had a different idea, and left that determination—**"on a case-by-case basis"**—to the States.

You can also end without quoting anything at all. In punching up this dry jurisdictional dispute in a patent case, is Morgan Chu, like MedImmune, trying to have his cake and eat it too?

Morgan Chu, *MedImmune v. Genentech*

At bottom, MedImmune is reluctant to breach its agreement for a simple reason: **MedImmune is trying to have its cake and eat it too** by continuing to lock in its low royalty rate while at the same time trying to invalidate the patent. The Federal Circuit in *Gen-Probe* disapproved of the sort of strategic positioning that MedImmune is attempting here. The Federal Circuit correctly noted that allowing such no-risk patent challenges would have the effect of discouraging the voluntary licensing of patents in the future.

Once in a while, the last paragraph of the argument hits a home run. Representing Hastings Law School in a dispute over student-group funding, Maureen Mahoney and Greg Garre use their adversary's words against it, include two short arresting sentences, and make their adversary's position sound absurd—all in just a few lines:

Maureen Mahoney and Greg Garre, *Christian Legal Society v. Martinez*

Hastings agrees with petitioner this far: "this case is most emphatically not a clash between religious freedom and rights pertaining to sexual orientation." Indeed, **as petitioner frankly admits**, "[t]he right that [the Christian Legal Student group] is asserting…is by no means limited to religious groups." **Far from it.** Petitioner claims that *every* "noncommercial expressive association []" in America has a First Amendment right *both* to demand access to public funds and benefits—indeed, even the right to use the State's own name—and to demand a special exemption from viewpoint-neutral non-discrimination provisions that apply to such public funds or benefits. This Court has never come close to adopting such a remarkable proposition. **And there is no reason to do so here.**

50

Wrap-Up: Recast your main points in a separate conclusion

Our fiftieth and final technique applies, appropriately enough, to your conclusion section.

Many great advocates are traditionalists on this front, presenting their last hurrah at the end of their argument and making their actual conclusion short and sweet:

Miguel Estrada, *Sanders v. Madison Square Garden*

For the reasons stated above, the punitive damages award on the hostile-environment claim against Madison Square Garden should be reduced to below the Title VII cap of $300,000.

But you may be inspired to end your brief with a bit more heft.

In the Harry Potter lexicon case, for example, Larry Lessig's clear summation distills a complex argument into a tight rebuttal to J. K. Rowling's claims:

Larry Lessig, *Warner Bros. Entertainment v. RDR Books*

Plaintiffs have not sustained any of their claims. The Lexicon **does not infringe** Plaintiffs' copyright and in any event **represents a fair use** of Ms. Rowling's novels. The current cover presents **no possibility of consumer confusion**, and **infringes no trademark** belonging to either Plaintiff. Plaintiffs' motion for a preliminary injunction should be denied.

Fred Bartlit's conclusion for a Tyco subsidiary is more daring. No matter what, Bartlit says, we win:

Fred Bartlit, *Stumpf v. Garvey*

Because there is no material fact in dispute as to statutes of limitations and the critical element of loss causation, summary judgment should be granted. **If summary judgment is not granted on both grounds, it must be granted on at least one.** Plaintiffs' attempt to keep alive a case filed years too late directly contradicts their argument on loss causation. If the March 2001 news establishes the loss causation necessary to defeat summary judgment on that score, then the statute of limitations has run. Plaintiffs cannot now maintain both positions.

If you've kept your emotions in check throughout your argument, let yourself vent a bit in your conclusion, as Brendan Sullivan does in his defense of the late Alaska Senator Ted Stevens:

Brendan Sullivan, *United States v. Ted Stevens*

In **a case awash with extraordinary revelations**, [FBI Special Agent] Joy's complaint is perhaps the most shocking and important. An FBI Special Agent has alleged that his colleagues engaged in **intentional constitutional violations** in the course of investigating and prosecuting this defendant and others. Because of their source, these allegations are highly credible. The misconduct is **utterly inexcusable**. The Court should dismiss the indictment or, at a minimum, grant a new trial and order discovery and an evidentiary hearing.

(A tighter version—stripped of "and important," "highly," and "utterly"—would have been even more effective.)

A little less fiery is this attack on the FCC from Dick Wiley and John Roberts. They round out their conclusion by quoting Arizona Senator John McCain, who once chaired the Senate committee that oversees the telecom industry:

Richard Wiley and John Roberts, *Advanced Communications Corporation v. FCC*

The agency's failure to address the impact on service to the public is particularly troubling given that the only operating DBS satellites are owned by Hughes (DIRECTV), and shared with USSB, who paid the government nothing for the use of spectrum. Not only has the Order **set back competition** to the DIRECTV/USSB service for years, but it will also **distort marketplace dynamics**, saddling the auction winner with substantial embedded costs which will not be incurred by its several competitors.

In short, the agency's proposed course of action will **thwart its stated goals**, a hallmark of arbitrary and capricious decisionmaking. The Commission's disregard of its historic DBS policies would be inexplicable if not for the agency's interests in raising revenues, **as Senator McCain candidly acknowledged** when he described the *Advanced* decision to Congress:

> The Bureau felt compelled to use a new, tougher definition of due diligence due to the congressional mandate regarding spectrum auctions. The Commission's blatant disregard for its precedents and its stated policy of expediting new DBS service, in order to generate auction revenues for itself and the Treasury, is the very antithesis of the reasoned decisionmaking that the Administrative Procedure Act requires.

Saving one last juicy quotation for the conclusion works well on appeal, too, suggests Nancy Abell—and even more so if you can pluck some language from the court below:

Nancy Abell, *Doiwchi v. Princess Cruise Lines*

The trial judge correctly observed: "There's absolutely no evidence at all that any discrimination was taking place." Doiwchi herself conceded that even she does not believe that she was let go because she has a learning disability. The record is devoid of substantial evidence of intentional discrimination. So, too, is it devoid of the requisite proof that those accused of failing to accommodate knew that Doiwchi had a covered disability and a disability-caused work-related limitation that required accommodation. Doiwchi never told them.

For our final example of this chapter, section, and book, I'll share an unusually ambitious conclusion. In this global warming case that pit General Motors against the State of California, former Solicitor General Ted Olson indulges in a long and detailed *Wrap-Up*, one that broadens the dispute while sounding expansive themes about good intentions run amok:

Ted Olson, *California v. GM*

The California Attorney General has **identified an admittedly important global environmental issue**—climate change associated with, among other things, greenhouse gases (mainly carbon dioxide). And he has selected a single one of the innumerable sources of such gases—internal combustion engines in motor vehicles—on which to focus his attention in seeking a partial solution to what he perceives to be the problem of global warming. And, **after having been rejected** in his efforts to commandeer the federal judiciary to address the climate change conundrum by targeting utility companies, he has brought this suit seeking essentially the same judicial intervention against automobile manufacturers.

But this is the wrong place, and the wrong process, for achieving the Attorney General's objectives. The issue he wishes to address is so vast and so complex that it must be redressed by governments acting through treaties, legislation, and political compromise. It simply cannot be done in the federal courts. This is a classic example of how taking a political issue and turning it into a tort lawsuit can only further complicate and disrupt the ongoing political process. Article III precludes federal courts from deciding such nonjusticiable issues.

Moreover, there is simply no such thing as a nuisance suit against manufacturers of lawful, indeed useful and absolutely invaluable, products. The manufacturer of a motor vehicle is no more guilty of creating a nuisance than the builder of a highway, such as the State of California, which, when used for its lawful and highly utilitarian purpose, results in the production of carbon dioxide. California, in particular, fosters a culture and identity that affirmatively encourages the use of the very product that it now seeks to brand as a nuisance. This makes no legal or logical sense.

Finally, of course, the political branches are assigned constitutional responsibility for dealing with national and global policy issues like global warming. And those branches have the institutional power to prevent state actors from interfering with national programs and objectives. That is precisely the case with automotive emissions and fuel economy. California is prohibited by federal law from interfering in this fashion.

Whatever its motivation, this suit is misconceived and pernicious and must be brought to a prompt and final termination.

With Olson's words, this book will be brought to a "prompt and final termination" of its own, though I'll leave you with one final thought.

Just days before he died in 1962, the great legal scholar Karl Llewellyn gave a speech in Indianapolis on advocacy. The job of a brief, he said, is "to provide the court with the technical wherewithal to be perfectly happy in deciding your way with no qualms of legal conscience at all." But first you have to get judges to approach your brief "with the favorable atmosphere you need":

> You need to interest them in that brief. You've got to make them feel that when they come to the brief, "Oh, baby; is it going to be hot."

I hope the techniques in this book will help fill your own readers with the burning desire that Llewellyn's ideal invokes. As you pursue that quest, I invite you to build on what we've begun here. For starters, turn to the end of the book, where you'll find fifty writing or editing challenges that track the fifty tips. Also visit http://www. LegalWritingPro.com and http://www.TheTopAdvocates.com for more tips and examples—and for a chance to interact with me, to share your own examples, and to discuss the techniques in the book. Sign up for my newsletter at http://www.LegalWritingPro.com/newsletter. Most of all, thank you—and happy writing!

PART SIX

APPENDICES

The Top Advocates: Biographies

Abell, Nancy

Nancy Abell is the Global Chair of Paul Hastings's Employment Law Department. *The International Who's Who of Business Lawyers* has recognized her as one of the world's best employment lawyers. In 2010, the *National Law Journal* named her one of the most influential lawyers of the past decade. In 2011 she was recognized by *Chambers USA* as one of the top four employment defense lawyers in California and by the Legal 500 as one of America's top six employment litigators and counselors. She also has been named by the *Daily Journal* as one of California's "Top 100" lawyers, Top Employment Lawyers, and Top Women Lawyers. She has also chaired the Board of Governors of the Institute for Corporate Counsel. Chambers ranks her as one of the nation's leading employment attorneys.

Abell graduated Order of the Coif from the UCLA School of Law.

Bartlit, Fred

Fred Bartlit is the founding partner of Bartlit Beck Herman Palenchar & Scott. The *ABA Journal* has named him as one of the Lions of the Trial Bar. He is also one of fourteen lawyers profiled in Don Vinson's "America's Top Trial Lawyers: Who They Are and Why They Win." Chambers ranks him as a Senior Statesman in the nationwide trial lawyer category. In 2013, the *National Law Journal* named him one of the 100 Most Influential Lawyers.

Bartlit graduated *magna cum laude* from the University of Illinois College of Law, where he graduated first in his class and was an editor of the law review.

Bennett, Bob

Bob Bennett is a partner at Hogan Lovells; he previously practiced at Skadden Arps and served as Assistant U.S. Attorney for the District of Columbia. The personal attorney for President Bill Clinton in the Paula Jones litigation, Bennett has also represented Enron, former *New York Times* reporter Judy Miller in the CIA leak investigation, former Secretary of Defense Clark Clifford in the Bank of Credit and Commerce International (BCCI) case, and former Secretary of Defense Caspar Weinberger in the Iran-Contra affair. Chambers ranks him as one of the nation's leading lawyers in white-collar crime and government investigations. In 2013, the *National Law Journal* named him one of the 100 Most Influential Lawyers.

Bennett graduated from Georgetown University Law Center and received his LL.M. from Harvard Law School. He clerked for district court judge Howard F. Corcoran.

Blatt, Lisa

Lisa Blatt chairs Arnold & Porter's Appellate and Supreme Court practice. She is a veteran Supreme Court advocate with thirty-three oral arguments before the Court. Since Blatt joined Arnold & Porter in November 2009, the *National Law Journal* has called her a "visionary" in the law, and Chambers rates her as one of the nation's top appellate lawyers. *Washingtonian* magazine has also named her one of the "100 Most Powerful Women in Washington." In 2013, the *National Law Journal* named her one of the 100 Most Influential Lawyers.

Blatt graduated *summa cum laude* from the University of Texas School of Law.

Boies, David

David Boies is the founder of Boies, Schiller & Flexner. Considered one of the greatest trial lawyers of his generation, he served as lead counsel for Vice President Al Gore in the 2000 presidential election dispute and as Special Trial Counsel for the Department of Justice in its antitrust suit against Microsoft. In the 1990s, Boies was counsel to the FDIC in its litigation to recover losses for failed savings and loan associations. He also served as Chief Counsel and Staff Director of the U.S. Senate Antitrust Subcommittee in 1978 and of the U.S. Senate Judiciary Committee in 1979. More recently, Boies has teamed up with Ted Olson to challenge California's Proposition 8. He is one of fourteen lawyers profiled in Don Vinson's "America's Top Trial Lawyers: Who They Are and Why They Win." In 2001, he was named "Lawyer of the Year" by both the *National Law Journal* and *Time* magazine. In 2013, the *National Law Journal* named Boies one of the 100 Most Influential Lawyers.

Boies graduated *magna cum laude* from Yale Law School and received an LL.M. from New York University School of Law.

Chu, Morgan

Morgan Chu chairs the litigation group at Irell & Manella. He was lead trial counsel in *City of Hope v. Genentech*, which generated the largest jury award ever affirmed on appeal by California courts. In

2013, the *National Law Journal* named him one of the 100 Most Influential Lawyers. He was also named "The Outstanding Intellectual Property Lawyer in the United States" in the first Chambers Award for Excellence in 2006.

Chu graduated *magna cum laude* from Harvard Law School. He clerked for Ninth Circuit Judge Charles Merrill.

Clarke, Judy

Judy Clarke is a prominent San Diego–based criminal defense attorney. She has represented clients in some of the most high-profile death penalty cases in the country and is considered a "master strategist" in death penalty cases. Her clients have included the "Unabomber," Ted Kaczynski; Susan Smith, who drowned her two children; Atlanta Olympics bomber Eric Rudolph; and Tucson, Arizona, shooter Jared Loughner. All received life sentences rather than the death penalty. In April 2013, Clarke was appointed to join the defense team representing Boston Marathon bombing suspect Dzhokhar Tsarnaev.

Clarke has served as President of the National Association of Criminal Defense Lawyers. She has also served as a Visiting Professor of Practice at Washington & Lee University School of Law.

Clarke received her J.D. from the University of South Carolina.

Clement, Paul

Paul Clement is a partner at Bancroft and was previously a partner at King & Spalding. He served as solicitor general for George W. Bush from 2005 to 2008. Clement has argued sixty-nine cases before the Supreme Court, including *Florida v. HHS* ("Obamacare"), *Arizona v. United States*, *McConnell v. FEC*, *Tennessee v. Lane*, *Rumsfeld v. Padilla*, *United States v. Booker*, *MGM v. Grokster*, and *McDonald v. Chicago*. Chambers ranks him as one of the nation's top appellate lawyers. In 2013, the *National Law Journal* named him one of the 100 Most Influential Lawyers.

Clement graduated *magna cum laude* from Harvard Law School, where he was the Supreme Court editor of the *Harvard Law Review*. He clerked for D.C. Circuit Judge Laurence Silberman and for Justice Antonin Scalia.

Corboy, Phil

Phil Corboy was the co-founder of Corboy & Demetrio. He represented plaintiffs in personal injury and wrong ful death actions; his only trial loss in three decades was reversed on appeal. Corboy was named one of the top 100 Most Influential Lawyers by the *National Law Journal* every year since the survey started in 1985, and he has been listed in *The Best Lawyers in America* since 1987. He served as president of both the Chicago Bar Association and the Illinois Trial Lawyers Association. Corboy is one of fourteen lawyers profiled in Don Vinson's "America's Top Trial Lawyers: Who They Are and Why They Win." Corboy passed away in July 2012.

Corboy graduated from Loyola University Chicago School of Law.

Craig, Greg

Greg Craig is a partner at Skadden Arps. Before joining Skadden, Craig was a partner at Williams & Connolly and served as a Senior Advisor to Senator Ted Kennedy, as Director of Policy Planning for Secretary of State Madeleine Albright, as Special White House Counsel in President Bill Clinton's impeachment proceedings, and as White House Counsel under President Barack Obama. Craig has taught trial practice at Yale Law School and Harvard Law School, and he is currently Skadden's lead counsel to Goldman Sachs. In 2013, the *National Law Journal* named him one of the 100 Most Influential Lawyers.

Craig graduated from Yale Law School.

Cruz, Ted

Ted Cruz is the thirty-fourth U.S. Senator from Texas. Before that, he served as Solicitor General of Texas and is the youngest person and the first Hispanic to have served in that role.

Cruz has signed more than 80 U.S. Supreme Court briefs and has argued 43 oral arguments, including nine before the Supreme Court.

The *American Lawyer* has named him one of the 50 Best Litigators under 45 in America, and the *National Law Journal* calls him one of the 50 Most Influential Minority Lawyers in America.

Cruz graduated *magna cum laude* from Harvard Law School, where he was an editor of the *Harvard Law Review*. He clerked for Fourth Circuit Judge Michael Luttig and for Chief Justice William Rehnquist.

Dellinger, Walter

Walter Dellinger chairs the appellate practice at O'Melveny & Myers. He served as an Assistant Attorney General of the United States and as head of the Office of Legal Counsel. As Acting Solicitor General for President Bill Clinton, Dellinger argued nine cases before the Supreme Court. Chambers ranks him as one of the leading lawyers nationwide for appellate law. Dellinger "played a key role," according to Chambers, "in convincing the U.S. Supreme Court that the $2.5 billion in punitive damages awarded to the victims of the *Exxon Valdez* oil spill was excessive." In 2013, the *National Law Journal* named him one of the 100 Most Influential Lawyers.

Dellinger graduated from Yale Law School, where he was an editor of the law journal. He clerked for Justice Hugo L. Black.

Dershowitz, Alan

Alan Dershowitz became at age 25 the youngest professor of law in the history of Harvard Law School, where he continues to teach as the Felix Frankfurter Professor of Law. Dershowitz has represented many high-profile criminal defendants, including O. J. Simpson, Patricia Hearst, Leona Helmsley, Jim Bakker, Mike Tyson, and Michael Milkin. Dershowitz is the author of more than twenty books, including *Blasphemy: How the Religious Right Is Hijacking the Declaration of Independence*, *The Case for Israel*, and *Reversal of Fortune*, which was made into an Academy Award–winning film.

Dershowitz graduated from Yale Law School. He clerked for former D.C. Circuit Chief Judge David Bazelon and for Justice Arthur Goldberg.

Easterbrook, Frank

Frank Easterbrook is the Chief Judge of the Seventh Circuit and is considered one of the best writers on the federal bench. He previously served as both assistant to the solicitor general and deputy solicitor general. He also teaches at the University of Chicago Law School and is the co-author of *The Economic Structure of Corporate Law*.

Easterbrook graduated Order of the Coif from the University of Chicago Law School, where he was an editor of the law review. He clerked for First Circuit Judge Levin Campbell.

Englert, Roy

Roy Englert is a name partner at Robbins, Russell, Englert, Orseck, Untereiner & Sauber. He previously worked as a partner at Mayer Brown and in the Office of the Solicitor General. He has won nearly all of the twenty cases he has argued at the Supreme Court. Englert is also an adjunct professor at the Georgetown University Law Center. Chambers ranks him as one of the nation's top appellate lawyers.

Englert graduated from Harvard Law School, where he was executive editor of the *Harvard Law Review*. He was a court clerk for the D.C. Circuit.

Estrada, Miguel

Miguel Estrada co-chairs Gibson Dunn's appellate and constitutional law practice. He represented President George W. Bush in *Bush v. Gore* and has handled a broad range of matters before the Supreme Court. Chambers ranks Estrada as one of the nation's top appellate lawyers. He was also profiled in the 2013 edition of *The Best Lawyers in America*.

Estrada graduated *magna cum laude* from Harvard Law School and served as an editor of the *Harvard Law Review*. He clerked for Second Circuit Judge Amalya Lyle Kearse and for Justice Anthony Kennedy.

Fitzgerald, Patrick

Patrick Fitzgerald is a partner at Skadden Arps, where he focuses on internal investigations, government enforcement matters, and civil litigation. He was previously the U.S. Attorney in Chicago, where he was the lead prosecutor in the Valerie Plame controversy and worked on the prosecutions of former Illinois Governor George Ryan, *Chicago Sun-Times* owner Conrad Black, and former Illinois Governor Rod Blagojevich. Fitzgerald also served for more than a decade as an Assistant U.S. Attorney in the Southern District of New York, where he helped prosecute twenty-three defendants in *United States v. Bin Laden*. In 2013, the *National Law Journal* named him one of the 100 Most Influential Lawyers.

Fitzgerald graduated from Harvard Law School. He teaches at the University of Chicago Law School.

Frey, Andy

Andy Frey is a partner at Mayer Brown. Frey has argued sixty-four cases before the Supreme Court. Before joining Mayer Brown, Frey served as deputy solicitor general. Chambers ranks him as one of the nation's top appellate lawyers. Frey was named as the "New York

City Appellate Practice Lawyer of the Year" by Best Lawyers 2012. He was also named one of *Benchmark's* 2013 Appellate National and New York Litigation Stars.

Frey graduated from Columbia Law School, where he was an editor on the law review. He clerked for D.C. Circuit Judge George T. Washington.

Garre, Greg

Greg Garre is a partner at Latham & Watkins. He served as Solicitor General for President George W. Bush. Garre has also served as Principal Deputy Solicitor General, as Acting Solicitor General, and as Assistant to the Solicitor General. Garre has argued 38 cases before the Supreme Court and has filed more than 100 briefs in cases before the Court. He has won major victories in such cases as *Ashcroft v. Iqbal*. Chambers ranks him as one of the nation's top appellate lawyers.

Garre graduated from the George Washington University Law School, where he was editor-in-chief of the law review. He clerked for Third Circuit Judge Anthony J. Scirica and for Chief Justice William H. Rehnquist.

Ginsburg, Ruth Bader

Ruth Bader Ginsburg is an Associate Justice on the U.S. Supreme Court. Before joining the bench, Ginsburg taught at Columbia Law School, where she was the first woman to receive tenure. As an advocate, she was renowned as the chief litigator of the ACLU's women's rights project. She served on the D.C. Circuit for thirteen years, beginning in 1980, until she was nominated to the Supreme Court.

After starting law school at Harvard, Ginsburg completed her studies at Columbia Law School. Ginsburg was the first woman to serve on both the *Harvard Law Review* and the *Columbia Law Review*. She clerked for district court judge Edmund L. Palmieri.

Goldstein, Tom

Tom Goldstein is a name partner at Goldstein & Russell. He has argued more than twenty-eight cases before the Supreme Court. Goldstein is also the founder and publisher of SCOTUSblog, the only blog ever to receive the American Bar Association's Silver Gavel Award for fostering the public's understanding of the law and our legal system. In 2010, the *National Law Journal* named him one of the most influential lawyers of the past decade. He has twice been named one of the leading attorneys under the age of 40 by the *National Law Journal*, and *The American Lawyer* named him one of the top 45 attorneys under 45. Chambers ranks him as one of the nation's top appellate lawyers. In 2013, the *National Law Journal* named Goldstein one of the 100 Most Influential Lawyers.

Goldstein graduated *summa cum laude* from American University's Washington College of Law. He clerked for former D.C. Circuit Chief Judge Patricia M. Wald.

Gorelick, Jamie

Jamie Gorelick is a partner at WilmerHale. Gorelick was also one of the longest-serving deputy attorneys general of the United States, and she has also served as the General Counsel for the Defense Department, as a member of the 9/11 Commission, and as president of the D.C. Bar. She was also vice chairman of Fannie Mae from 1997 to 2003. Chambers ranks her as one of the nation's top governmental-relations lawyers.

Gorelick graduated *cum laude* from Harvard Law School.

Holder, Eric

Attorney General Eric Holder began his career in the Justice Department's public integrity section, where he worked on the Abscam prosecutions and later oversaw the successful prosecution of Congressman Dan Rostenkowski in the Congressional Post Office scandal. Holder was also the first African-American deputy attorney general and is the first African-American attorney general. At Covington & Burling, he represented the NFL during the prosecution of Michael Vick on dog-fighting charges, defended Chiquita Brands in civil suits over murders by Colombian rebels, and filed an amicus brief in *D.C. v. Heller*, urging the Court to uphold the District's handgun ban. In 2013, the *National Law Journal* named him one of the 100 Most Influential Lawyers.

Holder graduated from Columbia Law School.

Jamail, Joe

Joe Jamail, also known as the King of Torts, masterminded the largest jury verdict in history: $11.12 billion in *Pennzoil v. Texaco*. He has been lead counsel in more than 200 personal injury cases with verdicts exceeding $1 million. All told, Jamail has generated more than $12 billion in jury verdicts and over $13 billion in verdicts and settlements.

Jamail graduated from the University of Texas Law School.

Kagan, Elena

Justice Elena Kagan is the fourth woman to serve on the Supreme Court and was the first female Solicitor General of the United States. She served as Associate White House Counsel under President Bill Clinton. Her article "Presidential Administration" was honored as the top scholarly article by the ABA's Section on Administrative Law and Regulatory Practice. In 2003, she became the first female dean of Harvard Law School. Before teaching at Harvard Law School, Kagan was a professor at the University of Chicago Law School.

Kagan graduated *magna cum laude* from Harvard Law School, where she was supervisory editor of the *Harvard Law Review*. She clerked for D.C. Circuit Judge Abner Mikva and for Justice Thurgood Marshall.

Lamm, Carolyn

Carolyn Lamm served as president of the American Bar Association (2009–2010) and is a partner at White & Case. She has also served as president of the D.C. Bar. She was named one of the 50 Most Influential Women in America by the *National Law Journal* in 2007 and one of Washington's Top 30 Lawyers by *Washingtonian* magazine in 2009. Chambers ranks her as one of the nation's top international-arbitration attorneys. In 2013, the *National Law Journal* named Lamm one of the 100 Most Influential Lawyers.

Lamm graduated from the University of Miami School of Law.

Lessig, Larry

Larry Lessig is director of the Edmond J. Safra Foundation Center for Ethics and is a professor at Harvard Law School. He has also been a professor at the University of Chicago Law School and at Stanford Law School, where he founded the school's Center for Internet and Society. In 2013, the *National Law Journal* named Lessig one of the 100 Most Influential Lawyers. He has won many awards, including the Free Software Foundation's Freedom Award, and he was named one of *Scientific American*'s top 50 visionaries. He has been a columnist for *Wired*, *Red Herring*, and *Industry Standard*.

Lessig graduated from Yale Law School. He clerked for Seventh Circuit Judge Richard Posner and for Justice Antonin Scalia.

Mahoney, Maureen

Maureen Mahoney is the founder of Latham & Watkins's U.S. Supreme Court and Appellate practice. She has also served as deputy solicitor general. As one of the most in-demand Supreme Court advocates, Mahoney represented the University of Michigan in its successful defense of its admissions programs; she also successfully argued Arthur Andersen's challenge to the firm's criminal conviction and, more recently, won a major First Amendment case for Hastings Law School. In 2007, the *National Law Journal* named Mahoney the runner-up for national Lawyer of the Year. In 2010, the same publication named her as one of the most influential lawyers of the past decade.

Mahoney graduated Order of the Coif from the University of Chicago Law School, where she was a member of the law review. She clerked for Seventh Circuit Judge Robert Sprecher and for then-Associate Justice William H. Rehnquist.

Maynard, Deanne

Deanne Maynard heads Morrison & Foerster's Appellate and Supreme Court Practice Group. She is also a former Assistant to the Solicitor General.

Maynard has argued thirteen cases before the Supreme Court of the United States and has filed more than 100 Supreme Court briefs in such key business cases as *RadLAX Gateway Hotel, LLC v. Amalgamated Bank*, and *Ransom v. FIA Card Services*.

Maynard served in the Solicitor General's office from 2004 to 2009. Before then, she was a partner at Jenner & Block.

Maynard graduated *magna cum laude* in 1991 from Harvard Law School, where she was an editor of the *Harvard Law Review*. After law school, Maynard clerked for both Justice Stephen Breyer and for retired Justice Lewis Powell.

Miller, Harvey

Harvey Miller, a partner at Weil Gotshal, is considered the leading bankruptcy lawyer in the nation. Recent representations include General Motors, Lehman Brothers, Pacific Gas & Electric, and Texaco. In 2010, the *National Law Journal* named him one of the most influential lawyers of the past decade. Describing him as "the greatest bankruptcy lawyer of all time," Chambers ranks him in the Star Individuals category for bankruptcy.

Miller graduated from Columbia Law School.

Millett, Patricia

Pattie Millett co-heads Akin Gump's Supreme Court practice, and she has had a total of thirty-one cases before the Supreme Court. As an Assistant to the Solicitor General, Millett argued twenty-five cases before the U.S. Supreme Court and briefed more than fifty cases. Before joining the Solicitor General's Office, Millett worked for four years on the Appellate Staff of the Justice Department's Civil Division, where she briefed and argued more than twenty cases before federal courts of appeals and state appellate courts. Chambers ranks her as one of the nation's top appellate lawyers. In 2013, the *National Law Journal* named Millett one of the 100 Most Influential Lawyers.

In 2013, President Obama nominated Millett to serve on the D.C. Circuit.

Millett graduated *magna cum laude* from Harvard Law School. She clerked for Ninth Circuit Judge Thomas Tang.

Nussbaum, Bernie

Bernie Nussbaum is a partner at Wachtell, Lipton, Rosen & Katz, where he focuses on corporate and securities litigation. In 1994, he served as Counsel to the President under President Bill Clinton. In 1974, he was a senior member of the staff of the House Judiciary Committee, which conducted the 1974 Watergate Impeachment Inquiry. Chambers ranks Nussbaum as a Senior Statesman in the nationwide trial lawyer category. Nussbaum led his firm's successful pro bono fight against the State of New York on behalf of Chief Judge Judith Kaye, who claimed that the state's failure to raise judicial salaries violated the state constitution.

Nussbaum graduated from Harvard Law School, where he was notes editor of the *Harvard Law Review*.

Obama, Barack

Barack Obama is the forty-fourth president of the United States. Before his election, Obama served as U.S. Senator for Illinois and as an Illinois state legislator. Earlier in his career, Obama turned down a prestigious judicial clerkship, practicing instead at the prominent civil rights firm Davis, Miner, Barnhill & Galland in Chicago, where he represented plaintiffs in housing and employment discrimination cases and participated in voting-rights cases and legislation. Obama has also taught constitutional law at the University of Chicago Law School.

Obama graduated from Harvard Law School, where he was the first African-American editor of the *Harvard Law Review*.

Olson, Ted

Ted Olson is a partner at Gibson, Dunn & Crutcher. He has argued fifty-nine cases before the Supreme Court, including *Bush v. Gore*. Olson served as Solicitor General for George H. W. Bush and as private counsel to Presidents Ronald Reagan and George W. Bush. While serving in the Reagan administration, Olson defended President Reagan during the Iran-Contra affair. From 1981 to 1984, he was Assistant Attorney General in charge of the Office of Legal Counsel in the Justice Department. Along with David Boies, Olson is currently challenging the constitutionality of California Proposition 8's ban on gay marriage. In 2010, *Time* magazine named Olson as one of the 100 most influential people in the world. In 2013, the *National Law Journal* named him one of the 100 Most Influential Lawyers.

Olson graduated Order of the Coif from the Boalt Hall School of Law, where he was a member of the law review.

Payton, John

John Payton was president and director-counsel of the NAACP Legal Defense Fund. Before joining the NAACP, Payton was a partner at WilmerHale, where he helped defend the University of Michigan's admissions practices. In 2010, the *National Law Journal* named Payton one of the most influential lawyers of the past decade. He has also served as Corporation Counsel for the District of Columbia.

Payton graduated from Harvard Law School. He clerked for district court judge Cecil Poole. Payton passed away in March 2012.

Phillips, Carter

Carter Phillips is a leading Supreme Court advocate and the managing partner of Sidley Austin's D.C. office. As Assistant to the Solicitor General, he argued nine cases before the Supreme Court. Since joining Sidley Austin, Phillips has argued fifty-seven other cases before the Supreme Court, including *Fox v. FCC*. Phillips was also named one of the 2012 Lawyers of the Year in the area of Litigation–Regulatory Enforcement by *Best Lawyers*. He was among *Super Lawyers* magazine's Top 100 lawyers in Washington in 2011 based on a vote of peers, and also earned a spot on *Law360*'s list of Appellate MVPs that year. In 2013, the *National Law Journal* named him one of the 100 Most Influential Lawyers. Chambers ranks him as a Star Individual for nationwide appellate law. "Peers envy his rapport with justices," notes Chambers.

Phillips graduated *magna cum laude* from Northwestern University School of Law. He clerked for Seventh Circuit Judge Robert Sprecher and for Chief Justice Warren E. Burger.

Quinn, John

John Quinn is a partner at Quinn Emanuel. Described by the *Los Angeles Daily Journal* as a "legal titan," and by Chambers as a "known litigation genius," he is one of the most prominent business trial lawyers in the country. Chambers ranks him as one of the leading lawyers for general commercial and trial litigation. In addition to representing the former director of Peregrine Systems, Quinn has represented international hedge funds and other global giants, including IBM, Google, and Mattel. In 2013, the *National Law Journal* named Quinn one of the 100 Most Influential Lawyers.

Quinn graduated *cum laude* from Harvard Law School, where he was a member of the *Harvard Law Review*.

Robbins, Larry

Larry Robbins is a trial and appellate litigator at Robbins, Russell, Englert, Orseck Untereiner & Sauber. He has argued eighteen cases in the U.S. Supreme Court, and has argued some forty others in the federal circuit courts of appeals.

He has served as an Assistant to the Solicitor General, an Associate Independent Counsel, and a partner at Mayer Brown.

Robbins graduated *magna cum laude* from Harvard Law School. He clerked for Third Circuit Judge John Gibbons.

Roberts, John

John G. Roberts Jr. has been Chief Justice of the United States since 2005. He previously served as Special Assistant to the Attorney General in the Justice Department, Associate Counsel to President Ronald Reagan, and Principal Deputy Solicitor General. He was appointed to the D.C. Circuit in 2003. Before that, he headed the appellate practice at Hogan & Hartson, now known as Hogan Lovells. During that time, he argued thirty-nine cases before the Supreme Court, prevailing in twenty-five of them.

Roberts graduated *magna cum laude* from Harvard Law School, where he was managing editor of the *Harvard Law Review*. He clerked for Second Circuit Judge Henry J. Friendly and for then-Associate Justice William H. Rehnquist.

Rosenkranz, E. Joshua

Joshua Rosenkranz heads Orrick's Supreme Court and Appellate Litigation practice. He has argued eight cases before the Supreme Court and has argued more than 170 times in the appellate courts.

The American Lawyer named him "Litigator of the Year" in its January 2012 edition.

Rosenkranz graduated *magna cum laude* from Georgetown University Law Center, where he was Notes and Comments Editor of the Georgetown Law Journal. He clerked for then-Judge Antonin Scalia on the D.C. Circuit and for Justice William J. Brennan Jr.

Seitz, Virginia

Virginia Seitz is the Assistant Attorney General in charge of the Office of Legal Counsel. Prior to joining the Department of Justice, Seitz was a partner at Sidley Austin. Seitz has filed many briefs in the U.S. Supreme Court, including an amicus brief on behalf of retired military officers in *Grutter v. Bollinger* that was cited by the Court in oral argument and in its decision. Chambers ranks her as one of the nation's top appellate lawyers.

A Rhodes Scholar, Seitz graduated first in her class from the University of Buffalo Law School. She clerked for D.C. Circuit Judge Harry T. Edwards and for Justice William J. Brennan Jr.

Seligman, Nicole

Nicole Seligman is the president of Sony Corporation of America and executive vice president and general counsel of Sony Corporation. Before joining Sony, Seligman was a partner at Williams & Connolly. She represented Lieutenant Colonel Oliver North during the Iran-Contra hearings. She also represented President Bill Clinton when he testified before the grand jury in the

Monica Lewinsky case and represented him before the Senate at his impeachment trial.

Seligman graduated *magna cum laude* from Harvard Law School. She clerked for D.C. Circuit Judge Harry T. Edwards and for Justice Thurgood Marshall.

Shapiro, Stephen M.

Stephen Shapiro is the senior member of the U.S. Supreme Court and Appellate Litigation practice group at Mayer Brown, the largest such practice in the country. Shapiro has briefed more than 200 cases and argued 30 cases before the U.S. Supreme Court. Chambers ranks him as one of the nation's top appellate lawyers. Before joining Mayer Brown, Shapiro served as Deputy Solicitor General and as Assistant to the Solicitor General.

Shapiro graduated from Yale Law School, where he was a member of the *Yale Law Journal*. After graduation, he clerked for Ninth Circuit Judge Charles Merrill.

Shapiro, Steven R.

Steven Shapiro is the legal director of the ACLU. He has been counsel or co-counsel on more than 200 briefs submitted to the U.S. Supreme Court. Shapiro is also an adjunct professor of constitutional law at Columbia Law School and a frequent speaker and writer on civil liberties. After joining the New York Civil Liberties Union in 1976, he served for twenty years as a member of the Board of Directors of Human Rights. He is now a member of the Policy Committee of Human Rights Watch and a member of the Advisory Committees of the U.S. Program and Asia Program of Human Rights Watch.

Shapiro graduated from Harvard Law School. He clerked for Second Circuit Judge J. Edward Lumbard.

Smith, Paul

Paul Smith is a partner in the Litigation Department of Jenner & Block. Smith has argued thirteen cases before the Supreme Court, including *Crawford v. Marion County Election Board, Lawrence v. Texas, Mathias v. WorldCom, and Schwarzenegger v. Entertainment Media Association.* In 2010, the *National Law Journal* named him one of the most influential lawyers of the past decade. Chambers ranks him as a leading attorney nationwide in First Amendment litigation and in nationwide appellate law. *Best Lawyers* named him the Washington DC First Amendment Lawyer of the Year for 2012.

Smith graduated from Yale Law School, where he was editor-in-chief of the *Yale Law Journal*. He clerked for Second Circuit Judge James L. Oakes and for Justice Lewis F. Powell Jr.

Srinivasan, Sri

D.C. Circuit Judge Sri Srinivasan was formerly the Principal Deputy Solicitor General of the United States.

Before that, he has also chaired O'Melveny & Myers's Appellate Practice Group and has served as an Assistant to the Solicitor General. He has argued before the Supreme Court twenty times.

Srinivasan graduated from Stanford Law School, where he was elected to Order of the Coif and served as an editor of the *Stanford Law Review*. He clerked for Fourth Circuit Judge J. Harvie Wilkinson and for Justice Sandra Day O'Connor.

Starr, Ken

Ken Starr is president of Baylor University and is also of counsel at Kirkland & Ellis. He has served as Counselor to U.S. Attorney General William French Smith, as Judge for the U.S. Court of Appeals for the D.C. Circuit, as Solicitor General of the United States, and as Independent Counsel in the Whitewater matter. As solicitor general, he argued twenty-five cases before the Supreme Court. Chambers ranks him as a Senior Statesman in nationwide appellate law.

Starr graduated from Duke Law School. He clerked for Fifth Circuit Judge David W. Dyer and for Chief Justice Warren E. Burger.

Sullivan, Brendan

Brendan Sullivan is a partner at Williams & Connolly. Notable representations include Lieutenant Colonel Oliver North, former HUD Secretary Henry Cisneros, New York Stock Exchange CEO Dick Grasso, and the late Alaska Senator Ted Stevens. In 2013, the *National Law Journal* named him one of the 100 Most Influential Lawyers. "A long list of trial successes in many different contexts," according to Chambers, "has ensured his legendary status."

Sullivan graduated from the Georgetown University Law Center.

Sullivan, Kathleen

Kathleen Sullivan has recently become a name partner at litigation powerhouse Quinn Emanuel Urquhart & Sullivan, making the firm the first Am Law 100 firm to have a female name partner. She won a landmark victory in the U.S. Supreme Court when it ruled in 2005 that states may not bar wineries from shipping to consumers out of state. Sullivan has taught at Harvard Law School and has served as Dean of Stanford Law School. Chambers ranks her as one of the nation's top appellate lawyers. Widely recognized as one of the nation's preeminent appellate litigators, in 2013, the *National Law Journal* named Sullivan one of the 100 Most Influential Lawyers. A *New York Times* editorial called her "a formidable advocate" and a *National Law Journal* article called her a Supreme Court "superstar." *Chambers USA* describes her as a "truly terrific" appellate lawyer who wins clients' approval as a "tremendously agile and a fabulous advocate."

Sullivan graduated from Harvard Law School, where she won the Ames Moot Court Competition. She clerked for Second Circuit Judge James L. Oakes.

Susman, Stephen

Stephen Susman is a name partner at Susman Godfrey. A pioneer in global warming litigation, Susman successfully represented a coalition of thirty-seven Texas cities opposing coal-fired electric generating plants. After this victory, the *National Law Journal* awarded Susman's firm the 2008 Pro Bono Award. His firm was also featured in Robert Redford's Sundance Preserve documentary, *Fighting Goliath: Texas Coal Wars*. Susman was also one of fourteen lawyers profiled in Don Vinson's "America's Top Trial Lawyers: Who They Are and Why They Win." In 2006, he was featured in the *National Law Journal* as one of the nation's top ten litigators. Chambers ranks him as a leading lawyer in nationwide trial litigation.

Susman graduated first in his class from the University of Texas Law School and was the editor-in-chief of the law review. He clerked for Fifth Circuit Judge John R. Brown and for Justice Hugo Black.

Taranto, Richard

Federal Circuit Judge Richard Taranto was a well-known Supreme Court advocate before his nomination and a partner at Farr & Taranto. He worked in the Solicitor General's Office and has taught at Georgetown and Harvard law schools. Chambers has ranked him as one of the nation's top appellate lawyers.

Taranto graduated from Yale Law School in 1981. He clerked for Second Circuit Judge Abraham D. Sofaer, for D.C. Circuit Judge Robert H. Bork, and for Justice Sandra Day O'Connor.

Tribe, Larry

Larry Tribe is a professor of constitutional law at Harvard Law School and is one of the nation's leading Supreme Court advocates. He represented Vice President Al Gore before the Supreme Court during the disputed 2000 presidential election. Tribe has written 115 books and articles, including his treatise *American Constitutional Law*, cited more often than any other legal book since 1950.

Tribe graduated *magna cum laude* from Harvard Law School. He clerked for Matthew Tobriner of the California Supreme Court and for Justice Potter Stewart.

Verrilli, Donald B.

Donald B. Verrilli Jr. is the forty-sixth Solicitor General of the United States.

He previously served as Deputy Counsel to President Obama and as an Associate Deputy Attorney General in the U.S. Department of Justice. Before that, he was a partner for many years at Jenner & Block, where he co-chaired the firm's Supreme Court practice. His matters there ranged from *MGM Studios, Inc. v. Grokster* to *Wiggins v. Smith*.

Verrilli graduated from Yale University and from Columbia Law School, where he served as editor-in-chief of the Columbia Law Review. He clerked for D.C. Circuit Judge J. Skelly Wright and for Justice William J. Brennan Jr.

Wachtell, Herbert

Herbert Wachtell is a founding partner of Wachtell, Lipton, Rosen & Katz. He has recently represented the National Football League and has represented Silverstein Properties in litigation arising from the 2001 World Trade Center attacks. In 2006, Wachtell received the Chambers Lifetime Achievement Award in Litigation. Chambers rates him a Senior Statesman in the nationwide trial lawyer category.

Wachtell graduated Order of the Coif from New York University Law School, where he was an editor of the law review and a Root-Tilden scholar. He also obtained an LL.M. from Harvard Law School.

Waxman, Seth

Seth Waxman chairs WilmerHale's Appellate and Supreme Court Litigation Practice Group. He served as solicitor general and has won landmark rulings in several major Supreme Court cases, including *Boumediene v. Bush*, which affirmed the right of foreign citizens held at Guantanamo Bay to challenge their detention in U.S. civilian courts; *Roper v. Simmons*, which declared the death penalty unconstitutional for juvenile offenders; and *McConnell v. FEC*, which affirmed the constitutionality of the Bipartisan Campaign Reform Act. Chambers ranks him in the Star Individuals category for nationwide appellate law.

Waxman graduated from Yale Law School. He clerked for district court judge Gerhard A. Gesell.

Wells, Ted

Ted Wells Jr. co-chairs the Litigation Department at Paul Weiss. In 2010, the *National Law Journal* named Wells one of "The Decade's Most Influential Lawyers"; the publication has repeatedly selected him as one of the 100 Most Influential Lawyers in America and as one of America's top white-collar criminal defense lawyers. Wells also has been recognized as one of the outstanding jury trial lawyers in the United States by many other publications, including *Chambers USA 2006*, which noted that he is recognized by many as "the greatest trial lawyer of our generation." Wells has represented

Citigroup, Michael Espy, Scooter Libby, and former Secretary of Labor Raymond Donovan.

Wells graduated from Harvard Law School. He clerked for Third Circuit Judge John J. Gibbons.

White, Mary Jo

Mary Jo White is the chair of the Securities & Exchange Commission.

Before that, she chaired the Litigation Department at Debevoise & Plimpton. As the first female U.S. Attorney for the Southern District of New York, White also supervised more than 200 Assistant U.S. Attorneys in successfully prosecuting many high-profile national and international cases. She has also served as director of the NASDAQ stock exchange and is a member of the Council on Foreign Relations. Chambers ranks her in the Star Individual category for white-collar crime and governmental investigation and as a leading attorney in nationwide securities regulation. In 2013, the *National Law Journal* named her one of the 100 Most Influential Lawyers.

White graduated from Columbia Law School, where she was a member of the law review.

Wiley, Richard

Richard Wiley heads Wiley Rein's eighty-attorney Communications Practice, the largest in the nation. He is also a past chair of the FCC. Chambers rates him as the nation's top telecommunications lawyer. In 2013, the *National Law Journal* named him one of the 100 Most Influential Lawyers.

Wiley graduated from Northwestern Law School and received an LL.M. from Georgetown University Law Center.

Annotated Models

Before-and-after section from *Jones v. Clinton*

I've included below a revised section from Paula Jones's summary judgment opposition in *Jones v. Clinton*.

Original	Revision
2. The Essential Elements of Plaintiff's Claim Under Section 1983 Are Not the Same as Those of a Claim Under Title VII and Do Not Include Proof of Tangible Job Detriment	**2. As a Section 1983 Plaintiff, Jones Need Not Prove Tangible Job Detriment[1]**
Even as to the "sexual harassment" form of gender-based discrimination, "tangible job detriment" is *not* an essential element of proof in an action under Section 1983 for denial of equal protection rights. Mr. Clinton's argument incorrectly assumes that every essential element of a sexual-harassment claim under Title VII is also an essential element of a sexual-harassment claim under Section 1983. This argument reflects a basic misunderstanding both of equal protection law (as explained in this section) and of Title VII (as explained in the following section).	Because Jones's Section 1983 equal-protection action requires her to prove intentional discrimination but not "tangible job detriment," the President cannot obtain summary judgment by claiming that he did not adversely affect her job status under Title VII.[2] In arguing otherwise, the President confuses a constitutional claim for a statutory one.[3]

1. *Russian Doll.*

2. *With You in Spirit.*

3. *Flashpoint* in the argument.

Original	Revision
In *Bohen v. City of East Chicago*, 799 F.2d 1180 (7th Cir. 1986), the court contrasted a claim of sexual harassment under the equal protection clause with a claim of sexual harassment under Title VII. In an equal protection case, the court said, "[t]he ultimate inquiry is whether sexual harassment constitutes intentional discrimination." 799 F.2d at 1187. "This differs from the inquiry under Title VII as to whether or not the sexual harassment *altered the conditions of the victim's employment*. That standard comes from the regulations promulgated under Title VII." *Id.* (emphasis supplied). Thus, a finding that the harassment altered the conditions of the victim's employment is *not* an essential element of an action under Section 1983 for violation of the right to equal protection. *See also Andrews v. City of Philadelphia*, 895 F.2d 1469, 1482, 1483 & n.4 (3d Cir. 1990) ("Section 1983 and Title VII claims are complex actions with different elements").	The federal courts have long distinguished Section 1983 claims such as Jones's from Title VII claims.[4] Under Section 1983, "[t]he ultimate inquiry is whether sexual harassment constitutes intentional discrimination." Under Title VII, by contrast, the inquiry is "whether or not sexual harassment altered the conditions of the victim's employment."[5] *Bohen v. City of East Chicago*, 799 F.2d 1180, 1187 (7th Cir. 1986); *see also Andrews v. City of Philadelphia*, 895 F.2d 1469, 1482, 1483 & n.4 (3d Cir. 1990) ("Section 1983 and Title VII claims are complex actions with different elements.").[6]

4. *Long in the Tooth.*

5. *Peas in a Pod; Mince Their Words.*

6. *Speak for Yourself.*

Original	Revision
Correct application of these principles is illustrated in *Ascolese v. Southeastern Pennsylvania Transportation Authority*, 925 F. Supp. 351 (E.D. Pa. 1996). *Ascolese* involved a claim by a female police officer who alleged three different forms of gender-based discrimination, one of which was sexual harassment. The harassment allegedly occurred during a medical examination by a male physician employed by the same agency. 925F. Supp. at 354, 358–59. The physician, who was named as a defendant, moved for summary judgment on the ground that the single medical examination could not have constituted a "hostile work environment" as defined by Title VII jurisprudence. The court rejected the defendant's argument specifically holding that the standard for actionable sexual harassment under Section 1983 is different from the standard for sexual harassment under Title VII:	Because of this distinction,[7] when public officials such as the President have cited the Title VII standard when seeking summary judgment in Section 1983 sexual-harassment cases, courts have denied the motion.[8] *See*, e.g., *Ascolese v. Southeastern Pennsylvania Transportation Authority*, 925 F. Supp. 351 (E.D. Pa. 1996) (denying summary judgment for state physician in Section 1983 case who claimed that conduct did not constitute "hostile work environment" under Title VII and finding "no need to consider the alleged discrimination in the context of [plaintiff's] entire work experience, as there would be under Title VII . . .; the relevant context is only that of the examination itself.").[9] *Id.* at 359–60 (citations omitted).
The present claim is brought under section 1983, and is therefore subject to a different analysis from the Title VII claim at issue in *Bedford [v. Southeastern Penn.*	

7. *Bridge the Gap.*

8. *Long in the Tooth.*

9. *Hybrid Model.*

Original	Revision
Transp. Auth.], 867 F. Supp. 288 (E.D. Pa. 1994). The focus of the analysis under section 1983 is on "whether the sexual harassment constitutes intentional discrimination," not on whether the "sexual harassment altered the conditions of the victim's employment," the standard under Title VII. In order to demonstrate that she has been subjected to sex discrimination under section 1983, Ascolese must show that she was treated differently than a similarly situated person of the opposite sex would have been. Moreover, the sex discrimination at issue in this case is discrimination by a public official in the course of performing his duties (in this case, a medical examination), rather than discrimination at Ascolese's workplace generally. Thus, there is no need to consider the alleged discrimination in the context of Ascolese's entire work experience, as there would be under Title VII...; the relevant context is only that of the examination itself.	

Original	Revision
925F. Supp. at 359–60 (citations omitted). Thus, the plaintiff in *Ascolese* was not required to prove that the acts of harassment had "altered the conditions of [her] employment" 925 F. Supp. at 359, but only that her one encounter with the defendant physician was "hostile" or "abusive." *Id.* at 360.	
The same principles apply here. Paula Jones is not required to prove that Governor Clinton altered the conditions of her employment (although she can and will do so), but only that, in the context of Plaintiff's public employment, Mr. Clinton, acting under color of state law, intentionally discriminated against Plaintiff because of her gender. Viewing the evidence in the light most favorable to Mrs. Jones (as is the Court's duty at this juncture), a jury might reasonably find—and indeed would likely find—that Governor Clinton's conduct was intentional, that it was based on Plaintiff's gender, and that it was both "hostile" and "abusive."	Here,[10] then, the "relevant context"[11] is what the President did to Jones, not, as the President suggests, Jones's "entire work experience." *See id.* To prevail, Jones need not prove[12] that the President's acts of harassment have "altered the conditions of [her] employment," but only that her encounter with the President was "hostile" or "abusive." *Id.* Put another way,[13] to defeat summary judgment, Jones need only proffer evidence that the President intentionally discriminated against her because of her gender.

10. *What a Breeze:* "here" rather than "in the instant case" or "in the present case."

11. *Bridge the Gap; Mince Their Words.*

12. *What a Breeze:* "need not prove" rather than "is not obligated to prove."

13. *Take Me by the Hand.*

Original	Revision
As supposed authority for the proposition that Plaintiff absolutely cannot recover under Section 1983 unless she proves every element of "sexual harassment" within the meaning of Title VII, Mr. Clinton's counsel cites two Seventh Circuit cases (and no Eighth Circuit cases), *Trautvetter v. Quick* and *King v. Board of Regents of the University of Wisconsin System*. See MEMORANDUM at 4. In fact, these cases make no such definitive pronouncement; to the contrary, they refute Mr. Clinton's suggestion that the essential elements of sexual harassment in a suit under Section 1983 are well defined to be identical to those in a suit under Title VII. In *King*, the court wrote: "We have held that sexual harassment is a violation of equal protection, *Bohen*, 799 F.2d at 1185, although the precise parameters of this cause of action have not been well defined." And in *Trautvetter* the court wrote:	Even if some cases suggest that Title VII sexual-harassment claims and Section 1983 sexual-harassment actions "generally follow the same contours," that hardly means that the two actions share the same elements.[14] *Cf.* Memorandum at 4, *citing Trautvetter v. Quick*, 916 F.2d 1140 (7th Cir. 1990); *King v. Board of Regents of the University of Wisconsin System*, 893 F.2d 533 (7th Cir. 1990). Both *Trautvetter* and *King* distinguish, in fact,[15] between the two types of claims. *See King*, 893 F.2d at 536 (noting that unlike Title VII sexual-harassment actions, "the precise parameters of [Section 1983 sexual-harassment actions] have not been well defined"); *accord Trautvetter*, 916 F.2d at 1149. Both cases even cite *Bohen* with approval in this regard, confirming that courts distinguish Title VII actions from Section 1983 actions.

14. *Rebound.*

15. *Take Me by the Hand.*

Original	Revision
"The parameters of a cause of action alleging sexual harassment as a violation of the equal protection clause have not been precisely defined. We have noted, however, that such a claim generally follows the contours of a Title VII allegation of sexual harassment." 916 F.2d at 1149 (citing *King*). Saying that sexual harassment under Section 1983 "generally follows the contours of" sexual harassment under Title VII is a far cry from saying that the required elements of proof are identical. Thus both cases explicitly note that the requirements for a sexual-harassment action under Section 1983 are *not* well defined. More importantly, both cases cite with approval *Bohen v. City of East Chicago*, wherein the same circuit court of appeals held that the elements of a sexual-harassment suit under Section 1983 are not the same as those in a suit under Title VII. 799 F.2d at 1187.	
Based as it is on a misreading of the two Seventh Circuit cases, the second premise of Mr. Clinton's argument is false. Significantly, Mr. Clinton has directed the Court to no Eighth Circuit or	For all these reasons, the President cannot seek summary judgment here by forcing Jones's Section 1983 claim into Title VII. What the President did to Jones is enough to sustain her claim.[16]

16. *What a Breeze.*

Original	Revision
Supreme Court cases holding that every element of a quid pro quo harassment claim under Title VII must be proven to maintain an action under Section 1983 for gender-based discrimination in the form of quid pro quo sexual harassment. More specifically, there is no Eighth Circuit or Supreme Court authority for the proposition that "tangible job detriment" is an essential element of a Section 1983 action based on quid pro quo sexual harassment.	

Alaska v. EPA

Excerpts from John Roberts's Supreme Court brief for the State of Alaska (most footnotes, definitions, and citations omitted for reading ease).

Introduction

Described as an "experiment in federalism,"[17] *Michigan v. EPA*, 268 F.3d 1075, 1078 (D.C. Cir. 2001), the Clean Air Act ("CAA") assigns to the States an important—indeed *primary*—[18] role in air pollution prevention and control. One of the States' principal responsibilities under the Act is to prevent the degradation of air quality in those areas where national clean air standards have been attained. To

17. *Leading Parts.*

18. *A Dash of Style.*

this end,[19] the CAA prohibits the construction or modification of a "major emitting facility" in any attainment area unless the facility is subject to the "best available control technology," or "BACT." BACT is defined in the CAA as "an emission limitation based on the maximum degree of reduction of each [regulated] pollutant...which *the permitting authority, on a case-by-case basis*, taking into account energy, environmental, and economic impacts and other costs, determines is achievable for such facility...." The "permitting authority" in this case—and in most cases arising under this provision—is the State.

The CAA by its terms thus[20] gives the States the authority to determine BACT for a particular source, and allows the States broad discretion in making that determination. This is confirmed by the Act's legislative history[21]: "The decision regarding the actual implementation of best available technology is a key one, and the committee places this responsibility *with the State*, to be determined in a case-by-case judgment. It is recognized that the phrase has *broad flexibility* in how it should and can be interpreted, depending on site."[22]

In this case, the State of Alaska issued a permit for the construction of a new electric generator at the Red Dog Mine, located in Northwest Alaska some 100 miles north of the Arctic Circle. In accordance with the CAA and the State's own regulations, the State determined that a particular technology—"Low NOx"—was BACT to control nitrogen oxide emissions from the new generator. In making that determination, the State spent eighteen months engaged in the permitting process—with required public comment and review—and

---

19. *Bridge the Gap* within a paragraph. Each sentence in this paragraph begins with something from the sentence before: States–States, prevent–prohibit, BACT–BACT, permitting authority–permitting authority.

20. *Take Me by the Hand.* "Thus" is moved inside the sentence, creating a smoother effect.

21. *Lead 'Em On.*

22. *The Short List*: the main reasons that (1) the statute and (2) the legislative history favor the States' position.

prepared extensive technical analyses specifically considering alternative technologies and their associated "energy, environmental, and economic impacts and other costs." The State considered but rejected an alternative technology—Selective Catalytic Reduction ("SCR")—primarily due to cost considerations. Nevertheless, the State's decision resulted in emissions levels that complied with all standards promulgated by the EPA. Moreover, because the operator of the mine had agreed to install Low NOx on other generators not subject to BACT review, the State's decision was likely to result in *lower* overall NOx emissions than if the more costly SCR had been selected as BACT for the new generator.[23]

The EPA, however, "disagree[d]" with the State's decision to select Low NOx, rather than SCR, as BACT for the new generator. Rather than challenge the State's decision through the available state review process, the EPA issued a series of orders prohibiting the construction of the generator. The EPA, however, had no authority to do so.[24] Because BACT is "key" to the States' ability to "manage their allowed internal growth" under the CAA, *Alabama Power Co. v. Costle*, 636 F.2d 323, 364 (D.C. Cir. 1980), Congress decided to make the determination of BACT "strictly a State and local decision."[25] Nothing in the Act gives the EPA the authority to override a State's discretionary judgment as to what constitutes BACT for a particular source.

The EPA has the authority[26] to issue orders to enforce any "requirement" of the Act, but the only pertinent "requirement" here is that the state-issued permit contain a BACT limitation, set by "the permitting authority, on a case-by-case basis, taking into account energy, environmental, and economic impacts and other costs." There is no dispute that the permit at issue here contains such a limitation, and

23. *Brass Tacks*: who, what, when, where, why, how.

24. *Size Matters*.

25. *Mince Their Words*.

26. *Bridge the Gap* through "authority."

no dispute that the limitation was determined by the State after considering the applicable factors. The EPA disagrees with the State's determination in this particular instance, and would set a different BACT limitation, but that does not mean that the State in any sense[27] violated a "requirement" of the Act in issuing the permit with the BACT limitation that it—"the permitting authority"—had selected.[28] The EPA's contrary view plainly usurps authority that the CAA vests with the States, upsetting the balance of power that Congress carefully sought to establish under the Act.[29] Because the Ninth Circuit below erred in sanctioning that result, the judgment below should be reversed.

Argument

I. The EPA Has No Authority Under The CAA To Invalidate A State BACT Determination That Is Based On Consideration Of The Statutory Factors.

We begin with first principles.[30] The EPA, a federal administrative agency, is "a creature of statute." As such, the EPA "literally has *no* power to act...unless and until Congress confers power upon it." Accordingly, "[i]f EPA lacks authority [to take particular action] under the Clean Air Act, then its action is plainly contrary to law and cannot stand."

The Ninth Circuit held that the CAA gives the EPA the "ultimate authority" to decide what constitutes BACT for a particular source. In its view, that conclusion is "compel[led]" by the plain language and legislative history of the Act. As we explain below, however,[31]

---

27. *What a Breeze*: note the one-syllable words.

28. *Flashpoint*: draw a line in the sand between a federal agency's "disagreeing" with a state agency and the state agency's violating statutory requirement.

29. *Why Should I Care?*

30. *Size Matters.*

31. *Take Me by the Hand.*

the plain language and legislative history of the CAA make clear that BACT is a determination to be made by the States, and the EPA has absolutely *no* authority to second-guess a State's BACT determination that—like Alaska's here—is based on consideration of the statutory factors. Because the EPA thus had no authority to invalidate Alaska's permit decision in this case, its action is "plainly contrary to law," and the Ninth Circuit decision below "cannot stand."[32] *Michigan v. EPA*, 268 F.3d at 1081.[33]

A. The Plain Language Of The CAA Makes Clear That BACT Is A Determination To Be Made By The States On A "Case-By-Case Basis."[34]

1. The CAA provides that no major emitting facility may be constructed or modified in a clean air area unless "the proposed facility is subject to [BACT] for each pollutant subject to regulation under [the Act] emitted from, or which results from, such facility." BACT is defined in the Act as "an emission limitation based on the maximum degree of reduction of each pollutant subject to regulation . . . , *which the permitting authority, on a case-by-case basis*, taking into account energy, environmental, and economic impacts and other costs, determines is achievable for such facility."

By its terms, the CAA squarely places the responsibility for determining BACT with "the permitting authority"—i.e., the State. As the plain language of the statute makes clear, a BACT determination is a discretionary judgment, involving the "case-by-case" weighing of several factors—"energy, environmental, and economic impacts and other costs." A BACT determination in any given case will thus[35] depend on how the State—"the permitting authority"—chooses to

32. *Mince Their Words.*

33. *Sneak Preview.*

34. *Russian Doll.*

35. *Take Me by the Hand.*

weigh the pertinent factors. Accordingly, the Act not only gives the States the authority to determine BACT for a particular source, but gives them broad discretion to do so.

The Ninth Circuit nevertheless held in this case that the EPA had the "ultimate authority" to invalidate Alaska's BACT determination. The court reasoned as follows: (1) Sections 113(a)(5) and 167 of the CAA give the EPA the authority to enforce any "requirement" of the Act; (2) "subjecting a facility to BACT" is a "requirement" of the Act; (3) the EPA found that the State had not complied with "the BACT requirement"; and (4) therefore, the EPA's invalidation of Alaska's BACT determination was authorized "by the plain language" of Sections 113(a)(5) and 167.[36]

The court's reasoning,[37] however, is fundamentally flawed. The only "BACT requirement" pertinent here[38] is that a state-issued PSD permit contain a BACT limitation, determined by the State "on a case-by-case basis, taking into account energy, environmental, and economic impacts and other costs." There is no dispute that the permit issued by Alaska to Cominco contains such a limitation or that the limitation was set by the State after considering the applicable factors. Thus, Alaska fully complied with "the BACT requirement," and the EPA had no authority under Section 113(a)(5) or Section 167 to override its decision. The EPA "disagrees" with Alaska's decision and regards SCR as "the control technology of choice," but that does not mean that the State has in any sense[39] violated a "requirement" of the Act.

There are many "requirements"[40] in the Act, including in the PSD provisions, that the EPA may enforce pursuant to Sections 113(a)(5)

---

36. *The Short List* with a twist. The list looks clean and fair, but it is meant to appear illogical on its face.

37. *Bridge the Gap* through "reasoning."

38. *What a Breeze*: "here," not "in the instant case" or some other bloated cliché.

39. *What a Breeze* through one-syllable words.

40. *Bridge the Gap* through "requirements."

or 167. The CAA provides that a facility's emissions may not exceed the NAAQS, PSD allowable increments, or other applicable emission standards. The provision defining BACT itself, while specifying that BACT is determined by "the permitting authority," goes on to provide that "[i]n no event" may application of BACT result in emissions exceeding any performance standards promulgated by the EPA or any limits on hazardous pollutants. Other requirements are that a PSD permit be issued in the first place; that the proposed permit be subject to review and required analysis; and that[41] interested persons—including "representatives of the Administrator"—be given an opportunity to submit written or oral presentations.

Should a State violate any of these requirements[42] or prohibitions, the EPA may take appropriate action pursuant to Sections 113(a)(5) or 167.[43] Such objective requirements, however, stand in sharp contrast to the determination of what BACT is for a particular source.[44] BACT is a discretionary judgment based on the case-by-case weighing of the applicable statutory factors. Accordingly, there is no single, objectively "correct" BACT determination for any particular source—[45] no "technology of choice" that applies without regard to case-specific policy judgments about how to[46] balance competing impacts and costs.

For example,[47] one State—experiencing little economic growth in the pertinent area and concerned about the impact of increased costs on a critically important employer—may select as BACT for

41. *Freight Train; Parallel Lives* through "that."

42. *Bridge the Gap.*

43. *With You in Spirit.* Note how the paragraph openers in this section fall in lockstep.

44. *Flashpoint* in the argument itself: "We're not saying the EPA has no remedies, just not this remedy."

45. *A Dash of Style* to elaborate or to recast an opening phrase or clause.

46. *What a Breeze*: "about how to," not "decision regarding the manner in which it implements."

47. *That Reminds Me.*

that employer a less stringent and less costly technology that results in emissions consuming nearly all of (but not more than) the available increment for growth. Another State—experiencing vigorous economic growth and faced with many competing permit applications—may select as BACT for those applications a more stringent and more costly technology that limits the impact of any particular new source on the increment available for development. A third State—in which ecotourism rather than more industrial development is the priority—may select as BACT an even more stringent and more costly technology, effectively blocking *any* industrial expansion.[48] In each case the State would have determined the maximum degree of pollution reduction achievable for the facility in question, given the priorities of the particular State and that State's decision about how to implement[49] those priorities in the case of that particular facility

Determining the "best" control technology is like asking different people to pick the "best" car. Mario Andretti may select a Ferrari; a college student may choose a Volkswagen Beetle; a family of six a mini-van. A Minnesotan's choice will doubtless have four-wheel drive; a Floridian's[50] might well be a convertible. The choices would turn on how[51] the decisionmaker weighed competing priorities such as cost, mileage, safety, cargo space, speed, handling, and so on.[52] Substituting one decisionmaker for another may yield a different result, but not in any sense a more "correct" one. So too here.[53] Because there is no

---

48. *Parallel Lives* throughout all three examples; use of antithesis.

49. *What a Breeze*: "decision about how to implement," not "decision regarding the manner in which it implements."

50. *Parallel Lives*. Also note his use of such rhetorical techniques as conjunction deviation (no "and") and verb elision (and the family of six doesn't "choose").

51. *What a Breeze*: "Turn on how," not "be contingent on the manner in which."

52. *That Reminds Me*: An example within an example within an example.

53. *Size Matters*.

"correct" BACT determination for any particular source, the EPA cannot conclude that a State failed to include the "correct" BACT limitation in a PSD permit, the way the EPA can conclude, say, that the State failed to require a PSD permit, that the State failed to include a BACT limitation at all in a PSD permit, or that the State issued a permit allowing emissions to exceed available increments.[54]

The Ninth Circuit's erroneous conclusion proceeded from a faulty premise—that the State is only the "initial" BACT decisionmaker under the Act. There is absolutely nothing in the CAA, however, that supports that notion. The statute expressly provides that *the permitting authority, on a case-by-case basis,"* shall determine BACT for a particular source. Except in one specified instance—not applicable here—[55] the Act nowhere requires the EPA to approve a State's BACT determination.

Indeed, that one instance[56] is the exception that proves the rule—that Congress otherwise did not intend the EPA to have the "ultimate authority" to determine BACT for particular sources. Section 165(a)(8) of the Act requires EPA approval of state BACT determinations for sources "in a class III area, emissions from which would cause or contribute to exceeding the maximum allowable increments applicable in a class II area where no standard under [42 U.S.C. § 7411] has been promulgated...for such source category." Thus, when Congress wanted to require EPA approval of a state BACT determination, it did so explicitly. *See,* e.g., *Barnhart v. Sigmon Coal Co.,* 534 U.S. 438, 452–453 (2002) ("Where Congress wanted to provide for successor liability in the Coal Act, it did so explicitly, as demonstrated by other sections in the Act"[57]).[58]

54. *Freight Train; Parallel Lives.*

55. *A Dash of Style.*

56. *Bridge the Gap:* "one instance."

57. *Speak for Yourself.*

58. *Race to the Bottom:* "Indeed, when Congress wanted to give the EPA *any* kind of role at all in the PSD permitting process, it did so explicitly. Section 165(a)(2), for instance, specifies that 'interested persons' who may submit concerns on a proposed permit include

MercExchange v. eBay

Excerpts from Seth Waxman's August 2006 Brief for MercExchange in Support of its Motion for Permanent Injunction (footnotes, definitions, and citations omitted for reading ease).

I. Introduction

The question in this case is whether equity favors granting injunctive relief to the patent holder, MercExchange, L.L.C., after a final judgment of willful infringement against the defendants, eBay, Inc., and its wholly-owned affiliate, Half.com.[59]

The equities strongly favor such relief.[60] This is a case of deliberate, and by eBay's own assertion, avoidable infringement.[61] eBay was not only well aware of MercExchange's patent, but eBay tried to purchase that patent before it started infringing. And[62] eBay deliberately chose to infringe when it could have (at least by its own contention), avoided infringement with a simple and inexpensive design-around. Under these circumstances, eBay can "make no claims whatsoever on the Chancellor's conscience."[63] *Albemarle Paper Co. v. Moody*, 422 U.S.

'representatives of the Administrator.' In a similar vein, Section 165(d) provides the EPA with a role in reviewing PSD permit applications to ensure that a proposed facility's emissions will not adversely impact air quality in class I areas. If the EPA files a notice alleging the potential for such an impact, the State may not only issue a PSD permit unless the facility demonstrates that its emissions will not cause or contribute to concentrations which exceed allowable increments for class I areas."

59. *Brass Tacks*: what sort of case is it?

60. *Bridge the Gap*.

61. Also an element of *Brass Tacks*: *what* sort of case is it?

62. *The Starting Gate*.

63. *Mince Their Words*.

405, 422 (1975). Indeed,[64] eBay[65] continues to proclaim to the investing public that an injunction would *not* harm it.[66]

MercExchange, on the other hand,[67] will continue to suffer irreparable harm in the absence of an injunction.[68] MercExchange, and MercExchange's licensees or potential licensees, are, or aspire to be, competitors of eBay. Permitting eBay to continue using MercExchange's technology would irreparably harm MercExchange's ability to market, sell, or license its technology to these existing or future competitors to eBay. Among other things,[69] if eBay cannot be enjoined, MercExchange is effectively denied the ability to maximize the value of its patents by exclusively licensing them. The value of MercExchange's lost opportunities to enter into these license relationships, and to take advantage of the further business those relationships might generate, is unquantifiable.

Moreover, the harm to MercExchange has only intensified in the three years since this case was last before this Court. eBay has solidified its market dominance, at least in part by infringing MercExchange's patent. MercExchange, on the other hand, is thwarted[70] in its efforts to market its invention because of its inability to prevent eBay—whose dominance squeezes out potential competitors—[71] from infringing.

---

64. *Take Me by the Hand.*

65. *Parallel Lives*: eBay is the subject of these last four sentences, giving the paragraph coherence.

66. *The Short List*: With well-known factors such as these, put the factors in the background, letting the facts establishing those factors take center stage.

67. *Take Me by the Hand.*

68. *Parallel Lives*: Through antithesis, this paragraph is the mirror image of the previous one.

69. *What a Breeze*: "Among other things," not "*inter alia.*"

70. *Zingers.*

71. *A Dash of Style.*

The public interest also favors injunctive relief. In addition to serving the strong public interest in maintaining the integrity of the patent system by enforcing patent rights, enjoining eBay also serves the public interest in promoting[72] competition. Without an injunction, eBay can further solidify its virtual monopoly power by impairing the development of potential online auction alternatives to eBay.[73]

The factors for evaluating injunctive relief all strongly favor granting that relief to MercExchange, and this Court should enter such an injunction without delay.[74]

II. Background

In April 1995, several months before eBay was incorporated,[75] Thomas Woolton filed his first patent application involving online marketing technology.[76] The family of patents that issued from this parent application includes the '265 patent.

A. The '265 Patent
As this Court is aware, the '265 patent, in general terms, describes an "electronic market" for the sale of goods. In such a market, sellers[77] can display their wares by posting pictures, descriptions, and prices of goods on a computer network, such as the Internet. A prospective buyer can electronically browse the goods on sale by connecting to the network. After selecting an item, the buyer can complete the

---

72. *Parallel Lives*: "public interest in maintaining" ... "public interest in promoting."

73. *Why Should I Care?* In this case, addressing the public-interest factor allows you to incorporate the *Why Should I Care?* technique at no extra cost.

74. *What a Breeze*: despite the technical material, the average sentence in this introduction is fewer than twenty words.

75. *Once Upon a Time.*

76. *Panoramic Shot.*

77. *Back to Life*: the sentences in this technical passage focus on actors: *sellers, buyer, a central authority.*

purchase electronically, with the "electronic market" mediating the transaction, including payment, on the buyer's behalf. The seller is then[78] notified that the buyer has paid for the item and that the transaction is final. A central authority within the market can police the obligations and performance of sellers and buyers over time, thereby promoting trust among participants.[79] In short, the invention provides a platform to offer goods for sale over the Internet in which the entire sales transaction, including the mediation of payment, is performed electronically.

B. Initial Efforts to Commercialize the Invention[80]

Mr. Woolston's goal from the outset was to commercialize his patented inventions. For that purpose, he founded MercExchange (as well as an earlier iteration of that company, called Fleanet) and assigned his patent rights to it. He developed a business plan and sought capital investment to commercialize his patents. He also hired a computer programming staff to write software to put his inventions into practice. In order to make the most of its limited resources,[81] MercExchange also entered into a licensing agreement with another company, Aden Enterprises, in October 1999. At that time,[82] Aden Enterprises was "embarking on a major industry initiative to build and deploy Internet Markets and Auctions," and MercExchange sought, through this license arrangement, to use its patent rights to develop its invention in ways that MercExchange could not accomplish with its own resources. MercExchange hoped to leverage the resources of these licensees to help develop and commercialize the invention.

78. *What a Breeze*: "then," not "subsequently"; "can," not "is able to"; "in short," not "in summary."

79. *Leading Parts.*

80. *Headliners.*

81. *Show, Not Tell.*

82. *Once Upon a Time.*

By the late 1990s, eBay was also looking for ways[83] to offer goods for sale with the entire sales transaction, including the mediation of payment, performed electronically. Accordingly, in June 2000, eBay approached MercExchange to discuss eBay's interest in buying MercExchange's patent portfolio. eBay had been aware of MercExchange's '265 patent and its technique for conducting electronic sales since the late 1990s; in fact, eBay had filed 24 patent applications citing the '265 patent as prior art from October 1998 through February 2002.[84] MercExchange was very interested in entering into a working relationship with eBay because MercExchange hoped that by so doing it could capitalize MercExchange into an operating company. In short,[85] MercExchange hoped that by partnering with eBay, MercExchange could convert the innovative ideas embodied in its patents into commercial reality. eBay, however, made clear that it was interested only in buying the patents, rather than entering into any[86] more extended business relationship.

. . . .

E. Current Impact of eBay's Continuing Infringement

Although MercExchange has a final judgment that eBay willfully infringed its valid patent, without an injunction ordering eBay to stop infringing the '265 patent, the prospect that eBay will persist in its infringement has continued to make MercExchange's effort

---

83. *What a Breeze*: "hoped," not "remained hopeful that it could"; "help develop," not "assist in developing"; "looking for ways to offer," not "seeking methods by which it could offer."

84. *Good Bedfellows.*

85. *Take Me by the Hand.*

86. *Show, Not Tell*: A good example of using the facts to develop legal themes and to put the client in a favorable light (or the adversary in an unfavorable one.) Note the lack of editorial commentary: you read nothing about eBay's being "mercenary" or "greedy." The facts, if true, should speak for themselves.

to commercialize its invention extremely difficult, and may doom it entirely.[87]

First, it is difficult for MercExchange to enter into license arrangements because potential licensees have little incentive to adequately compensate MercExchange for the use of its patented technology so long as eBay is infringing.[88]

Second, the prospect of eBay's ongoing infringement continues to make it very difficult for MercExchange to do what it has wanted to do from the outset—fully exploit its patented invention . . . .

Third, MercExchange has lost other business opportunities to compete with eBay, at least in part because eBay is not enjoined from infringing the '265 patent. Although eBay is a virtual monopolist in the Internet auction market, several other companies that each have a large presence in other fields of Internet commerce have expressed interest in—and are quite capable of—presenting significant competition to eBay through use of the '265 patent. MercExchange has tried to pursue such ventures, but its efforts have not come to fruition, at least in part because of its current inability to enjoin eBay from continued infringement of the '265 patent.[89]

. . . .

ARGUMENT

. . . .

87. *Show, Not Tell*: *Show, Not Tell* doesn't mean that you avoid strong language or dramatic facts. It simply means that you rely on facts not rhetoric. Here, MercExchange appropriately treats as facts the difficulties it faces in commercializing its invention and the possibility that those difficulties might doom the company entirely.

88. *The Short List* in a factual setting: note the interesting use of a list to organize difficult or diffuse factual material.

89. *End with a Bang.*

III. *The Equities Entitle MercExchange to a Permanent Injunction Enjoining eBay from Infringing MercExchange's Patent*

. . . .

B. Absent an Injunction, MercExchange Will Suffer Immediate Irreparable Harm for Which There Is No Adequate Remedy at Law

Absent an injunction, eBay's infringement will continue to cause MercExchange irreparable harm, i.e., harm that cannot be adequately compensated by money damages. The essence of the patent right is the right to exclude others from using one's invention for a limited time. The mere passage of time during which that right is deprived, therefore, can work an irremediable harm.

It is for that reason[90] that, once infringement and validity have been established, the patent holder is generally presumed to have suffered irreparable harm. The Supreme Court's decision in *eBay* did not alter that presumption.[91] In *eBay*, the Supreme Court explained that a plaintiff seeking a permanent injunction must demonstrate irreparable harm. But,[92] as the Federal Circuit has suggested in at least one post-*eBay* case, the plaintiff can do so where the defendant fails to rebut the presumption of irreparable harm that arises from a showing of success on the merits of validity and infringement.[93] *Cf. Abbott Labs v. Andrx Pharms., Inc.*, 452 F.3d 1331, 1347 (Fed. Cir. 2006) (holding that, because plaintiff

---

90. *Bridge the Gap.*

91. *Long in the Tooth* with a twist: a case that might appear to change the legal landscape does not in fact do so.

92. *The Starting Gate.*

93. *Long in the Tooth*: Putting a positive spin on an adverse Supreme Court case and then on a Federal Circuit case that went the wrong way.

seeking preliminary injunction failed to establish likelihood of success on merits, plaintiff was not entitled to presumption of irreparable harm).[94] And[95] eBay cannot rebut that presumption here; MercExchange's "willingness to license" should not diminish MercExchange's right to exclude, nor the harm that befalls MercExchange through its deprivation.

Even if this Court concludes that MercExchange is not entitled to a presumption of irreparable harm, however, MercExchange will unquestionably suffer such harm, in numerous ways, absent an injunction.

1.Depriving MercExchange of the right to choose to whom it licenses its patented technology is a harm that cannot be remedied with money damages.[96]

The[97] necessary corollary to the right to exclude is the patent holder's right to decide if, when, and to whom[98] to license its patented invention. Absent an injunction to enforce that right here, MercExchange would, in effect,[99] be forced to license its technology to eBay. Such a forced license is "antithetical to a basic tenet of the patent system... that the decision whether to license is one that should be left to the patentee."[100]

94. *Ping Me.*

95. *The Starting Gate.*

96. *Russian Doll.*

97. *With You in Spirit.*

98. *What a Breeze; Parallel Lives.*

99. *Take Me by the Hand.*

100. *Mince Their Words.*

Forcing MercExchange to license its patent to someone not of its choosing[101] is an irreparable harm—[102] once lost it cannot be retroactively restored nor remedied with money. That is true whether[103] MercExchange uses its patented invention itself in a commercial enterprise, licenses the invention, or even refuses to license or make any other use at all of the patent.[104]

But[105] the harm to MercExchange is particularly severe on the record here. MercExchange, and MercExchange's licensees or potential licensees, are (or aspire to be) *competitors* of eBay—[106] an entity that commands 90% of the relevant market. Money damages are therefore[107] particularly inadequate to compensate MercExchange for eBay's unauthorized use of the patented invention. Not only[108] is MercExchange forced to license someone *not* of its choosing, which negates an essential and irremediable aspect of MercExchange's patent rights, but MercExchange's ability to license its patent to those of its *own* choosing is degraded. A potential licensee might be undeterred from taking a license if the unenjoined competitor is a small part of the market but would have little incentive to adequately

101. *Bridge the Gap.*

102. *A Dash of Style.*

103. *What a Breeze.*

104. *Parallel Lives*: "uses," "licenses," "refuses."

105. *The Starting Gate.*

106. *A Dash of Style.*

107. *Take Me by the Hand*: *Therefore* is moved inside the sentence rather than stuck at the beginning.

108. Like many *not only... but also* sentences (including the fourth sentence in this excerpt), this one is cumbersome. The double negative of "not" and "negates" is jarring. "Which negates" is also a remote relative—the "someone not of its choosing" is not doing the negating. Perhaps something like this: "In the end, MercExchange loses more than just its right to avoid licensing to those it does not choose: It also loses its right to license to those it does choose."

compensate MercExchange for the use of its technology where the unenjoined competitor so dominates[109] the market.

And as this court explained in *Odetics*, the argument that future royalty payments ameliorate such harm to a patent holder is untenable.[110] The court observed that "[d]efendants are incorrect that absent an injunction Odetics will not suffer irreparable harm simply because it will be paid royalties for all future infringement. If no injunction issues, Odetics effectively will be forced to license [its] patent to [the infringer], a result antithetical to a basic tenet of the patent system, namely that the decision whether to license is one that should be left to the patentee." In addition, a compulsory license denies the inventor the opportunity to take an active role in the exploitation of his invention. Permitting eBay to continue using MercExchange's technology without authorization is antithetical to the patent law and irreparably harmful to MercExchange....

Fifty Writing Challenges

Introductions

1. *Brass Tacks.* In one sentence each, answer these five questions about a dispute: Who are the parties and what is their relationship? What question does the dispute seek to answer? When did the dispute arise? Where did the dispute arise? Why is your client in the right? Now mold those answers into a short narrative that explains your case and puts your client in the best light.

2. *The Short List.* List three or four reasons a court should do what you want the court to do about the narrative you just shared.

---

109. *What a Breeze; Why Should I Care?* in the argument itself.

110. *The Starting Gate.*

Now type the word "because" after each reason and add one more layer of specificity.

3. *Why Should I Care?* Without citing any case law or other authorities, explain in your own words why it would be bad in the long run if your adversary won the dispute.

4. *Flashpoint.* Fill in these blanks for two different cases. The dispute is about _____, not _____. To decide this motion, the Court need not decide _____; it need only decide _____.

Fact Sections

5. *Panoramic Shot.* Pick a dispute with complicated facts. Write a short opening overview paragraph that sets the stage.

6. *Show, Not Tell.* Think of a quality or trait that you'd like the court to associate with you—or with your adversary. Now write two or three facts that "show" that trait in action. Use no adjectives or adverbs, and do not "tell" the court what to conclude about those facts.

7. *Once Upon a Time.* In a fact section, find at least one date that could be cut, and at least two dates that could be replaced with a phrase like "two days later."

8. *Headliners.* Write a series of at least four fact-section headings, all in the present tense, that flow from the one before, and that favor the party you represent.

9. *Back to Life.* Pick a technological device. Write a paragraph describing how it works. Anchor your sentences on the phrase "the user" rather than on various features of the technology itself.

10. *Poker Face.* Write two sentences about two unfavorable facts. Start each sentence with "Although" or "Even though," and end each sentence by putting the bad fact in the best possible light.

11. *End with a Bang.* Rewrite the end of a fact section by leaving the court with a final image or thought.

Structure

12. *Russian Doll.* Draft a series of headings and subheadings that consist of complete thoughts and that form logical units.

13. *Heads I Win, Tails You Lose.* Draft a series of three headings in which the second and third headings start with the phrase "Even if."

14. *Sneak Preview.* Take a section of an argument in which the lawyer jumps from Argument to the first roman numeral, or from a roman numeral to the letter A. Now add a short umbrella passage to introduce the headings or subheadings to come.

15. *With You in Spirit.* Take a heading you've drafted and ask yourself what questions the court would need answered before endorsing that heading. Put those questions in the most likely logical order. Now answer each question, and make those answers the openings of your paragraphs.

16. *Sound Off.* Take another heading you've drafted that lends itself to a numbered list of points in support. Draft that list, and make the enumerated reasons the openings of your paragraphs.

Working with Authorities

17. *Long in the Tooth.* Find three different ways to complete this sentence: "Courts have long held that in cases such as this one, _____."

18. *Peas in a Pod.* Take a case you want to analogize. In a single paragraph, compare every key point of similarity and difference. Use both "like this case" and "unlike this case."

19. *Mince Their Words.* Find a sentence in a motion or brief that's really just a sentence quoted verbatim from an opinion or judgment. Rewrite the sentence by starting with your own words, and only then weaving in some short phrases from a quoted passage.

20. *One Up.* Complete this sentence: "[Opponent] cites [case], but that case applies even more to [client] because _____."

21. *Interception.* Complete this sentence: "Although [opponent] cites [case] in its favor, if anything that case helps [client] because _____."

22. *Rebound.* Complete this sentence: "[Opponent] claims that [the case I have cited] is distinguishable, but [the distinction] does not matter: _____."

23. *Not Here, Not Now.* Complete this sentence: "[The case that opponent cites] is different from this case: _____."

24. *One Fell Swoop.* Complete this sentence: "In all these [cases that my opponent cites], the court _____, not _____."

25. *Not So Fast.* Complete this sentence: "Although [the case that my opponent cites] might have suggested that _____, it did not hold that _____."

26. *Authority Problems.* Complete this sentence: "The Court should not follow [old or illogical case that cuts against you] here: _____."

27. *Ping Me.* Draft a series of three or more case parentheticals that begin with a participle like "affirming" or "awarding" and that then explain how the reason the court did what it did there proves a broader point you're making about the law here.

28. *Speak for Yourself.* Reduce a long quotation to a parenthetical that consists solely of a single-sentence quotation.

29. *Hybrid Model.* Draft at least two parentheticals that combine a participle like "affirming" or "awarding" with key quoted language.

30. *Lead 'Em On.* Rewrite the introductions to three block quotes by introducing them not with the topic of the quotation but with the gist of the quotation.

31. *Race to the Bottom.* Take several motions or briefs in which the attorneys used footnotes for something other than case citations. Decide whether you think that the material in each

footnote should have been (1) in the body itself, (2) as is, in footnote form, or (3) nowhere at all.

Style

32. *Zingers*. Take a motion or brief. Replace at least five of the original verbs or verb phrases with new verbs that are shorter, more vivid, or both.
33. *What a Breeze*. Read a page of an argument section out loud. Each time the writing sounds heavy or awkward, imagine how you'd make the same point orally. Transcribe the results.
34. *Manner of Speaking*. Enliven a dull passage by incorporating a metaphor or a figure of speech.
35. *That Reminds Me*. Pick a legal concept or doctrine that is difficult to explain or understand. Write a passage explaining it that begins with the word "Take" or "Suppose" or "Consider" and that then develops the point through a hypothetical.
36. *The Starting Gate*. Find at least ten sentences beginning with "However," "Nevertheless," "Accordingly," "Moreover," "Additionally," or "Consequently." Recast those sentences by beginning with a short transition word or by moving a short transition word inside the sentence near the verb.
37. *Size Matters*. Find three different sentences that last for more than a line, and then shorten each one to seven words or fewer.
38. *Freight Train*. Find a passage in which an attorney writes several sentences in a row that each begin with something a court did. (Example: "The Court noted...The Court added...Additionally, the Court emphasized...") Turn the list into a single Freight Train sentence.
39. *Leading Parts*. Find a few sentences that begin with "Therefore" or "Accordingly." Now look at the preceding sentence and combine the two into a single *Leading Parts* sentence.

40. *Talk to Yourself.* Draft two rhetorical questions that go to the core of a key legal or factual issue in your case.

41. *Parallel Lives.* Complete this sentence: "In [doing something that my client doesn't like], [my opponent] _____, _____, and _____." Make sure that the language in the three blanks is all in parallel form.

42. *A Dash of Style.* Draft two sentences with a pair of internal dashes to emphasize a word or phrase, and then draft a single sentence with a dash at the end to introduce a trailing thought.

43. *Good Bedfellows.* Draft two sentences in which you use a semicolon to highlight a likeness or a contrast.

44. *Magician's Mark.* Draft two sentences in which you use a colon rather than language like "because" or "since" or "due to the fact that."

45. *Take Me by the Hand.* Pick ten transition words or phrases. Write a passage that uses all ten.

46. *Bridge the Gap.* Find some paragraph openers that do not follow logically from the end of the paragraph before. Recast those paragraph openers by repeating a word, phrase, or idea from the end of the previous paragraph.

47. *Join my Table.* Transform an ordinary prose passage into a table or chart.

48. *Bullet Proof.* Transform a dense paragraph into a series of bullet points or a numbered list.

Conclusions

49. *Parting Thought.* Find a conclusion that consists of a throwaway line beginning with such language as "For all of the foregoing reasons." Consider whether the end of the argument serves the function of a conclusion, and if not, rewrite it so that it does.

50. *Wrap-Up.* Draft a conclusion for a motion or brief that incorporates a final thought or a new quotation.

Index